Heritage Conservation and Social Engagement

Heritage Conservation and Social Engagement

Edited by
Renata F. Peters, Iris L. F. den Boer,
Jessica S. Johnson and Susanna Pancaldo

First published in 2020 by
UCL Press
University College London
Gower Street
London WC1E 6BT

Available to download free: www.uclpress.co.uk

A CIP catalogue record for this book is available from The British Library.

ISBN: 978-1-78735-922-2 (Hbk.)
ISBN: 978-1-78735-921-5 (Pbk.)
ISBN: 978-1-78735-920-8 (PDF)
ISBN: 978-1-78735-923-9 (epub)
ISBN: 978-1-78735-924-6 (mobi)
DOI: https://doi.org/10.14324/111.9781787359208

Contents

List of figures	vii
List of tables	ix
Notes on contributors	x
Preface	xiii
Acknowledgements	xiv

Introduction 1

Renata F. Peters

1. Conservation and engagement: transforming and being transformed 6

   Renata F. Peters

2. Conservation and collaboration: a discussion 30

   Miriam Clavir

3. The role of conservation education in reconciliation: the example of the Iraqi Institute for the Conservation of Antiquities and Heritage 46

   Jessica S. Johnson, Kim Cullen Cobb and Brian Michael Lione

4. Community involvement in built heritage conservation: the case study of the Birzeit Historic Centre Project, Palestine 66

   Anna Teresa Ronchi

5. Putting sustainability into practice: the use of locally available materials in conservation 85

   Flavia Ravaioli

6. The 'Open Lab Project': addressing the skills deficit
   of volunteer community archaeologists in
   Lincolnshire, UK   105

   Craig Spence

7. Cultural heritage conservation and public benefits:
   effectiveness of Kenya's legal and administrative framework   125

   Gilbert Kituyi Wafula

8. Learning from archives: integrating preservation and access   141

   Nancy Bell and Dinah Eastop

9. Objects and wellbeing: a personal view   155

   Elizabeth Pye

Index   178

List of figures

Figure 1.1   Some of the recursive stages that may be involved
             in contemporary decision-making processes
             in conservation. © the author.   9
Figure 2.1   Bronze representation of Vishnu in 'visible storage'
             at the UBC Museum of Anthropology. Photographer
             Heidi Swierenga. Courtesy of UBC Museum of
             Anthropology, Vancouver, Canada.   38
Figures
2.2 and 2.3 A Hindu bronze statue at MOA is celebrated by its
             Vancouver community in 2010. Photographer
             Heidi Swierenga. Courtesy of UBC Museum of
             Anthropology, Vancouver, Canada.   38, 39
Figure 3.1   Outline for the Final Report for Visiting Instructors
             in the University of Delaware Conservation Programs
             at the Iraqi Institute for the Conservation and
             Preservation of Antiquities and Heritage. Courtesy of
             Iraqi Institute for the Conservation and Preservation
             of Antiquities and Heritage.   54
Figure 4.1   Aerial view of the historic centre of Birzeit.
             © Digitalglobe 2014.   73
Figure 4.2   View of El Etem courtyard, Al Ein Road.
             © Mutual Heritage 2009.   76
Figure 4.3   Intervention of street paving. © Mutual Heritage 2009.   77
Figure 4.4   Saadeh House, rehabilitated in 2011–13, hosts
             an interactive centre for Science and Technology.
             © the author 2016.   81
Figure 5.1   The multi-period tell site of Gurga Ciya, in the
             Sharizor Plain, Iraqi Kurdistan. © the author 2014.   87
Figure 5.2   Respondents to a survey of heritage professionals in
             2013 were split almost equally into three groups: those
             who bought most or some materials locally, those who
             shop within the country and those who look abroad.

'Locally' was defined as 'within one hour's drive from the workplace'. © the author 2014.   92

Figure 5.3   Respondents to a survey of heritage professionals were asked to rate the importance of different characteristics of packaging materials. © the author 2014.   92

Figure 5.4   Diagram summarising the proposed methodology. © the author 2014.   94

Figure 5.5   A model matrix for comparing the benefits of various options in the selection of locally available storage materials (after Cassar 1998, 43). © the author 2014.   95

Figure 5.6   Packaging materials at the Suleymaniya market. © the author 2014.   98

Figure 6.1   Volunteers take part in a typical 'Open Lab' session to process and catalogue their finds. © the author 2013.   111

Figure 6.2   Participants in a skills workshop take a closer look at some examples of Roman ceramics. © the author 2013.   112

Figure 8.1   Design for a kerchief commemorating Field Marshal Garnet Joseph Wolseley, 1st Viscount Wolseley and the razing of Coomassie in the Gold Coast (now Kumasi, Ghana) in 1887 (Design 282367). © The National Archives.   147

Figure 8.2   A volunteer inspecting designs and transcribing information written on or alongside the Representations. © The National Archives.   149

Figure 9.1   Two South African pennies dated 1898, showing the effects of very different lives. © Stuart Laidlaw 2011.   158

Figure 9.2   Carved wooden beam, sixteenth century. © Nick Balaam 2011.   161

Figure 9.3   (a) Traditional Windsor chair, probably eighteenth century; (b) Ercol chair made by using similar materials and techniques, twentieth century. Photographs © Nick Balaam 2011.   163

Figure 9.4   Victorian pennies showing the effects of handling and use for over a century. © Stuart Laidlaw 2011.   165

Figure 9.5   (a) Front page of eighteenth-century Greek/Latin lexicon, with nineteenth-century schoolboy doodles; (b) Back page of lexicon. Photographs © Stuart Laidlaw 2011.   166

List of tables

Table 3.1   Other institutions that have used Iraqi Institute
             facilities for research and education programmes.
             Source: the authors.   59

Notes on contributors

Nancy Bell is currently acting as a preservation consultant for The National Archives, USA. Formerly she was Head of Collection Care, The National Archives, UK (2008–17). She also headed The National Archives Research and Development team that delivered an integrated research programme for The National Archives which included conservation science research. She was awarded the Plowden Medal in 2015 for her work on developing revised environmental standards for museums, libraries and archives.

Iris L. F. den Boer has an MA in Classical Archaeology from Leiden University and an MA in Principles of Conservation from UCL. She currently lives and works in the Netherlands. She is a board member of a regional department of the AWN, a national archaeological society for volunteers in the Netherlands. She also works as a co-editor of the department's archaeological magazine, *Grondig Bekeken*.

Miriam Clavir, Conservator Emerita at the UBC Museum of Anthropology, Canada, has won awards for her work focusing on conservators' relationship with Indigenous material heritage and the need to understand that conservation preserves cultural belongings with which the originators have ongoing relationships, and so hold key roles in conservation decisions.

Kim Cullen Cobb is a conservator in private practice in the Washington, DC area and Research Associate with the Smithsonian's Museum Conservation Institute. She holds a Master's in Art Conservation from Queen's University, Canada. Prior to entering the field of conservation she was a practising goldsmith, artist and teacher. Cullen Cobb began working as a visiting teacher at the Iraqi Institute for the Conservation of Antiquities and Heritage in the spring of 2011.

Dinah Eastop PhD, FIIC, ACR has 40 years' experience in conservation. She has worked at the Textile Conservation Centre (UK), The National Archives (UK), the University of Melbourne and with ICCROM, notably for CollAsia. She holds honorary posts at three UK universities: Glasgow, UCL and Southampton. Publications include *Chemical Principles of Textile Conservation*, co-authored with Ágnes Tímár-Balázsy (1998); *Upholstery Conservation*, co-edited with Kathryn

Gill (2001); *Changing Views of Textile Conservation* (2011) and *Refashioning and Redress* (2016), co-edited with Mary Brooks.

Jessica S. Johnson is Head of Conservation at the Smithsonian's Museum Conservation Institute. Previously she worked with the University of Delaware and helped to establish the Iraqi Institute for the Conservation of Antiquities and Heritage. She was Senior Conservator at the National Museum of the American Indian in Washington, DC and Conservator for the Museum Management Program of the National Park Service. She has worked for many years with the Penn Museum's Gordion Archaeological Project in Turkey.

Brian Michael Lione is the International Cultural Heritage Protection Program Manager for the Smithsonian's Museum Conservation Institute, the lead for MCI projects in Erbil (Iraq) and an instructor at the Iraqi Institute for the Conservation of Antiquities and Heritage (IICAH). Before joining the Smithsonian he helped to establish the IICAH, serving as Director and Executive Director from 2009 until 2017. His work at the Smithsonian focuses on capacity building and sustainability for the IICAH.

Susanna Pancaldo is an objects conservator, specialising in archaeological materials. She received an MA in Art History and Diploma in Conservation from New York University and has worked on numerous short-term contracts and excavations, the latter mainly in Italy. She was Conservation Manager for the Petrie Museum of Egyptian Archaeology and Senior Conservator for UCL Museums and Collections before taking up her current post as Conservator of Objects (Metals) at the Fitzwilliam Museum, Cambridge.

Renata F. Peters is Associate Professor in Conservation at the UCL Institute of Archaeology. She is also Chair of the Conservation Higher Education Institutions Network of the Institute of Conservation (ICON CHEIN), Conservation Lead of the Olduvai Geochronology Archaeology Project in Tanzania and Principal Investigator of the research project 'Fibres of Resistance: Tikuna barkcloth and identity in the Amazon'.

Elizabeth Pye is Emeritus Professor of Archaeological and Museum Conservation at the UCL Institute of Archaeology, where she taught both theoretical and practical aspects of heritage conservation. Her current interests focus on access to museum and heritage objects. She is author of *Caring for the Past: Issues in conservation for archaeology and museums* and editor of *The Power of Touch: Handling objects in museum and heritage contexts*.

Flavia Ravaioli is an objects conservator and research associate at the Fitzwilliam Museum, Cambridge. She previously worked as a researcher at University College London Qatar from 2015 to 2017, where she focused on the preservation of religious heritage in Islamic contexts and data analysis in conservation. She has fieldwork experience as an archaeological conservator in Egypt, Turkey, Iraqi Kurdistan and Italy.

Anna Teresa Ronchi is an architect and has a PhD in Technology and Design for the Built Environment from the Polytechnic of Milan, Italy. From 2009 to 2015 she worked at the Polytechnic of Milan, developing research projects in the field of built heritage conservation. She is currently responsible for R&D and EU projects at the Center for Cultural Heritage of the University of Milan. She also collaborates as a consultant in rehabilitation and regeneration projects of the historical built heritage.

Craig Spence FSA, FRHistS, MCIfA is Senior Lecturer at Bishop Grosseteste University, Lincoln. He initially worked as a field archaeologist in the UK and abroad, during which time he directed a number of excavations. At the Museum of London he led the revisions to the internationally renowned MoLAS Site Manual, including the pioneering use of multi-sheet single context recording. More recently he has undertaken historical research at several universities and published monographs on the social and cultural history of early modern London. He has interests in community archaeology and heritage management.

Gilbert Kituyi Wafula is a Lecturer in the Department of History and Archaeology, University of Nairobi, Kenya. He teaches Archaeology and Tourism. His interests and research work are in the areas of ceramic technology, ethnoarchaeology, Swahili Coastal Archaeology and natural and cultural heritage conservation.

Preface

This publication explores different kinds of social engagement motivated by the practice of heritage conservation, especially in areas of the world where heritage and museum collections show potential for use as tools for social empowerment. The topics and ideas discussed here were introduced in the conference 'The Social Impact of Cross-disciplinary Conservation' in 2014. It was organised by the UCL Conservation and Development Research Network (CDRN) in collaboration with the Heritage Conservation and Human Rights Network (University of Nairobi) and the Iraqi Institute for the Conservation of Antiquities and Heritage (University of Delaware).

The nine chapters of this book explore different aspects of cross-disciplinary conservation work. They offer ethical and practical perspectives from which to approach cultural heritage projects and preservation, with a focus on engagement, participation, access and the creative use of resources. As such, *Heritage Conservation and Social Engagement* is relevant to a broad range of heritage practitioners, local governments and heritage management authorities, as well as to graduate and postgraduate students interested in cross-disciplinary conservation perspectives.

Acknowledgements

We are grateful to the UCL Grand Challenges Small Grant (Intercultural Interaction) and the UCL Institute of Archaeology for generously funding the event that inspired this publication. We would like to extend our gratitude to the authors of this volume for their valuable contributions and to Anne-Marie Deisser for contributing to 'The Social Impact of Cross-disciplinary Conservation' conference and the first stages of the publication. Thanks are also due to William J. Mastandrea for editorial management assistance; to Eleni Asderaki for logistical support; and to the following UCL conservation graduates for their help during different stages of this project: Irene Capasso, Jan Cutajar, Abigail Duckor, Harald Fredheim, Anna Funke, Sarah Giffin, Kathleen King, Jamie McGuire, Megan Narvey, Eri Ohara-Anderson, Letty Steer, Seiko Tokuda, Karin Walda and Qifan Wang.

Introduction

Renata F. Peters

Professionals working with cultural heritage preservation have had to respond to difficult challenges in the last few decades, mainly brought about by globalisation, armed conflicts, natural disasters and the use of heritage as an ultimate resource to redress injustices of the past. The topics and experiences discussed in this book demonstrate that conservators may play important roles in facilitating and enhancing understanding between different cultural groups or groups with different interests. Though commonly associated with the sciences through interventive and preventive practices, we here discuss other possible perspectives for conservation-related activities. As will be seen, conservation practice may bring opportunities for redressing past and present injustices, healing, reconciliation, social cohesion and the strengthening of socio-cultural identities, as well as facilitating new ways of interaction between individuals and communities.

Conservation was already crossing boundaries between science and craft by the second half of the twentieth century – a time when the dominant structure of knowledge was based on division and disciplinary specialisation. Around the 1980s heritage and museum professionals started reviewing the objectives of their disciplines and the policies of access to collections or sites. Increasingly they became more open to sharing decision-making processes with groups related to originators, or descendants of originators, of material culture. Although such reviews did provoke shifts in the way in which museums and heritage institutions operate, real changes have been slow and are still in motion (see chapters 1 and 2 for further discussion). Nonetheless, the roles of conservators have started to become consistently more cross-disciplinary, dynamic and flexible. As a consequence, the discpline's boundaries have become more complex and new challenges and variables have arisen.

Collaboration is a strong aspect of cross-disciplinary work. In fact, such work cannot exist without collaboration. As will be seen in the following chapters, collaborative processes in conservation are not uncommon. That being said, there is no definitive evidence as to how far or how often they occur in conservation practice. The 2013 survey 'Participatory Processes and Conservation Practice' (Peters 2019) was disseminated in international conservation discussion lists and blogs in an attempt to bridge this gap. The results revealed that 76.2 per cent of the 168 respondents had participated in such projects at least once in their careers. The survey also indicated that a large majority of these professionals worked for museums or educational institutions completely or partially funded by public money. This predominance may suggest, among other things, that these projects may have been motivated by governmental policies of social inclusion or by ethical issues flagged up by educational institutions. The survey also revealed that most respondents worked in collaborative projects in North America and Europe (58 in the USA, 15 in Canada, 3 in Mexico, 14 in the UK and 27 in other European countries, 6 in Australia and 1 in New Zealand).[1]

Today museum professionals, and conservation staff in particular, increasingly endeavour to develop collaborative and inclusive approaches to all aspects of the material under their care. These collaborations are complex and often influenced by the colonial legacy of museums. Moreover, despite the high number of projects that may have attempted engagement and representation of different interest groups in decision-making, the effectiveness of the engagement varies according to the context, objectives, methods and resources available. Given the non-quantifiable – and often uncontrollable – nature of the variables involved in cross-disciplinary efforts, providing evidence for their beneficial impacts is not always very straightforward. In fact, neither the benefits nor the challenges encountered can always be tackled within well-established structures of knowledge and methodologies. In order to form a strong body of evidence, it is essential that conservators continue to create spaces in which to debate methods that may open new frontiers – the main objective of this book.

Efforts to promote inclusion and engagement in museums are likely to become even more socially relevant in the near future, as in recent years we have observed a rise in intolerance towards minority groups in traditionally democratic societies. This is illustrated, for example, by the election of divisive or authoritarian political representatives in different parts of the world. Some of these seem specifically to target human rights or attempt to normalise prejudices, segregation and further marginalisation of ethnic or religious minorities, Indigenous nations, the LGBTQ+ community, refugees and women. With dismay, we notice an increasing number of people expressing backward sentiments in relation to inclusion, diversity and the most basic human rights. These sentiments, often stimulated by biased opinion-makers or even fake news, are frequently underpinned by socio-economic problems provoked by austerity. The heritage sector is responding strongly, however, as it has the tools and ability to help fight prejudices invariably based on ignorance, misinformation or manipulation of facts. This book enthusiastically joins these efforts, in the knowledge that nothing can be done without dialogue and engagement.

Heritage Conservation and Social Engagement is structured around the themes of engagement and participation, as well as the significance of working collaboratively across disciplines. The contributors offer original analyses and present international perspectives that may be relevant and adaptable to different contexts. They also provide socio-cultural perspectives on conservation practices and explore development, engagement, wellbeing, recovery and reconciliation. Their underlying commonality is the emphasis on the value of cross-disciplinary collaborations and the adoption of more encompassing approaches to decision-making.

In chapter 1 Renata F. Peters introduces the topic of conservation and engagement by examining how museums and heritage institutions have responded to challenges posed by a postcolonial world. Ultimately it means decision-making about material held by these institutions has become more democratic and inclusive, and that conservation has incorporated a more social orientation rather than remaining purely technical and scientific. The main premise is that because conservation decision-making is central to how collections can be accessed, interpreted and used, conservators are in ideal places to facilitate or even to trigger these engagements. The chapter uses Paulo Freire's dialogical method to explore reasons for and challenges involved in using collaborative and engaged models, and to elaborate the need for constant evaluation of, and reflection upon, what is being thought and done.

In chapter 2 Miriam Clavir reviews changes over the last 30 years that have prompted conservation's material-based field to incorporate values related to the intangible attributes of objects in museum collections. In addition, these changes extend to an understanding that conservation practice brings together people with people, not just people with objects. Is collaboration considered a necessary competency in the field, however, and is it recognised as such – both by the conservation profession as a whole and by workplace colleagues and administrators? Do conservation training programmes adequately address the concerns voiced by Indigenous people in relation to the preservation of their belongings? The author suggests that the goals of conservation practice include recognition of the larger context of 'human wellbeing'.

This is followed in chapter 3 by Jessica S. Johnson, Brian M. Lione and Kim Cullen Cobb's elaboration on the role of conservation education in reconciliation. Drawing upon Iraq and the Iraqi Institute for the Conservation of Antiquities and Heritage in Erbil as a case study, the authors discuss the use of cultural heritage education in support of reconciliation and redevelopment. Collaboration among teachers and trainers, and a recursive approach to curriculum review, is central to the evolution of the Institute's educational programme, conceived to support a renewed community of heritage professionals in Iraq.

In chapter 4 Anna Teresa Ronchi explores the topic of community involvement in built heritage conservation. Her aim is to identify the main weaknesses and success factors that can restrict or emphasise mutual potentialities between conservation processes and local sustainable development. The rehabilitation of the old town of Birzeit, Palestinian Authority is explored, especially in relation to the role played by the local community in various strategies of engagement.

In chapter 5 Flavia Ravaioli discusses the use of locally accessible materials for use in preventive conservation, especially in contexts where resources are very limited and specialised materials unavailable. In such circumstances the attempt to apply Western standards of best practice may not be sustainable and can in fact disempower practitioners. Ravaioli considers the causes for some of the major challenges found in these contexts and suggests measures to overcome them.

In chapter 6 Craig Spence discusses the 'Open Lab Project' – a programme of practical support, skills training and awareness raising among local community archaeology groups developed by a team of academics and archaeologists at Bishop Grosseteste University, Lincoln. The programme successfully engaged with five local groups from across Lincolnshire, a geographically extensive and primarily rural county, supporting them in archiving their archaeological finds assemblages. The aim was to provide participating volunteers with the knowledge, skills and resources to do such work in an independent manner. Equally important outcomes were an increased sense of self-worth and physical and mental wellbeing among a number of the participants.

In chapter 7 Gilbert Kituyi Wafula considers the African context and persistent social and economic challenges, including poverty, illiteracy and disease. He argues that despite these Africa possesses resources of different natures that could positively impact people's livelihoods, archaeological heritage being one of them. In a changing world where people are increasingly recognising their democratic and human rights, the moral and legitimate rights of ordinary citizens in exploiting heritage cannot be taken for granted. The main focus of Wafula's discussion is who archaeological heritage benefits in Kenya and how effective the country's legal, administrative and policy frameworks are in addressing public interests and needs in the exploitation of archaeological heritage.

In chapter 8 Nancy Bell and Dinah Eastop present the interdisciplinary approach to conservation (understood as investigation, preservation and presentation) adopted at The National Archives (UK) and link it to the democratic mandate of the institution. The essay highlights the underpinning conceptual and practical approaches used to make conservation sustainable by integrating strategies for preservation and access. It demonstrates the engagement of local groups in the development of archival records, the democratic ethos of The National Archives and the ways in which this ethos is manifested in practice.

Chapter 9 presents Elizabeth Pye's personal views and experiences with objects, and investigates the many ways in which people may value and enjoy them. Pye also explores stories that objects may prompt and reflects on how these stories may affect conservation processes. She argues that artefacts should not be frozen into inactivity, but rather be enabled to continue providing enjoyment to people on many different levels.

Note

1. For more details see: Peters, R. 2019. 'Participatory Processes and Conservation Practice: a 2013 survey', *Conversations on Conservation of Cultural Heritage*. Accessed 18 August 2020. https://uclconversationsonconservation.blogspot.com/p/the-survey-participatoryprocesses-and_30.html.

1
Conservation and engagement: transforming and being transformed

Renata F. Peters

Introduction

It is widely known that Western museums have both validated and profited from structures of colonial domination and imperialism for at least the last two hundred years (Haas 1996; Ames 1992; Clifford 2004). Besides playing important roles in the structures of ideas, concepts and interpretations that reinforced the hegemony of the Western world[1] (for example Fanon 1963 [1961], 210–11; Said 2003 [1978], 6; Chakrabarty 1998; Spivak 2011 [1995]), many of these institutions also benefited from colonial structures to form their formidable collections. Even after such structures had been dismantled, many Western museums continued colonial strategies by retaining all the power to decide how to interpret and use these collections, without attempting to include the views or voices of the people they were trying to interpret and/or represent (Haas 1996, S1; Clifford, 2004; Howe 2005; Sillar 2005; Atalay 2006, 280–5). These practices have come under increasing scrutiny in the last few decades.

Towards the end of the 1970s the impact of political activism and the different narratives aimed at revising the norms and practices of colonial domination started to be felt in the world of museums. Groups previously considered marginal to central societies then started to find channels to voice their opinions about a range of subjects, including the stewardship of the collections originated by them or their ancestors (Clifford 1999; Haas 1996; Howe 2005; Atalay 2006). This process has been slow and is far from completion, as demonstrated by Felwine Sarr and Bénédicte Savoy's report (2018). This questions the legitimacy of holding collections with disputed provenance, such as African heritage looted during the colonial era. Although the report focuses on sub-Saharan material heritage, it finally brought the topic to the forefront of museums' agendas and to public attention.

This chapter discusses the development of conservation in relation to the changes that museums have experienced in the last 30 years. It considers how these have affected the discipline and explores reasons for more democratic and engaged practices, as well as some of the challenges involved. The main premise is that because conservation decision-making is cross-disciplinary and central to defining how objects[2] can be accessed, interpreted and used, conservators are able to facilitate or even trigger these engagements. Processes of empowerment and their potential impacts are explored through the lenses of Paulo Freire's dialogical method (1996 [1970]); 1972 [1970]) and, to a lesser extent, the work of Participatory Action Research (PAR) advocates and postcolonial theorists in order to show how structures of power are formed and maintained, and how to attempt to deconstruct them.

Despite the different terminologies and elaborations, Freire, PAR advocates and some postcolonial theorists show similarities and complement one another. For example, all aim to bring more equality and justice to the different peoples of the world and advocate that this can only be achieved through a bottom-up, participatory approach. They focus on the production of knowledge and the fact that practice may generate theory through critical reflection. Finally, they all emphasise the benefits of cross-disciplinary work and collaboration.

Contemporary conservation

Conservation started to be organised as a discipline when, as Muñoz Viñas (2005, 2) observes, 'it became clear that the views, approaches and skills required to treat a painting were different from those required to treat the walls of a common peasant house' (Muñoz Viñas 2005, 2). Clavir (2002, 4–5) underlines the differences by highlighting the non-utilitarian reasons for these interventions – which may include changes in social context or the desire to return the object to what is believed to have been its original appearance. For most of the twentieth century the conservation discipline was associated with arts and crafts traditions; it was supported by scientific methods and scientific knowledge of materials and deterioration mechanisms, and by certain aspects of their materiality (Brandi 2005 [1963]; Conti 2007 [1988]; Caple 2000, 46–58; Pye 2001, 51; Jokilehto 2009). Within that context conservators used to be mostly concerned about longevity or aesthetic aspects of the material fabric of objects.

The theoretical basis of Western conservation started to be problematised more strongly with Brandi's *Teoria del Restauro* (1963; 2005 [1963]). In this work conservation was articulated as a critical process based on academic knowledge and through which subjectivity should be minimised. Later in the twentieth century the conservation process also incorporated the need to integrate other aspects of objects such as intangible meanings, objects' biographies (Kopytoff 1986; Gosden and Marshall 1999; Seip 1999) and the values of people associated with them (Bernstein 1992; Heald 1997; Clavir 1998; Avrami et al. 2000; Peters et al. 2008; Avrami 2009).

Today the conservation process entails a continuous, non-linear, recursive and cross-disciplinary process. It includes tangible and intangible features, all of which have to be understood in relation to one another and never separated; separating tangible from intangible invariably limits the understanding of material heritage (Fig. 1.1). The process is documented using traditional and innovative methods and includes a broad range of recursive stages. These usually start with an understanding of the raw materials and manufacturing techniques used in objects, then considers the changes of these materials related to where the objects have been and how they have been used, which also includes current contexts. It also entails several activities related to preventive conservation, such as monitoring or managing the environment or material changes of objects, risk assessments and disaster preparedness – as well as a variety of interventive measures that could be applied to their material fabric.

All these stages need to be related to the provenance of the objects, their history and biographies and the different uses that have been given to them in different periods of the past and present. These will inevitably be associated with the interest groups surrounding these objects throughout their histories and uses (past, present and possibly future), which will define their values and significance to different groups of people. It should also be highlighted that the conservation process never ends. The variables defining conservation actions are dynamic; they never cease to evolve and may be influenced by a range of factors such as the mission of holding institutions or the art/antiquity markets, among others.

Thus understanding layers of history and values, the ways in which they are shaped, their contexts, motivations and impact combine to form the fundamental basis for effective decision-making processes in conservation today (Avrami et al. 2000; Mason 2002; de la

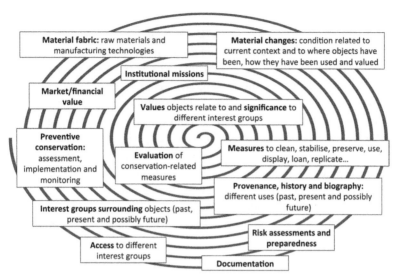

Fig. 1.1 Some of the recursive stages that may be involved in contemporary decision-making processes in conservation. © the author.

Torre 2002; Peters 2008; Avrami 2009; Russell and Winkworth 2009; Owczarek et al. 2017). Further complexity may be added when, for example, the same object reveals different or conflicting layers of significance and values, depending on who it is associated with and who is interpreting it, as well as where, when and why (Hooper-Greenhill 2000, 3–5; Eastop and Brooks 2011; Shih 2019). In practice this means that contemporary conservation is inherently cross-disciplinary, context-dependent and value-driven. As a consequence, decisions need to be based on robust reasoning, as different courses of action could be taken. These are some of the reasons why conservators, especially those dealing with Indigenous or ethnographic collections, have endeavoured to engage in reflective practices and open up decision-making to participation of more interest groups that are traditionally related to conservation objects.

Conservation and participation

Incorporating knowledge exchange and the interests of different groups into conservation decision-making processes, however, has the potential to suggest unpredictable paths of actions or even clashes with hitherto established conservation principles. Despite the challenges, the literature shows that conservators have been promoting collaboration and participation for a few decades now. For example, the Museum of New Mexico (Santa Fe, New Mexico, USA) had already established by 1991 that conservation treatments should not be performed on culturally sensitive materials without prior consultations with 'concerned parties'. The Museum defined culturally sensitive materials as 'religious objects, human remains, funerary objects, photographs and other depictions of sensitive materials, and documents about sensitive material' (Bernstein 1992, 25). One of the reasons given for this policy was a concern that because conservation was traditionally focused on the long-term preservation of material, it was not always sympathetic to the values of people associated with such objects (Bernstein 1992, 25–6).

In 2002 Clavir published *Preserving What Is Valued: Museums, conservation, and First Nations*, a work based on her life-long commitment to carry out collaborations between conservators and representatives from Indigenous groups. Clavir's most notable contribution relates to the elaboration of how the values entrenched in the conservation discipline and the views of non-professional groups may conflict due to the prioritisation of Western perspectives in decision-making processes. Her thinking undermines old conservation assumptions related to preservation of heritage materials by bringing human relationships to the fore of the discussion.

The Smithsonian National Museum of the American Indian (NMAI) should have prominence here, as it has been working in collaboration with Indigenous nations from the Americas since the 1990s (Atalay 2006; Johnson et al. 2005; Kaminitz et al. 2008; 2009; McHugh and Gunnison 2016). After so many years of experience and strong focus on the voices and views of Indigenous peoples of the American continent, NMAI's policies have become examples of best practice. Many conservators have championed similar views in other parts of the world. While a comprehensive list of participatory conservation projects would be too long to include here, the projects below illustrate the geographic spread of these practices.

In Sri Lanka, Wijesuriya (2000) coordinated the conservation of the *Temple of the Tooth Relic*, badly damaged by terrorist bombing in 1998. The project engaged various sectors of society, including politicians, religious leaders, users of the temple, the media and the general public. Deisser (2007; 2008) conducted a conservation project in Ankober, Ethiopia in which values and uses of artefacts were highlighted by integrating traditional local practices of preservation with the preventive conservation approaches mostly used in Western museums.

Gordon and Silva (2005) were engaged with representatives from the Xikrin-Kayapó in Brazil to curate and conserve a collection housed at the *Museu de Arqueologia e Etnologia, Universidade de São Paulo* (Museum of Archaeology and Ethnology, University of São Paulo) in São Paulo, Brazil. This has been followed by other projects that included Indigenous participation in various aspects of museum work (Delgado Vieira et al. 2017). For over ten years Sully (2007) has promoted the conservation of *Hinemihi, a Maori Meeting House* in London, working in collaboration with Maori living in the UK and New Zealand. Peters (Peters et al. 2008; Salomon and Peters 2009) has conducted a cross-disciplinary participatory project in San Cristobal de Rapaz, in the high Andes of Peru, in which conservation played an important role in the materialisation of the expectations of the local community. In Australia conservators have likewise been working in close collaboration with Aboriginal Australians to conserve Aboriginal art (Thorn 2006; 2008; Agnew et al. 2015).

Because of the intricacies and the range of values and interests involved, discussions on why and how to conduct collaborative projects and partnerships continue to be highlighted on the agenda of various conservation specialisms (Chitty 2017; Owczarek et al. 2017; Hornbeck and Moffett 2016; McHugh and Gunnison 2016; Peters 2016). Some of the practicalities of these processes will be explored later in this chapter. First, however, it is necessary to consider some concepts commonly embedded in conservation discourse and practice.

Implicit ideas of truth and neutrality

Despite all the developments seen in the last 30 years, the material and scientific focus that dominated conservation practice in the twentieth century is still the basis of the discipline. Thus it is perhaps more accurate to say that the conservation mandate has become more intricate and cross-disciplinary. Conservators today use the scientific process as a springboard to find strategies to conserve material fabric while ensuring that the process and the resulting conserved material respect the object's history and its layers of significance in the past, present and possible future (Clavir 1998; Avrami et al. 2000; Mason 2002, 5–8; de la Torre 2002). Such processes are further complicated by the fact that even though notions of 'neutrality' associated with the discipline have been deconstructed in the last two decades, they still emerge as justifications for conservation approaches in informal conservation discourse. I discuss a few of them below.

Artist's intention

'Artist's intention' (which could be understood here as the more generic 'maker's intention' in order to avoid value added by the word 'art') is often informally evoked in conservation decision-making to justify conservation approaches – in particular those that disregard later additions or ways in which the history of objects and the corresponding values associated with different events may have affected their material fabric. However, a short investigation into the concept reveals its inherent intricacy. It was already provoking a lot of discussion in the mid-twentieth century, following the publication of Wimsatt and Beardsley's 'The Intentional Fallacy' (1946). Here Dykstra (1996) summarises the ideas raised by the work:

> Mistaken justification occurs when readers or beholders attribute scientific, critical, or historical interpretations to the mentality of the author or artist. This justification appears mistaken because these interpretations have sources that are several steps removed from the artist's thought. Only the work was directly created by the artist, not the interpretations derived from it by beholders. The intentional fallacy applies when critics, historians, or conservators associate their analyses and interpretations with the artist's work and equate their conclusions with the artist's aims. Simply stated, the intentional fallacy insists that our interpretations are our own and we are mistaken if we identify them with the artist instead of ourselves. (Dykstra 1996, 204)

Moreover, intention is not the same as having a plan. Artists may do things without intending them or they may achieve things that were not intended. They may be unaware of exactly what they want to achieve – or even change their mind during and after the creative process (Bass 1989; Dykstra 1996; Livingston 2007 [2005], 3; Gordon and Hermens 2013; Wharton 2015). In addition, it is impossible for artists to predict how their work will be perceived, or even whether any kind of value will be associated with it. As seen in the quotation below, 'interpretation' is a concept that is often related, contrasted or compared to 'intention'. Works of art may trigger unforeseen meanings to different groups of people in different times and places, as both intention and interpretation are context-dependent and interdependent (Mele and Livingston 1992, 933–5).

Different conditions of the artist, the perceiver, and variations in historical precedents and cultural milieu as well as variations among a work's potential for affording various kinds of experiences may all figure in determining what in that particular case will determine the applicability of a given interpretation. (Feagin 1982, 73)

Furthermore, in contexts where the views and values of different groups are taken into account, artist's intention – or even interpretations made by professional experts – may not take priority unless they correspond to the reason why the material is valued or considered significant by key interest groups. In some contexts the events that take place *after* the creation of the material, their 'life histories' or 'biographies', may be at least as important (Smith 1989; Kopytoff 1986, 64–91; Gosden and Marshall 1999; Seip 1999).

Reversibility

The principle of 'reversibility' developed from ideas introduced by the Murray Pease Report (Murray Pease Committee 1964) – a set of influential standards of practice elaborated to prevent damage and promote professional standards among the profession. In that context reversibility was understood as the ability to bring the conserved object back to the state it was in before conservation took place. That is, the conservator would work in such a manner that all the actions implemented during the conservation process could be reversed, if so wished, and the object would go back to the state it was in before conservation (Oddy and Carroll 1999). In ideal terms, such a process would measure '... the capability of a conservator to remove any residue or effect introduced or caused in or on an object by a conservation treatment, either at the time of treatment or subsequently' (Smith 1999, 99).

The power to 'undo' is obviously desirable, as it implies unique skills and knowledge. As such it contributed to the development of the discipline during the 1970s and 1980s, becoming entrenched in conservation practice. However, in the late 1990s its feasibility came under scrutiny until the concept was finally deemed unattainable (Oddy 1999; Oddy and Carroll 1999; Smith 1999; Caple 2000, 64). Reversibility today is still considered useful as a parameter or reference to which to compare interventions – but not as an objective itself. The focus today is upon the ability of re-treating objects (re-treatability) (Appelbaum 2007, 353–9; Smith 1999; Muñoz Viñas 2005, 183–8).

Minimum intervention

The concept of minimum intervention started to be used more frequently at the same time as 'reversibility' declined (Caple 2000, 65). Acting 'minimally' means that only strictly necessary conservation interventions should be carried out, so as to achieve the objectives of the conservation treatment (Pye 2001, 32–3).

Objectives of conservation treatments, however, are always context-dependent. They will vary, for example, according to who is involved in the decision-making process, what the material is going to be used for, how and for how long it is required, why it is valued and what the resources available may be. Thus deciding what is strictly 'necessary' or the 'minimum' required to achieve a particular objective is essentially a relative process that is calibrated by the context. Moreover, Appelbaum (2007, 305) warns about using this concept as a blanket approach that ignores the uniqueness of the material fabric and values related to each object:

> Using minimal intervention as a guide in all cases disregards the individual needs of the object and its custodians, its interpretation, and its longevity. It would seem to rely at least partially on the unwarranted assumption that all objects live in sheltered environments where they can survive happily in whatever state they are in already. Given an object's physical state, its use, its context, and its likely future, an optimal treatment may be anything *but* minimal. (Appelbaum 2007, 305, original emphasis)

The concept, however, is extremely important as it acknowledges the potential destructive power of conservation and, as Muñoz Viñas (2005, 188–90) put it, introduces a sense of 'relativity' to conservation.

Condition

Even the apparently straightforward 'condition' of material fabric reveals complexity when looked at more closely. All material things will go through changes during their existence, but deciding what kind of change constitutes damage (or undesirable change) may become subjective unless the values attached to this judgement are thoroughly clarified (Ashley-Smith 2009; Clavir 2009, 140–4). For example, while some may look at signs of use as poor condition, others may interpret them as added value: they may provide information about the past or give the material the aged aspect of antiquities. In a similar way to minimum conservation, the conclusions will depend on who is conducting the assessments, how they are being calibrated, why and where they are taking place and for what the material will be used.

All the concepts discussed above, and some others too, are to some degree related to expectations of 'truth' or 'neutrality'. These expectations may stem from Viollet-le-Duc's attempts to reveal what material was meant to be (its 'true form') (Viollet-le-Duc 1996 [1854], 314), even if this form had never existed. But they may also arise from Ruskin's contrasting willingness to allow material to age and decay (Ruskin 1996 [1849]). They may have even been intensified by Brandi's understanding of the aim of conservation as being 'to re-establish the potential oneness of the work of art, as long as this is possible without committing artistic or historical forgery, and without erasing every trace of the passage through time of the work of art' (Brandi 2005 [1963], 50).

More crucially, these concepts and principles may also stem from the belief that conservation, because it is based on scientific methods, should always achieve truth (Muñoz Viñas 2005, 89–90). It is illogical, however, to believe that the conservation process may reveal, recover or enhance truth embodied in the materiality of objects, yet not interfere with it. As Avrami et al. (2000, 8) elaborate below, the mere fact that something has been considered worthy of becoming part of a collection already affects how it is valued.

> Conservation (narrowly defined) has commonly been viewed as that which follows the act of heritage designation – that is, a technical response after a place or object has already been recognized as having value. The underlying belief has been that preservation treatment should not, and would not, change the meaning of the heritage object, yet the traditional practice of conserving – of preserving the physical fabric of a heritage object – does in fact actively interpret and valorize the object. Every conservation decision – how to clean an object, how to reinforce a structure, what materials to use, and so on – affects how that object or place will be perceived, understood and used, and thus transmitted to the future. Despite such postulated principles as minimum intervention, reversibility, and authenticity, a decision to undertake a certain conservation intervention gives priority to a certain meaning or set of values. (Avrami et al. 2000, 8)

Conservation actions (or the deliberate absence thereof) may help to put forward preferences, opinions or even political statements. That is, conservation actions have the power to *materialise* and communicate choices, and may be influenced by socio-political contexts that go far beyond those of the museum.

Visibility and neutrality

In general terms, conservators did not always have channels to voice their opinions and reach decision makers until the end of the twentieth century. Despite their long and demanding training, and the important roles they played within the cultural heritage sector, it was common until then for conservators to operate in relative professional invisibility (Pye 2001, 155; Brooks 2008; Jones and Holden 2008; Koutromanou 2017).

It takes a lot of orchestrated effort to break out of old hierarchical patterns, especially for professionals who carry out actions that need to be *imperceptible* in order to be considered effective (Brooks 2008). Even if unwittingly, some might by association confuse 'imperceptible actions' with 'lack of agency'. Moreover, not very long ago, it was mainly up to other professionals – curators, anthropologists, archaeologists, historians, scientists or even politicians – to make final decisions on how the material fabric of objects should look, what values they should highlight and how these artefacts should be used. Although this relative distance from final decisions did not redeem conservators from responsibility, it may well be one of the reasons they started to acquire, and at times even to believe in, an 'aura of neutrality'. Some might also argue that the need to be perceived as 'professionally impartial' may have added to this.

Other factors to be considered include the relatively low esteem associated with the artistic and craftsmanship roots of conservation, as opposed to disciplines perceived as being more intellectual or scientific. As well as the relatively lowly positions which conservators have traditionally enjoyed in museum hierarchies, they have suffered from insufficient professional mobility, low salaries (Keene 1996, 113; Brooks 2008, 1137; Aitchison 2013, 8) and a perceived need to communicate more effectively (Henderson 2001; Schadla-Hall 2001; Jones 2002; Brooks 2008, 1136; Frame 2008, 1149; Jones and Holden 2008, 16; Koutromanou 2017).

Notions of neutrality, however, are widely contested – especially in political realms. The political philosopher Noriaki Iwasa (2010), for example, uses established philosophical work to demonstrate that it is almost impossible to achieve political neutrality; to be truly neutral one would need neutral grounds to operate on (Iwasa 2010, 155). Following Iwasa's (2010, 150–1) elaboration, whenever a conflict occurs one is confronted with the options of engaging or not engaging with different aspects of this conflict, and with different needs of the parties involved in the conflict, directly or indirectly. Failing to engage with either party may entail a kind of neutrality, but is likely to benefit the stronger. Intervening equally with both parties usually has the same effect: that is, the stronger will probably profit more from the help than the weaker. Being 'neutral' in relation to cultural material is an equally frustrating struggle. In addition, as Sloggett points out:

> It is impossible for a conservator to be 'detached' or 'impartial' when dealing with cultural material. Detachment may be possible with the 'material' part of the descriptor, but the 'cultural' prefix requires very clear identification of prejudices, frameworks, allegiances and preferred outcomes. (Sloggett 2009, 178)

In short, by displaying a particular object, by preserving, revealing, enhancing, recovering, interpreting or even ignoring a given aspect of this object, museum professionals make choices that carry messages from the context of these decisions. More crucially, these decisions may not only affect and politically charge the way in which the past is perceived, but also influence what people do, feel and think in the present.

Conservation might perhaps be neutral if conservators were able to operate in neutral frameworks. But this is hardly the case in a context where the removal of specimens from less powerful countries or cultures continued to be acceptable, especially in Western countries, until not very long ago. As already mentioned, the restitution debate is only recently coming higher up on the museum agenda, forcing museum directors, for example, to discuss it more openly (Hunt et al. 2018; Hunt 2019). Claiming neutrality could perhaps be acceptable if conservation decision-making processes were not informed by socio-political contexts, or if these decisions did not affect socio-political contexts in which objects and the people associated with them circulate. For here it suffices to say that acknowledging the potential impact of conservation, and consequently its lack of neutrality, makes it even more crucial to ensure conservation decision-making processes are open, democratic, well informed and engaged with different interest groups.

Transforming and being transformed

I have already acknowledged the complexity of collaborative processes and indicated their geographic spread among the conservation discipline – especially the sub-disciplines that deal directly with collections formed as a consequence of colonial power, such as those originating from Indigenous nations of various parts of the world. Regardless of some underlying and unspoken reasons for setting up participatory projects (no one wishes to be labelled as old-fashioned, for example, nor to be associated with colonial or non-democratic practices) and of the fact that Indigenous involvement does not necessarily entail collaboration (McMullen 2008, 55; Boast 2011), consultations, collaborations and partnerships with originators of artefacts and/or their descendants have been conducted extensively during the last 30 years. These processes need careful preparation, however. Not only may it be difficult to deal with the views and interests of many different groups and still come up with a consensus that satisfies everyone: it may also be challenging to make sure that the voices of everyone with an interest in the conservation of a particular object are represented. More crucially, it may be difficult to make sure that these voices and opinions are truly considered before decisions are taken. Below we explore Paulo Freire's dialogical method to discuss how to approach these processes, as well as their possible impacts.

Since it was published, Freire's *Pedagogy of the Oppressed* (1996 [1970]) has been used as a platform to implement more engaging and democratic practices in a range of education sub-disciplines. However, the work has also impacted other disciplines. It provided, for example, the foundations for Participatory Action Research (PAR) theories which have been applied to a diversity of contexts (Gustavsen 2001; Brydon-Miller et al. 2003). Freire's text focuses on the concept of *conscientização*, translated as *conscientisation* (also known as 'dialogical method') – an elaboration on how critical reflection can play essential roles in individual and social changes (McIntyre 2008, 3). Freire argued for an ethical responsibility to provide people with tools to reveal and understand situations of oppression, in order to enable them to create the means to act towards change. The method does not simply strive to provide the means to ask people what they think, however. It also seeks to empower them to formulate their own opinions through reflection and dialogue, and to transform all who are involved in the process. 'Dialogue', in short, is seen as an essential tool for empowerment.

Although not always explicitly, Freire's thinking has influenced museum anthropology and theoretical articulations around the possible beneficial impacts of museum practices on less privileged sectors of societies (Ames 2006), heritage language education (Gounari 2014), visual and digital participatory research (Gubrium et al. 2015) and critical heritage studies (Harrison 2010; Harrison and Hughes 2010), among others. His thinking also shows synergies with conservation collaborative projects (Johnson et al. 2005; Wharton 2008; 2012; Pouliot et al. 2017; Williams 2017), as well as established conservation-teaching methodologies (Henderson 2016; Pearlstein 2016).

Freire's work is devoted to those in society who have no power or cannot effectively influence decision-making processes – groups that work for the benefit of others and as defined by others (Freire 1996 [1970], 55). This is entrenched in a system of domination, in which education is a powerful instrument. Instead of preparing people to transform the reality of oppression, Freire believes that this system stimulates groups to adapt to the world around them (Freire 1996 [1970], 59). In education terms it consists of teachers *educating* and students passively *being educated* – the former are the thinkers and the latter the object of such 'thinking'. Educators choose the content with which the educated are *filled* (Freire 2001 [1998], 45). Educators are the *subject* and the educated the *object*, creating what Freire named 'banking education' (Freire 1996 [1970], 52–9) – a process in which one end deposits knowledge and the other end receives it, leaving no space for critical or creative thinking. Similar relationships have often been seen in museums, for example, in relation to how collections have been interpreted and controlled (Haas 1996; Ames 1992; 1994; Clifford 2004; Atalay 2006).

One of the effects of this 'banking system' is that the educated will often tend to internalise the ideas of others, notably of those in power or closer to decision-making (Freire 1996 [1970], 29). The lack of dialogue and critical thinking generates what Freire calls a 'culture of silence'. This tends to repeat itself ad infinitum, as those who internalise the perceptions and interests of others become fearful of thinking differently. In the contemporary context we could also draw a link to the damaging role that 'fake news' may play in this picture; the lack of training in critical thinking generates apathetic acceptance of information, even when this is obviously manipulated. Edward Said (2003 [1978]) famously showed that domination does not always have to rely on explicitly violent methods to succeed. For example, he explains the roles that 'knowledge' plays in the success of British imperial dominance, emphasising that 'knowing' defines dominance:

Knowledge means rising above immediacy, beyond self, into the foreign and distant. The object of such knowledge is inherently vulnerable to scrutiny; this object is a 'fact' which, if it develops, changes, or otherwise transforms itself in the way that civilizations frequently do, nevertheless is fundamentally, even ontologically stable. To have such knowledge of such a thing is to dominate it, to have authority over it. (Said 2003 [1978], 32)

It is also pertinent to note that the European museum model implemented in the nineteenth century was conceived to play a public role on behalf of the state and dominant systems of knowledge. Through the organisation, interpretation and presentation of their collections, these institutions validated and disseminated views from the dominant groups (Hooper-Greenhill 2000, 151). This model is still prevalent in many institutions today. Freire's (1972 [1970], 16–29) elaborations on cultures of silence are pertinent here, especially in relation to how 'silence' is generated and perpetuated by lack of dialogue and reflection. For example, perhaps the lack of representation of conservators in higher instances of decision-making in museums and heritage institutions has persisted because of a work culture based for a long time on invisibility and relative silence. Among many other effects, this has allowed conservation concerns to be used to justify or legitimise a number of actions that may have had little to do with conservation. Such concerns include access to objects, restrictions on how they can be used, loans or even repatriation disputes.

Action and reflection

The dialogical method proposed by Freire (1996 [1970], 76) is grounded in respect for people's knowledge and for their perceptions of the world. The process starts by an examination of the present context and its concrete situations, and should reflect the aspirations of all groups involved. There is little point in carrying out collaborative projects if they are not grounded in willingness to reassess established positions and opinions. This may apply to requests revealed during collaborations, but also to the way in which the projects themselves are conducted. Regardless of the topic under discussion, all the participants in a collaboration that aims to be a democratic partnership should carefully consider their own motivations for participation. In practice, however, these processes may not always be straightforward, as not all involved may be prepared for it, or even committed to share a common goal. In order to prevent conflicts from undermining engagement and knowledge exchange, it would therefore be advisable to start partnerships by discussing what each group expects to get out of the process. This would allow participants to adjust their expectations (or make them more realistic) according to the expectations of other participants.

Another challenge entails the creation of an environment in which people are able to think critically and creatively, and in which all participants act as both *subject* and *object* of inquiries (Brydon-Miller et al. 2003, 14). The de-hierarchisation of 'knowledge' or 'expertise' allows space for further reflection on everyone's ability to understand and address the issues under discussion. Nevertheless, the process starts with the identification and inclusion of representatives from different groups of knowledge holders. Besides affecting the outcome of the dialogues, these choices may also reflect back on the represented groups themselves. McMullen (2008, 70), a curator at the NMAI, has discussed the impact of individuals chosen by a museum to participate in such processes and highlighted difficulties that may be brought about when the choices happen in contexts where friction already exists – or where, as in the examples she uses, tribes may seek some kind of governmental acknowledgement.

> Additionally, individuals chosen by the museum – and potentially the lineages or tribal factions that they represent – may gain significant validation as cultural authorities based on their selection. Where intra- and intertribal frictions exist, as in situations in southeastern New England where groups lacking federal acknowledgment as 'tribes' vie with those who have achieved that status to be heard and involved, being asked to the museum table is a significant validation. (McMullen 2008, 70)

Freire (1996 [1970], 77) warns against the danger of presenting preconceived views during collaborations. This may happen when, for example, conservators (or other museum professionals) participate in international projects and impose guidelines from their own countries or institutions. It may also occur when these professionals expect all project partners to have the same priorities, follow the same procedures or use the same material resources that they would. A more productive alternative here would be to discuss different perceptions, objectives and resources available until all points defining the collaboration are carefully considered. Clearly, in order to do that, one has to be able to communicate effectively. A lot of progress has been made in that respect in the last decade, as a result of orchestrated efforts to improve conservators' communication skills and conservation public outreach (Jones 2002; Calver 2006; Frame 2008; Ternisien 2009; Drago 2011; McClure 2013; Watts et al. 2013; Williams 2013; Hykin et al. 2019).

Effective communication includes finely tuned listening. Naturally, this is even more fundamental for communication between groups from different cultural backgrounds – in such circumstances understanding what things really mean may not be entirely straightforward. This corresponds to Kaminitz's observations (Kaminitz et al. 2009), based on her extensive experience at the NMAI:

> Most Western cultures have very different styles of approaching the handing down of cultural knowledge when compared to those of indigenous communities where particular knowledge is often restricted to specific individuals. Learning methods are also different. Asking questions directly and outright is often considered impolite; rather, students learn by watching and listening carefully. (Kaminitz et al. 2009, 202)

Clavir elaborates on how the use of vocabulary, for example, is not always definitive, as the assumed meanings of words may be misleading and need to be related to their contexts (Clavir 2002, 211). She quotes Howard Grant (from the Musqueam First Nation of Canada) to show that effective communication does not end in what is being said, but is rather a process that needs to be nurtured.

> Stronger communication. I would say to any museum or to any institute that as part of the curriculum they should visit First Nations communities, to talk, as you are doing right now … and to maintain posts, linkages, in respect to communicating with the public that someone owns the art pieces. Because too often we make academic decisions that are very logical and very real and albeit the right one, but people get offended. Almost all the right decisions are so debatable and so controversial, you know? And my thoughts are, this should have been done twenty years ago and not for a thesis paper but just general care of the object. (Howard Grant, quoted in Clavir 2002, 212)

Freire talks of human beings as creatures of action and reflection, and of animals as creatures of pure activity. Action unaccompanied by reflection would probably effect what he calls 'activism'. That is, by acting without reflecting conservators would probably merely follow models that have been perceived as desirable, without really examining their meanings or implications. On the other hand, if there is an excess of discussion but no action, the process could fall into the category of 'verbalism' (1996 [1970], 68). An example of verbalism in the contemporary museum could be illustrated by a project that claims to engage with different interest groups, but does not allow appropriate time or conditions for dialogue to develop and for its effects to be felt. In these instances participation only happens 'in theory' or 'on paper'. The basic premise here is that for a process of inquiry to become truly collaborative all participants must be encouraged to inquire into the nature of the problems in question, and be given opportunities to understand causes and implications for different contexts.

As per McIntyre (2008, 1–6), this may be achieved through a recursive and continuous process of exploration, knowledge construction, reflection and action. Here it is worth repeating that the conservation process also never ends, deterioration agents never cease to change and values associated with cultural material never cease to evolve. As in the model suggested by McIntyre, the conservation process of inquiry includes questioning particular issues, reflecting upon and investigating them, developing action plans and implementing, refining and reassessing these plans. The cycle can be resumed at any of these stages, whenever necessary. But all of these stages depend on the relationships between practice and theory, and may generate new knowledge through reflection.

This collaborative and engaged model emphasises the need for constant evaluation of, and reflection upon, what is being thought and done. It also emphasises that *all* different groups involved in the inquiry engage in *all* stages of the process, not only 'experts' and not only in the stages that the 'experts' have defined. Discrepancies may occur even between groups from the same discipline or institution. But people build trust through dialogue, action and reflection – and the more trust they build, the more productive the discussions will become.

Finally, reflective processes focus on transformation. When people transform the world with their work or the theory and policies generated by their work, they are also transformed themselves (Freire 1996 [1970], 106). This is especially significant for conservation, as conservators act in the crossroads of many disciplines and may find themselves in strategic positions to trigger dialogues affecting not only conservation actions but also relationships of power inside and outside the museum. The aim should always be to work *with* others, not only *for* others.

Conclusions

The rise of the postcolonial world challenges the authority that museums and heritage institutions hold to represent the past of others. Ultimately it means decision-making about material held by these institutions ought to be shared with larger and more diverse groups of people. Accordingly, the discipline of conservation has incorporated a more social orientation, rather than remaining purely technical and scientific. The conservation process is becoming increasingly more inclusive and focused on the people related to the material under conservation, rather than solely on the material itself. This could not be more appropriate, as conservation has the power to materialise, consolidate and communicate specific views of history, tastes and opinions. Conservation actions may vary according to the groups involved in decision-making, the character of the input, the political context in which they operate and the overall agenda of the professional and non-professional groups involved. Working in these contexts requires innovative methods of engagement. It is no longer enough to assume neutrality when confronted with a changing global landscape – particularly in terms of social identities, political and cultural values in contemporary circumstances.

As proposed by Freire, in order to transform something one has to be transformed as well. This means that when conservators engage with other knowledge holders, they should be ready to go through a process of reflective transformation. Not only does this affect the conservation process and the conserved object. It may also influence conservation theory and how people related to the process or the object perceive themselves: by acting and reflecting, conservators can generate new theory through practice. The consistent problematisation of knowledge exchange, practical skills and their impacts helps the effective creation of independent knowledge. It also strengthens knowledge that can be applied to specific problems or contexts and that can, in turn, reflect back on the discipline, its practitioners and all other groups involved.

Notes

1. Concepts such as 'West' or 'Western' are defined here by socio-political and economic conditions rather than by geographical locations. They usually refer to powerful nations in Western Europe and the United States of America.
2. For ease of communication, in this chapter the word 'object' will be used to refer to anthropological, archaeological and artistic works/pieces without distinction.

References

Agnew, Neville, Deacon, Janette, Hall, Nicholas, Little, Terry, Sullivan, Sharon and Taçon, Paul. 2015. *Rock Art: A cultural treasure at risk*. Los Angeles, CA: Getty Conservation Institute. Accessed 23 September 2020. http://www.getty.edu/conservation/publications_resources/pdf_publications/rock_art_cultural.html.

Aitchison, Kenneth. 2013. *Conservation Labour Market Intelligence 2012–2013*. London: ICON. Accessed 24 September 2018. http://icon.org.uk/system/files/documents/conservation_labour_market_intelligence_2012-2013.pdf .

Ames, Michael M. 1992. *Cannibal Tours and Glass Boxes: The anthropology of museums*. Vancouver: UBC Press.

Ames, Michael M. 1994. 'The Politics of Difference: Other voices in a not yet post-colonial world', *Museum Anthropology* 18 (3): 9–17.

Ames, Michael M. 2006. 'Counterfeit Museology', *Museum Management and Curatorship* 21: 171–86.

Appelbaum, Barbara. 2007. *Conservation Treatment Methodology*. Oxford: Butterworth-Heinemann.

Ashley-Smith, Jonathan. 2009. 'The Basis of Conservation Ethics'. In *Conservation: Principles, dilemmas and uncomfortable truths*, edited by A. Richmond and A. Bracker, 6–24. Oxford: Butterworth-Heinemann, in association with the Victoria and Albert Museum.

Atalay, Sonya. 2006. 'Indigenous Archaeology as Decolonizing Practice', *The American Indian Quarterly* 30 (3 and 4): 280–310.

Avrami, Erica. 2009. 'Heritage, Values, and Sustainability'. In *Conservation: Principles, dilemmas and uncomfortable truths*, edited by A. Richmond and A. Bracker, 177–83. Oxford: Butterworth-Heinemann in association with the Victoria and Albert Museum.

Avrami, Erica, Mason, Randall and de la Torre, Marta. 2000. *Values and Heritage Conservation. Research Report*. Los Angeles, CA: Getty Conservation Institute. Accessed 23 September 2020. https://www.getty.edu/conservation/publications_resources/pdf_publications/pdf/value-srpt.pdf.

Bass, Walter. 1989. 'Art and the Unintended', *British Journal of Aesthetics* 29: 147–53.

Bernstein, Bruce. 1992. 'Collaborative Strategies for the Preservation of North American Indian Material Culture', *Journal of the American Institute for Conservation* (31): 23–9.

Boast, Robin. 2011. 'Neocolonial Collaboration: Museum as contact zones revisited', *Museum Anthropology* 34 (1): 56–70.

Brandi, Cesare. 1963. *Teoria del Restauro*. Rome: Nardini Editore.

Brandi, Cesare. 2005 [1963]. 'Theory of Restoration'. In *Theory of Restoration*, edited by G. Basile. Florence: Nardini Editore.

Brooks, Mary M. 2008. 'Talking to Ourselves. Why do conservators find it so hard to convince others of the significance of conservation?' In *Diversity in Heritage Conservation: Tradition, innovation and participation – Preprints of the ICOM-CC 15th Triennial Conference*, edited by J. Bridgland, 1135–40.

Brydon-Miller, Mary, Greenwood, Davydd and Maguire, Patricia. 2003. 'Why Action Research?' *Action Research* 1 (1): 9–28. Accessed 20 June 2017. http://arj.sagepub.com/content/1/1/9.

Calver, Andrew. 2006. 'Yes, We Can Help You Do That: Communicating a positive conservation message'. In *ICOM-CC Newsletter of ICOM-CC Taskforce on Public Engagement in Conservation*. Accessed 5 July 2019. http://www.icom-cc.org/54/document/newsletter-2006-1-july-2006/?action=Site_Downloads_Downloadfile&id=217.

Caple, Chris. 2000. *Conservation Skills: Judgement, method and decision making*. London; New York: Routledge.

Chakrabarty, Dipesh. 1998. 'Minority Histories, Subaltern Pasts', *Postcolonial Studies* 1 (1): 15–29.

Chitty, Gill, ed. 2017. *Heritage, Conservation and Communities: Engagement, participation and capacity building*. London; New York: Routledge.

Clavir, Miriam. 1998. 'The Social and Historic Construction of Professional Values in Conservation', *Studies in Conservation* 43 (1): 1–8.

Clavir, Miriam. 2002. *Preserving What is Valued: Museums, conservation, and First Nations*. Vancouver; Toronto: UBC Press.

Clavir, Miriam. 2009. 'Conservation and Cultural Significance'. In *Conservation: Principles, dilemmas and uncomfortable truths*, edited by A. Richmond and A. Bracker, 139–49 Oxford: Butterworth-Heinemann, in association with the Victoria and Albert Museum.

Clifford, James. 1999. 'Museums as Contact Zones'. In *Representing the Nation: A reader. Histories, heritage and museums*, edited by D. Boswell and J.D. Evans, 435–57. London; New York: Routledge.

Clifford, James. 2004. 'Looking Several Ways: Anthropology and native heritage in Alaska', *Current Anthropology* 45 (1): 5–30.

Conti, Alessandro. 2007 [1988]. *A History of the Restoration and Conservation of Works of Art*. Translated by Helen Glanville. Amsterdam: Elsevier.

Deisser, Anne-Marie. 2007. *Investigating Partnership Between Local and Institutional Communities for the Preventive Conservation of Cultural Heritage in East Africa*. PhD thesis, unpublished. Southampton: University of Southampton.

Deisser, Anne-Marie. 2008. 'Community Management of Cultural Heritage at Ankober, Ethiopia: A partnership in preventive conservation'. In *Diversity in Heritage Conservation: Tradition, innovation and participation – Preprints of the ICOM-CC 15th Triennial Conference*, edited by J. Bridgland, Vol. 2, 1029–34.

de la Torre, Marta, ed. 2002. *Assessing the Values of Cultural Heritage. Research Report*. Los Angeles, CA: Getty Conservation Institute.

Delgado Vieira, Ana Carolina, Xavier Cury, Marília and Peters, Renata F. 2017. 'Saving the Present in Brazil: Perspectives from collaborations with indigenous museums'. In *ICOM-CC 18th Triennial Conference Preprints, Copenhagen, 4–8 September 2017*, edited by J. Bridgland, art. 1201. Paris: International Council of Museums.

Drago, Amy. 2011. '"I feel included": The Conservation in Focus exhibition at the British Museum', *Journal of the Institute of Conservation* 34 (1): 28–38.

Dykstra, Steven W. 1996. 'The Artist's Intentions and the Intentional Fallacy in Fine Arts Conservation', *Journal of the American Institute for Conservation* 35 (3): 197–218.

Eastop, Dinah and Brooks, Mary M., eds. 2011. *Changing Views of Textile Conservation*. Readings in Conservation Series. Los Angeles, CA: Getty Conservation Institute.

Fanon, Frantz. 1963 [1961]. *The Wretched of the Earth*. Translated from French by Constance Farrington. [Original title *Les damnés de la terre*]. New York: Grove Press.

Feagin, Susan L. 1982. 'On Defining and Interpreting Art Intentionalistically', *British Journal of Aesthetics* 22: 65–77.

Frame, Kate. 2008. 'Communicating Conservation at the Historic Royal Palaces'. In *Diversity in Heritage Conservation: Tradition, innovation and participation – Preprints of the ICOM-CC 15th Triennial Conference*, edited by J. Bridgland, 1147–53.

Freire, Paulo. 1972 [1970]. *Cultural Action for Freedom*. London: Penguin Books.

Freire, Paulo. 1996 [1970]. *Pedagogy of the Oppressed*. Translated by Myra Bergman Ramos. London: Penguin Books.

Freire, Paulo. 2001 [1998]. *Pedagogy of Freedom: Ethics, democracy, and civic courage*. Lanham, MD: Rowman & Littlefield.

Gordon, Cesar and Silva, Fabíola A. 2005. '*Objetos vivos: a curadoria da coleção etnográfica Xikrin-Kayapó no Museum de Arqueologia e Etnologia – MAE/USP'*, *Estudos Históricos* 36: 93–110. Accessed 21 September 2020. http://bibliotecadigital.fgv.br/ojs/index.php/reh/issue/view/303.

Gordon, Rebecca and Hermens, Erma. 2013. 'The Artist's Intent in Flux', *CeROArt*. Accessed 21 September 2020. https://journals.openedition.org/ceroart/3527.

Gosden, Chris and Marshall, Yvonne. 1999. 'The Cultural Biography of Objects', *World Archaeology* 31 (20): 169–78.

Gounari, Panayota. 2014. 'Rethinking Heritage Language in a Critical Pedagogy Framework'. In *Rethinking Heritage Education*, edited by P. Trifonas and T. Aravossitas, 254–68. Cambridge: Cambridge University Press.

Gubrium, Aline, Harper, Krista and Otañez, Marty, eds. 2015. *Participatory Visual and Digital Research in Action*. Walnut Creek, CA: Left Coast Press.

Gustavsen, Bjørn. 2001. 'Theory and Practice: The mediating discourse'. In *Handbook of Action Research: Participatory inquiry and practice*, edited by Peter Reason and Hilary Bradbury, 18–26. London: Sage.

Haas, Jonathan. 1996. 'Power, Objects, and a Voice for Anthropology', *Current Anthropology* 37, supplement: 1–22.

Harrison, Rodney. 2010. 'Heritage as Social Action'. In *Understanding Heritage in Practice*, edited by S. West, 240–76. Manchester: Manchester University Press.

Harrison, Rodney and Hughes, Lotte. 2010. 'Heritage, Colonialism and Postcolonialism'. In *Understanding the Politics of Heritage*, edited by R. Harrison, 234–69. Manchester: Manchester University Press.

Heald, Susan. 1997. 'Compensation/Restoration of a Tuscarora Beaded Cloth with Tuscarora Beadworkers', *Textile Specialty Group Postprints. American Institute for Conservation 25th Annual Meeting, San Diego*, 35–8. Washington, DC: AIC.

Henderson, Jane. 2001. 'New Skills, New Influence'. In *Past Practice – Future Prospects*, edited by A. Oddy and S. Smith, 103–8. British Museum Occasional Paper 145. London: British Museum Press.

Henderson, Jane. 2016. 'University Teaching in the Development of Conservation Professionals', *Journal of the Institute of Conservation* 39 (2): 98–109.

Hooper-Greenhill, Eilean. 2000. *Museums and the Interpretation of Visual Culture*. London; New York: Routledge.

Hornbeck, Stephanie E. and Moffett, Dana L. 2016. 'Altered Surfaces, Taking the Long View: Applications of ethnographic conservation practices to the conservation of contemporary art', *Studies in Conservation* 61 (Iss. Supp. 2): 84–90.

Howe, Craig. 2005. 'The Morality of Exhibiting Indians'. In *Embedding Ethics: Shifting boundaries of the anthropological profession*, edited by Lynn Meskell and Peter Pels, 219–37. Oxford; New York: Berg.

Hunt, Tristram. 2019. 'Should Museums Return Their Colonial Artefacts?' *Guardian*, 29 June 2019. Accessed 5 July 2019. https://www.theguardian.com/culture/2019/jun/29/should-museums-return-their-colonial-artefacts.

Hunt, Tristram, Hartmut, Dorgerloh and Thomas, Nicholas. 2018. 'Restitution Report: museum directors respond'. *The Art Newspaper*. Accessed 5 July 2019. https://www.theartnewspaper.com/comment/restitution-report-museums-directors-respond.

Hykin, Abigail, Siegal, Matthew and Uyeda, Tanya. 2019. 'Conservation in Action: Object treatment as public programming'. In *What is the Essence of Conservation?*, edited by François Mairesse and Renata F. Peters, 70–5. Paris: ICOM. Accessed 21 September 2020. http://network.icom.museum/fileadmin/user_upload/minisites/icofom/images/Icofom-EssenceofConservation-FINAL.pdf?fbclid=IwAR0NUhq52SGOSvhHZXDnkevvI79i1QYaZzBABgSstvW41y6dHviEBhdc5rI.

Iwasa, Noriaki. 2010. 'The Impossibility of Political Neutrality', *Croatian Journal of Philosophy* X (29): 148–55.

Johnson, Jessica, Heald, Susan, McHugh, Kelly, Brown, Elizabeth and Kaminitz, Marian. 2005. 'Practical Aspects of Consultation with Communities', *Journal of the American Institute for Conservation* 44 (3): 203–15.

Jokilehto, Jukka. 2009. 'Conservation Principles in the International Context'. In *Conservation: Principles, dilemmas and uncomfortable truths*, edited by A. Richmond and A. Bracker, 73–83. Oxford: Butterworth-Heinemann, in association with the Victoria and Albert Museum.

Jones, Helen. 2002. 'The Importance of Being Less Earnest: Communicating conservation', *V&A Conservation Journal* 41. Accessed 5 July 2019. http://www.vam.ac.uk/content/journals/conservation-journal/issue-41/the-importance-of-being-less-earnest-communicating-conservation/.

Jones, Samuel and Holden, John. 2008. *It's a Material World: Caring for the public realm*. London: Demos.

Kaminitz, Marian, Mogel, Barbara S., Cranmer, Barb, Johnson, Jessica, Cranmer, Kevin and Hill, Thomas V. 2008. 'Renewal of a Kwakwaka'wakw Hamsamł Mask: Community direction and collaboration for the treatment of cultural heritage at the National Museum of the American Indian – A panel presentation'. In *Proceedings of Symposium 2007 Preserving Aboriginal Heritage: Technical and traditional approaches, Ottawa, Canada, September 24–28, 2007*, edited by Carole Dignard, Kate Helwig, Janet Mason, Kathy Nanowin and Thomas Stone, 75–88. Ottawa: Canadian Conservation Institute, 75–88.

Kaminitz, Marian and West Jr., Rick, with contributions from Enote, Jim, Quam, Curtis and Yatsattie, Eileen. 2009. 'Conservation, Access and Use in a Museum of Living Cultures'. In *Conservation: Principles, dilemmas and uncomfortable truths*, edited by A. Richmond and A. Bracker, 197–209. Oxford: Butterworth-Heinemann, in association with the Victoria and Albert Museum.

Keene, Susanne. 1996. *Managing Conservation in Museums*. Oxford: Butterworth-Heinemann and The Science Museum.

Kopytoff, Igor. 1986. 'The Cultural Biography of Things: Commodization as a process'. In *The Social Life of Things: Commodities in cultural perspective*, edited by Arjun Appadurai, 64–91. Cambridge: Cambridge University Press.

Koutromanou, Danai. 2017. 'Developing Evaluation Strategies for Engagement Projects in Museum Conservation'. In *Heritage, Conservation and Community: Engagement, participation and capacity building*, edited by Gill Chitty. London; New York: Routledge.

Livingston, Paisley. 2007 [2005]. *Art and Intention: A philosophical study*. New York; Oxford: Clarendon Press.

McClure, Ian. 2013. 'Making Exhibitions of Ourselves'. In *The Public Face of Conservation*, edited by E. Williams, 163–9. London: Archetype.

McHugh, Kelly and Gunnison, Anne. 2016. 'Finding Common Ground and Inherent Differences: Artist and community engagement in cultural material and contemporary art conservation', *Studies in Conservation* 61 (Iss. Supp. 2): 126–9.

McIntyre, Alice. 2008. *Participatory Action Research*. London: Sage.

McMullen, Ann. 2008. 'The Currency of Consultation and Collaboration', *Museum Anthropology Review* 2 (2): 54–87.

Mason, Randall. 2002. 'Assessing Values in Conservation Planning: Methodological issues and choices'. In *Assessing the Values of Cultural Heritage. Research Report*, edited by M. de la Torre, 5–30. Los Angeles, CA: Getty Conservation Institute.

Mele, Alfred R. and Livingston, Paisley. 1992. 'Intentions and Interpretations', *MLN* 107 (5): 931–49.

Muñoz Viñas, Salvador. 2005. *Contemporary Theory of Conservation*. Oxford: Elsevier Butterworth-Heinemann.

Murray Pease Committee. 1964. 'The Murray Pease Report', *Studies in Conservation* 9 (3): 116–21.

Oddy, Andrew. 1999. 'Does Reversibility Exist in Conservation?' In *Reversibility – Does it exist?*, edited by Andrew Oddy and Sara Carroll, 1–6. British Museum Occasional Paper 135. London: British Museum Press.

Oddy, Andrew and Carroll, Sara, eds. 1999. *Reversibility – Does it exist?* British Museum Occasional Paper 135. London: British Museum Press.

Owczarek, Nina, Gleeson, Molly and Grant, Lynn A. 2017. *Engaging Conservation: Collaboration across disciplines*. London: Archetype.

Pearlstein, Ellen. 2016. 'Conserving Ourselves: Embedding significance into conservation decision-making in graduate education', *Studies in Conservation* 62 (8): 435–44.

Peters, Renata. 2008. 'The Brave New World of Conservation'. In *Diversity in Heritage Conservation: Tradition, innovation and participation – Preprints of the ICOM-CC 15th Triennial Conference*, edited by J. Bridgland, Vol.1, 185–90. New Delhi: Allied Publishers.

Peters, Renata. 2016. 'The Parallel Paths of Conservation of Contemporary Art and Indigenous Collections', *Studies in Conservation* 61 (Iss. Supp. 2): 183–7.

Peters, Renata, Salomon, Frank, González, Rosa and González, Rosalía. 2008. 'Traditional Use and Scholarly Investigation: A collaborative project to conserve the Khipu of San Cristóbal de Rapaz'. In *Proceedings of Symposium 2007 Preserving Aboriginal Heritage: Technical and traditional approaches, Ottawa, Canada, September 24–28, 2007*, edited by Carole Dignard, Kate Helwig, Janet Mason, Kathy Nanowin and Thomas Stone, 95–100. Ottawa: Canadian Conservation Institute.

Pye, Elizabeth. 2001. *Caring for the Past: Issues in conservation for archaeology and museums*. London: James & James.

Pouliot, Bruno, Rofkar, Teri, Bright, Lea and Pack, Crista. 2017. 'Learning From an "Old One": A Tlinglit basket makes its journey home'. In *Engaging Conservation: Collaboration across disciplines*, edited by Nina Owczarek, Molly Gleeson and Lynn A. Grant, 115–21. London: Archetype.

Ternisien, Virginie. 2009. 'Conservation in Action: Welcome to the "CSI" Lab', *E-conservation Magazine* 12: 25–35. Accessed 5 July 2019. https://documents.pub/document/e-conservation-magazine-12.html.

Ruskin, John. 1996 [1849]. 'The Lamp of Memory, II'. In *Historical and Philosophical Issues in the Conservation of Cultural Heritage*, edited by Nicholas Stanley Price, M. Kirby Talley Jr. and Alessandra Melucco Vaccaro, 322–3. Los Angeles, CA: Getty Conservation Institute.

Russell, Roslyn and Winkworth, Kylie. 2009. *Significance: A guide to assessing the significance of collections* [2nd ed.]. Collections Council of Australia. Accessed 25 March 2018. http://www.environment.gov.au/heritage/publications/significance2-0/pubs/significance20.pdf.

Said, Edward. 2003 [1978]. *Orientalism*. London: Penguin. First published by Routledge & Kegan Paul.

Salomon, Frank and Peters, Renata. 2009. 'Governance and Conservation of the Rapaz Khipu Patrimony'. In *Intangible Heritage Embodied*, edited by Helaine Silverman and D. Fairchild Ruggles, 101–25. Frankfurt; New York: Springer Verlag.

Sarr, Felwine and Savoy, Bénédicte. 2018. 'The Restitution of African Cultural Heritage. Toward a new relational ethics'. In *Restitution Report 2018*. Accessed 10 April 2019. http://restitutionreport2018.com/sarr_savoy_en.pdf.

Schadla-Hall, Tim. 2001. 'Death by a Thousand Cuts? Conservation in museums', *Museum Archaeologists' News* 33: 6–11.

Seip, Lisa P. 1999. 'Transformations of Meanings: The life history of a Nuxalk mask', *World Archaeology* 31 (2): 272–87.

Shih, Jian-Pai (also known as Hsin-Hui Hsu). 2019. 'Museality, Authenticity and Religious Reality: A Buddhist view on the conservation and exhibition of Buddhist objects'. In *What is the Essence of Conservation?*, edited by François Mairesse and Renata F. Peters, 134–40. Paris: ICOM. Accessed 21 September 2020. http://network.icom.museum/fileadmin/user_upload/minisites/icofom/images/Icofom-EssenceofConservation-FINAL.pdf?fbclid=IwAR0NUhq52SGOSvhHZXDnkevvI79i1QYaZzBABgSstvW41y6dHviEBhdc5rI.

Sillar, Bill. 2005. 'Who's indigenous? Whose archaeology?', *Public Archaeology* 4: 71–94.

Sloggett, Robyn. 2009. 'Expanding the Conservation Canon: Assessing cross-cultural and interdisciplinary collaborations in conservation', *Studies in Conservation* 54 (3): 170–83.

Smith, Charles Saumarez. 1989. 'Museums, artefacts and meanings'. In *The New Museology*, edited by P. Vergo, 6–21. London: Reaktion Books.

Smith, Richard D. 1999. 'Reversibility: A questionable philosophy'. In *Reversibility – Does it exist?*, edited by A. Oddy and S. Carroll. British Museum Occasional Paper 135. London: British Museum Press.

Spivak, Gayatri Chakravorty. 2011 [1995]. 'Can the subaltern speak?' In *The Post-Colonial Studies Reader*, edited by Bill Ashcroft, Gareth Griffiths and Helen Tiffin, 28–37. London; New York: Routledge.

Sully, Dean, ed. 2007. *Decolonising Conservation: Caring for Maori meeting houses outside New Zealand*. Walnut Creek, CA: Left Coast Press.

Thorn, Andrew. 2006. 'Tjurkulpa; A conservator learns respect for the land, the people and the culture'. In *IIC Munich Congress. The Object in Context: Crossing conservation boundaries*, edited by David Saunders and Joyce Townsend, 133–7. London: James & James.

Thorn, Andrew. 2008. 'The Yuwengayay Preservation Project'. In *Proceedings of Symposium 2007 Preserving Aboriginal Heritage: Technical and traditional approaches, Ottawa, Canada, September 24–28, 2007*, edited by Carole Dignard, Kate Helwig, Janet Mason, Kathy Nanowin and Thomas Stone, 333–9. Ottawa: Canadian Conservation Institute.

Viollet-le-Duc, Eugène Emmanuel. 1996 [1854]. 'Restoration'. In *Historical and Philosophical Issues in the Conservation of Cultural Heritage*, edited by N. S. Price, M. K. J. Talley and A. M. Vaccaro, 314–18. Los Angeles, CA: Getty Conservation Institute.

Watts, Siobhan, Baumber, Eleanor, La Pensée, Annemarie and Yates, Sally Anne. 2013. 'Liverpool's Conservation Centre: Fourteen years of public access'. In *The Public Face of Conservation*, edited by E. Williams, 16–25. London: Archetype.

Wharton, Glenn. 2008. 'Dynamics of Participatory Conservation: The Kamehameha I Sculpture Project', *Journal of the American Institute for Conservation* 47: 159–73.

Wharton, Glenn. 2012. *The Painted King: Art, activism, and authenticity in Hawaii*. Honolulu: University of Hawai'i Press.

Wharton, Glenn. 2015. 'Artist Intention and the Conservation of Contemporary Art'. In *Objects Specialty Group Postprints, Volume Twenty-Two*, edited by Emily Hamilton and Kari Dodson. Washington, DC: The American Institute for Conservation of Historic & Artistic Works. Accessed 21 September 2020. http://resources.conservation-us.org/osg-postprints/wp-content/uploads/sites/8/2015/05/osg022-01.pdf.

Wijesuriya, Gamini. 2000. 'Conserving the Temple of the Tooth Relic, Sri Lanka', *Public Archaeology* 1: 99–108.

Williams, Emily, ed. 2013. *The Public Face of Conservation*. London: Archetype.

Williams, Lucy. 2017. 'Supporting Community Revitalization: Curatorial and conservation stewardship at the Penn Museum'. In *Engaging Conservation: Collaboration across disciplines*, edited by Nina Owczarek, Molly Gleeson and Lynn A. Grant, 109–14. London: Archetype.

Wimsatt, William K. and Beardsley, Monroe C. 1946. 'The Intentional Fallacy', *Sewanee Review* 54: 468–88.

2

Conservation and collaboration: a discussion

Miriam Clavir

Introduction

The conservation of historic and artistic works focuses on the preservation of material culture. Equally, though, examining questions such as 'what is being preserved?', 'for whom?' and 'how?' brings the importance of cultural values, and of people themselves, into any conservation discussion. This chapter will highlight a continuing evolution in the field: the recognition that conservation brings together people with *people*, not just people with objects.

To examine this evolution, I will begin by discussing conservation practice in museums beginning in the 1980s that is related to the material culture of Indigenous peoples, using examples primarily from Canada. The conservation codes of ethics, and their inclusion of intangible as well as tangible heritage, will form part of the discussion. In addition, conservation values and practices will be examined in the context of changing museum values during the later twentieth and early twenty-first centuries. After this review of museum conservation history, the discussion will broaden to consider the conservation profession as a whole, asking all conservation subfields 'how the practice of conservation can promote human wellbeing' (the subject, albeit condensed in my own words, of the conference at which this text was first presented). The conclusion of this chapter will centre on three Canadian examples of collaborative preservation projects where the process, not just the outcome, was intended to promote respect and wellbeing.

A brief history of conservation and Indigenous concerns

In this overview I make particular reference to Canada and the question of using museum collections. In Canada the context of Aboriginal peoples' concerns began radically to affect the conservation field in the 1980s. In 1986 the Canadian Conservation Institute (CCI) organised a seminal conference on 'the care and handling of ethnological materials' (Organising Committee 1988, 1). CCI's goal was both innovative and reflective of the increasingly politicised museum environment of the period. The organisers in 1986 had in fact stated that 'Conferences related specifically to this class of materials had been infrequent' (Organising Committee 1988, 1).

One Indigenous curator presented at the conference. She is Gloria Cranmer Webster, a member of a chiefly 'Namgis (Kwakwaka'wakw) family in British Columbia, the first director of the U'mista Cultural Centre and responsible for many repatriations. Cranmer Webster has later commented, 'Of particular interest to me were the papers which dealt with the conservation of cultural property in association with the original owners. This kind of dialogue is to be increasingly encouraged in the future' (Cranmer Webster 1988, 78). In her own presentation she had affirmed to the audience, composed mainly of conservators, that, 'The objects themselves are not important; what matters is what the objects represent' (Cranmer Webster 1988, 77). The audience had clapped politely.

Two curators from Vancouver's University of British Columbia Museum of Anthropology (MOA) and myself, MOA's conservator, gave a joint paper on the pros and cons of MOA's policy of loaning back contemporary pieces from our collection to their makers for ceremonial use. In the early 1980s MOA occasionally received one but not more than three requests per year for use of collections related to the objects' meaning, although the number of requests doubled to six during Vancouver's World's Fair in 1986. After listening to our talk at the CCI conference, one audience member responded:

> I'm so upset about this whole thing. ... I'm a generalist conservator in a fine art museum and I fought a similar battle with a decorative arts curator. ... A lot of decorative arts pieces are made for utilitarian uses and they were being constantly pressed into utilitarian uses in the museum. ... [I]t is [the curator's] decision what kind of legacy they want to pass on as a professional curator. Now if they want

to pass on a bunch of altered, mutilated, damaged objects, they're fooling themselves if they think that the museum is going to let them have those choices. (Clavir et al. 1988, 87–8)

Codes of ethics

Let me open a parenthesis here and say that even today conservation codes of ethics, such as the American Institute for Conservation's (AIC), succinctly state 'The field of conservation deals with the physical aspect of cultural property' (AIC 1994a). The Canadian (CCI) and the International Institute for Conservation's (IIC) codes are similar.[1,2] The early history of professional conservation emphasised, among other stipulations, that conservators treat objects so that their physical fabric is stabilised and practitioners are not adding to deterioration or loss. As early as 1959, in fact, the IIC stated that its members should 'take any action necessary to further the understanding and controlling of the causes of deterioration of Historic and Artistic Works'.[3]

In the United States the Murray Pease Report and the Code of Ethics formulated and published in the years 1960 to 1968 not only adopted the IIC's objectives but also declared, for instance, 'It must be axiomatic that all professional actions of a conservator be governed by unswerving respect for the integrity of works of art' (IIC 1968).[4] At this time, and in the 1960s in North American conservation, the integrity of contemporary and historic materials was formally defined using the words 'physical, historic and aesthetic'. Phrases such as 'conceptual integrity' or 'unique character and significance' were not codified until the mid-1980s or even later.

Concerning the question of use of museum collections, in 1986 the Canadian code did begin by stating that conservators must 'strive constantly to maintain a balance between the need of society to use a cultural property and the preservation of that cultural property' (CAC and CAPC 2000, 1). This clause has remained unchanged.

In summary, it is certainly true, especially today, that the conservation profession acknowledges that attributes or dimensions other than the physical are important in preserving the significance of an object's meaning. Equally, however, conservation has long defined itself as being focused on those expressions of meaning that can be found in the physical materials. And with good reason: the conservation profession has a necessary, highly specialised, applied focus. The AIC code states:

> While recognizing the right of society to make appropriate and respectful use of cultural property, the conservation professional

shall serve as an advocate for the preservation of cultural property. (AIC 1994b)

Readers may understand why, in 1983, three years before the CCI symposium mentioned earlier, I felt very conflicted when MOA's director asked me to approve the loan of an *older* piece – one from the permanent MOA collection – for use at a potlatch by a First Nations family that had the traditional rights and privileges to it. Apart from MOA in Vancouver and the Royal British Columbia Museum (then the British Columbia Provincial Museum) in Victoria, which had commissioned a dedicated collection of contemporary Northwest Coast regalia, virtually no museum at that time considered that loaning out objects for use was professional practice.

How was I expected to balance out the values of my conservation profession and the values of my museum? As Gloria Cranmer Webster (1988, 72) said in 1986:

> We know what conservators do or try to do; that is, preserve objects for as long as possible. But, diametrically opposed to this is the general Indian view as I know it, which is that objects are created to be used and when those objects are damaged or worn out, they are thrown away and new ones are made.

Cranmer Webster also understood very well what art galleries and museums did. The traditional gallery perspective privileged its concept of the aesthetics of the works and, as well, 'the masterpiece'. In museums curators had most often written their labels in an anonymous, timeless style. In both instances the museum voice was the omniscient narrator, the author and authority. Now this was beginning to be challenged and to change.

Changing priorities in conservation and museums in response to stakeholders

Some of the most significant museum changes in the last few decades have come about because of the activism of Indigenous communities. Even in the 1970s and earlier, a few communities such as Zuni had called for repatriation of their sacred belongings. In the 1980s, in North America at least, the traditional museum functions of collecting and classifying began to be firmly challenged by more requests for repatriation and for Indigenous cultural values to be respected.

In Canada the first joint meeting between the national museum organisation, the Canadian Museums Association, and the national Aboriginal organisation, the Assembly of First Nations, was held in 1988 – in response to an effective First Nations and partial international boycott of a major museum exhibit over the actions of its sponsor.[5] Whether a particular museum might be considered conventional or progressive, all members of both national organisations had now become involved in the dialogue and the relationship between Canadian museums and Canada's Indigenous peoples. Museum rules evolved into museum questions. For instance, whether loaning Indigenous heritage objects out of a museum's permanent collection for use or in the example given by the deeply worried conservator at the CCI symposium mentioned above, the process became in many ways a question of resolving whether the use was necessary or unnecessary and according to whom – and of whether it was possible to mitigate deterioration of the museum object's physical fabric during the use.

Let me mention here another changing context at the time. In the museum world, 'stakeholders' became a word widely used for people with a particular interest in the museum enterprise. As readers know, Indigenous or other originators of museum collections are not the only museum stakeholders. What is interesting to note is that relationships, not just collections, were already being emphasised in certain places. For instance, both the 'new museology' that began in the 1960s and the 'eco-museum' involved 'community participation in all aspects of museum operations' (Kreps 2008, 28).[6]

As a second example of stakeholders, in the 1980s, museums had begun to see themselves as being not just about art or about stories, but also about entertainment. Entertainment in one sense was also about relationships – and not just those between the museum and its visitors. Exhibition designers created spaces and ways not only for enjoyment, but also for interaction between people, encouraging people to bring their family and friends and to interact with them while in the museum.

The end result of acknowledging the importance for the museum of promoting relationships for or with all 'stakeholders' was that museums listened in new ways to voices beyond those of the museum professional. And the museum's voice and authority began to be shared, including with the originating communities of their collections. Many areas of museum practice felt the effects of this reconceptualisation of power and authority – although, notably, this was implemented to greater or lesser extents in various museums. Indigenous people became not merely informants for exhibit content, but partners in the whole exhibit development process from the start – including the use of agreed-upon direct quotations as the exhibit labels and the negotiated rights to copyright of information coming from Indigenous participation. Many curators no longer did their research to accumulate knowledge in specialist subject areas so they could curate 'their exhibit'; instead they worked as facilitators to present first-hand perspectives and voices from the communities whose cultural history or contemporary realities were being shown. A curator's specialist knowledge certainly is important, but often now it is shared knowledge: an exhibit reflects and acknowledges extensive collaboration. A project may well have begun with a negotiated mutual protocol agreement between equal exhibit partners. Museums have now come to see themselves as having a primary responsibility to people and their values rather than to the value of objects.

In the 1990s one American museum specialist observed 'The increasing presence of Native American[s] … in mainstream museums is challenging … western, scientifically based museological paradigms' (Kreps 1998, 3). Readers will appreciate that conservation is one of these scientific paradigms. This evolution in museums has meant that conservation's stated primary interest in preserving the physical object has not only been displaced as a priority in many museums, but has in some places been seen as fundamentally incompatible with their major commitments.

At the same time, these changing priorities have helped museum staff to see certain assumptions and values embedded in their own practices more clearly. The same museum specialist also acknowledged '[W]e … see how professional … practices, regarded as "natural" and "logical," are cultural constructs and products of our own museum culture' (Kreps 1998, 3). In addition, certain subfields of conservation, such as the conservation of material belongings from Indigenous and world cultures, have evolved new paradigms that fit well with the contemporary contexts that have developed – and, additionally, with the new technologies that increase access to information.

For instance, by the mid-1990s and certainly in the twenty-first century, conservation professionals in various countries – and especially but by no means exclusively in countries with Indigenous populations – have worked more and more often with Indigenous and minority communities on preservation projects. Knowledge gained from these projects has then been shared more broadly in conservation: at various conferences, workshops and in articles and books published in the conservation and museum literature. In addition, museums and their organisations have provided an expanding context for this work. The Collections Council of Australia (CCA), for example, published guidelines for assessing the significance of collections (Russell and Winkworth 2009), and the much smaller Museums Association of Saskatchewan (Canada) investigated standards for the care of First Nations and Metis collections (Fiori 1999). The legal profession has also written increasingly on repatriation for both legal and general audiences.

Throughout all of the work in these areas, projects have directly involved First Nations; they were done in collaboration with them and responding to their requests. Much of this varied work on preservation is now available on the internet, allowing access for anyone – students, Indigenous communities, museums outside the originating country, etc. Conservators have been fundamental initiators and resource people for many of these developments. More and more, conservation professionals have good access to information on many aspects of the preservation of world and Indigenous heritage including, importantly, from the websites of Indigenous organisations and individuals.

Relationships between the conservation field as a whole and community stakeholders

This discussion will now focus on conservation's sub-disciplines – because even though conservators have increasingly participated in collaborative projects conserving Indigenous heritage, what meaning has this had for the profession as a whole? Is the contemporary context of 'preserving conceptual integrity' and collaboration with originating communities relevant to the practice of conservators of European oil paintings or decorative arts, for example? Certainly conservation's subfields have different concerns and contexts, and focus on different materials. But we work under essentially similar professional ethics.

Do we ask whether a student in a conservation programme's paintings' stream could be arguing why an art museum will not lend an icon or an altarpiece for use? Do conservators of Euro-American pieces discuss whether the term 'source community' should be used for the West? Or the fact that many copyright laws may protect artists, but offer less security if you happen to be defined as a craftsperson?

I believe that the conservation profession as a whole does not engage enough in these debates. I have the impression that questions can be sidestepped by the fact that different compromises are made all the time in conservation, a situation that is considered allowable in different subfields. But what I am addressing here is not compromise. Not, at least, in the negative sense that means one has settled for less. Instead, it can mean a goal of maximising the benefits for all concerned, even though no single party achieves one hundred per cent. I would like to make sure that the conservation profession as a whole appreciates that words such as 'standards' and 'codes of ethics' encompass both the ideal in relation to the object and the real, daily world of context, and thus strive to maximise the ideal for the individual object in relation to the whole context. So-called compromises from ethical standards can allow a 'win–win' situation, for example maximising physical preservation during use that is a necessary part of the object's significance. Yet does this bring us back to the conservator of decorative arts quoted earlier? In his field, what is 'necessary'?

In any case, do questions pertaining to use of museum collections or relationships with originating cultures concern the conservation profession as a whole? Conservators have more than enough to do in their own focus on physical materials, especially in today's world of cutbacks, and the profession as a whole is concerned with other contemporary issues, such as sustainability. Is it not enough that at least the sub-specialty of conserving objects from world cultures is active in, and publishes on, museum–community relationships?

There *are* substantive concerns, though. In saying this, I acknowledge that my reasons may be personal: I may merely be trying to defend my own areas of interest. But to give one example: conservators in private practice can overprotect the physical object – they have to protect their businesses as well. As more museums hire private conservators rather than maintain in-house departments, the stringent conditions that these private conservators stipulate for a loan, for instance, may leave little flexibility for the receiving museum to let the originating people be comfortably close to their heritage belongings without breaking the loan conditions.

A second illustration is the Hindu bronze statue at MOA being celebrated by its Vancouver community in 2010 (Figs 2.2 and 2.3). An article in the *New Yorker* on repatriation had stated:

> For religious Hindus, images of the gods are not merely representational; they can be inhabited by the deity they depict. The faithful anoint the statues with oils, camphor, and sandalwood, garland them with flowers, and make offerings of food, incense, and music. .... When, in 1986, the Indian government sued for the return of a twelfth-century bronze Shiva that had been looted from a village in Pathur, it did so on behalf of the offended god himself. Shiva was named as a plaintiff in the case. 'In the south, people still don't tell lies in Shiva's temple,' Ashok Shekhar, a former state arts and culture official in Rajasthan, told me. 'These are very hotheaded deities.' (Keefe 2007, 60)[7]

In a non-anthropology museum, the MOA-owned bronze statue of Vishnu might be in a department that sees it chiefly as an art object. What would be the relationship between the museum and the community?

Fig. 2.1 Bronze representation of Vishnu in 'visible storage' at the UBC Museum of Anthropology. Photographer Heidi Swierenga. Courtesy of UBC Museum of Anthropology, Vancouver, Canada.

Fig. 2.2

(continued)

Figs 2.2 and 2.3   A Hindu bronze statue at MOA is celebrated by
its Vancouver community in 2010. Photographer Heidi Swierenga.
Courtesy of UBC Museum of Anthropology, Vancouver, Canada.

The preservation of heritage

This discussion could include an examination of fundamental definitions
surrounding heritage preservation, a topic that concerns all conservators.
For example, the word 'preservation' applies to skills as well as to
materials. Anupam Sah, Head of Art Conservation at the Chhatrapati
Shivaji Maharaj Vastu Sangrahalaya (CSMVS) in Mumbai, has discussed

the conservation of heritage wall paintings in the state of Orissa (Stoner 2009). In this project conservation meant preserving the traditional skills of the local artists by having them reconstruct wall paintings that had deteriorated and in places disappeared. The old paintings were not necessarily saved; preservation meant new images on new walls. These paintings sustain local economic wellbeing.

Conservators have often been compared to doctors – not just because of their white lab coats, but because they are seen as specialists in diagnosing and healing the 'diseases' of heritage materials. I was particularly interested to hear a medical doctor declare that he no longer wanted to be a specialist. He acknowledged that 'It's something I wanted to do since the beginning of meds school, to be a specialist and have all the information…' But as he practised this physician decided to become an Emergency Room doctor, realising that he 'wanted to be the one discovering what the issues were' (Knowledge Network 2014). As I understand his words, the doctor preferred the challenge not only of continual new cases that needed quick resolution, but also of what this situation involved: the need to analyse a whole complexity of factors to help his patients most successfully, as opposed to repeating treatments in his one, particular specialty. Does this have any resonance in conservation practice?

Collaboration in heritage preservation: three examples

This chapter concludes with three Canadian examples of collaboration related to heritage preservation. What interested me especially about these examples was how, by recognising and working with the underlying issues, the people involved promoted more respect within the preservation projects. The projects recognised the context of 'human wellbeing' as a goal of the process.

The first example is the process that the Canadian Conservation Institute used with its Indigenous Advisory Board for their landmark 2007 conference, 'Preserving Aboriginal Heritage: Technical and Traditional Approaches'. The conference proceedings have been published, with CCI's Tom Stone contributing a further analysis (Dignard et al. 2008; Stone 2009). This chapter will summarise just one aspect, the Advisory Board meetings themselves.

The Indigenous Board members used a modified Aboriginal circle process in the meetings. CCI, as proposers of the conservation conference, drafted the meeting agenda, but only the Board discussed its items. CCI people sat and listened. My understanding is that the discussion might go around the table more than once, until consensus was reached. Then CCI summarised what they had heard. They might also present their side and listen to more round-table discussions or, more usually, wait until the next meeting to give themselves the time to discuss the topics raised internally. The point I want to emphasise here is that the CCI people spent a lot of time truly listening.

Listening in an open-minded way to grasp someone else's emphasis is hard. Consciously or not, our professional, cultural or other mindsets filter what we hear. To quote from a very different context, from an aid agency that works internationally 'The difference between hearing and listening is paying attention, finding and living that elusive element of real connection' (Messinger 2014).

The second example is about a collaboration that grew from a firm base in *mistrust*. It concerns a tract of land in Ontario whose location had made it, for millennia, a water and land transportation gateway. The land and its portage had played a huge role historically as a place of both meeting and conflict for peoples and cultures.

This land had come under the ownership of a pulp and paper company that in recent years had shut down its mill. Kenora, the small city next to the land, wanted to make new use of the area; so did other levels of government. However, the city and the land are both located in the traditional and treaty territory of three Anishnaabe First Nations. Add pollution, clear cutting (razing a large area of forest) and other issues, and the result was a huge legacy of mistrust on all sides – including an earlier (1970s) First Nations armed occupation of municipal land in Kenora, as well as court battles over Aboriginal rights.

All the local leadership, then, was aware that a dispute could create serious conflict. The issue became the best way in which 'to settle the future of this historic piece of land'. The leaders on all sides decided:

> I won't own the land, but neither will you. In recognition of our contentious past, let's move forward with a common purpose of respect for the land and mutual benefit, and give everyone access to the land as a park called 'Common Ground'. (Cuyler Cotton, Dovetail Resources, pers. comm., 2011)[8]

The land was then donated by the pulp and paper company. It has since been managed by a stewardship group with representatives from the municipality, the Grand Council of Treaty 3 and the three local First Nations. Success was not described as being measured by a utopian end at the project's finish, but by the on-going process – by the health, the wellbeing, of both the land and the relationship. Success in these terms has now existed for over a decade. Several academics commented about the expectations raised by the phrase 'Common Ground', however, saying:

> [W]hile the 'Common Ground' land management initiative requires them to negotiate diverse and sometimes conflicting objectives in their pursuit of a potentially unifying goal, tensions still exist between people's views, interests and values. (Robson et al. 2013, 18)

The third example illustrates collaboration using social media. I have had a small part in a university-funded project where my role was to offer conservation advice for people in two First Nations villages who had heirlooms or contemporary pieces at home that they wished to preserve.[9] The project was concerned primarily with repatriation. Preservation was thus configured rather metaphorically here, as an extension of repatriation, in the sense that it was helping to ensure objects were at home.

The project's leaders envisioned, as a first step, two pilot videos on conservation, about 4 to 5 minutes in length, to go up on the project's website – for example, discussions with a family about a piece they wanted to preserve. But then Duncan McCue, a First Nations journalist working in Canadian television news, advised against this idea. He explained to me that 'People in the villages might look at that once. The site would be static'. Instead he recommended a page on Facebook, a platform that people in the First Nations communities were already using. McCue said that Facebook's importance is that it hands control over to people, to a community of engaged sharers, not just to a project or author.

> And people enjoy it, so they'll use it over and over again, sharing information, both their own, and preservation information, and opinions. It's a two-way street. … Think of your project as not just linking people and collections, or people and information, but linking people and people. (Duncan McCue, pers. comm., 22 November 2011)[10]

Let me open a brief parenthesis here with information about a different Canadian First Peoples' context.

A northerner has pointed out that low internet bandwidth in parts of Nunavut in the far north of Canada has forced those living in remote Inuit communities to communicate through text. This has meant that even fluent speakers of Inuktitut often use English and a Roman alphabet keyboard. He described the potential consequence:

Languages that have survived 4,000 years, through whalers, traders, priests, government, residential schools and cable TV, will not survive 20 years of a literary internet forcing everybody to communicate in their second language. ... We're trying to build an internet that people can use in their own oral languages, and to do that it has to work *audio-visually*. (Everett-Green 2014)

It is time to return to Duncan McCue and his advice that the project adopt the internet platform that people in the two Quebec villages – Kitigan Zibi and Mashteuiatsh, First Nations communities with reasonably good internet access – are already enjoying.

From the project's perspective, one big negative in having an interactive site is that it needs to be monitored continually for nasty or otherwise undesirable postings. In addition, the project's goal should ideally ensure that someone can get an answer to a conservation question months or years from now. This particular project is grant funded and therefore time-limited. At the end of the project, then, can there be anything other than a static site? In my opinion, one resolution might come through the conservation interaction being part of an on-going relationship between one of the First Nations cultural centre museums and a conservation training programme with its continual new influx of students. I am grateful to Dr Joyce Helmer (Anishinaabe) for supplying medical information which provided a catalyst for this conservation analogy (pers. comm., 30 May 2016).[11]

Duncan McCue, with his expertise as a professional journalist, advised other changes to the project's media plans. He suggested, for example, that a video of 4 or 5 minutes' duration is too long, instead recommending short segments, just 1 or 2 minutes in length, on different but pertinent aspects of the subject matter. Both Kitigan Zibi and Mashteuiatsh have cultural centres. Staff there knew that these subject segments could include traditional language use, for example, or cultural or archival information related to the family's heritage piece, not only discussions on preservation. Each segment, McCue recommended, should highlight no more than two points; it should also be possible to access the segments separately so that people can choose which one(s) they want to look at. This not only suits the media platform and how people use it, but it also gives the users, not the project, control. This design would help to ensure that the segments are useful for the communities, rather than simply looking good for the project's mandate and to its funders.

Conclusion

The points raised in these discussions lead back to the importance, in my opinion, for the conservation field to have an interest in the whole, larger picture, and to foreground the building of good, respectful, relationships as a goal. By adopting such strategies conservation *can* link people to people, as well as helping to preserve their material biographies.

Notes

1. The Canadian document states that 'The purpose of conservation is to study, record, retain and restore the culturally significant qualities of the cultural property as embodied in its physical and chemical nature, with the least possible intervention' (CAC and CAPC 2000).
2. Memorandum and Articles of Association of the International Institute for Conservation of Historic and Artistic Works, section 3: 'The objects for which The Institute is established (c), p. 16, 1959'. The IIC also stated as point (d) that it was an object of The Institute 'to take any action conducive to the bettering of the condition of Historic and Artistic Works' (IIC 1968).
3. Memorandum and Articles of Association of the International Institute for Conservation of Historic and Artistic Works, section 3: 'The objects for which The Institute is established (c), p. 16, 1959'. The IIC also stated as point (d) that it was an object of The Institute 'to take any action conducive to the bettering of the condition of Historic and Artistic Works' (IIC 1968).
4. In addition, the Single Standard of care was in the 1968 Code of Ethics. 'With every work of art he undertakes to conserve, regardless of his opinion of its value or quality, the conservator should adhere to his highest and most exacting standard of treatment.' While this clause had the positive effect of valuing all material heritage equally, from fine arts to baskets, it implies that the same high standard of care and preservation from further deterioration should be applied to all works.
5. For more information on this, as well as an extensive analysis of – and developments in – modern and postmodern museums, see Phillips (2011).
6. See also de Varine (2008). In this reference Hugues de Varine, former Director of ICOM (1965–1974), describes 'new museology' as follows: 'A new concept on the involvement of museums in regional development emerged in the 1970s (Santiago 1972; Le Creusot-Montceau 1975–1980). The 1980s saw the appearance of initiatives resulting from this movement, henceforth known as "the new museology", in Canada (Haute Beauce, Fier Monde), Sweden (Bergslagen), Norway (Toten), and Portugal (Seixal). In the 1990s, this new museology was universally adopted and the terms eco-museum or community museum coined to distinguish these "heretical" or, quite simply "heterodox" museums from the traditional institutions [...]'.
7. For information on the exhibition at MOA see https://moa.ubc.ca/exhibition/border-zones-new-art-across-cultures/. Accessed 31 July 2019.
8. See also reports available on the internet, for instance under Common Land, Common Ground or Common Ground Kenora. One example may be found at http://www.mah.gov.on.ca/Page6054.aspx. Accessed 31 July 2019.
9. The project is called TSHIUE-NATUAPAHTETAU-KIGIBIWEWIDON, or 'Exploring new alternatives concerning restitution/reappropriation of native heritage' (Ilnu and Anishinabeg). Information can be found at: http://nikanishk.ca. Accessed 17 September 2020.
10. See also McCue (2018).
11. Consultation over long distances, for example for remote communities, is already in use in health care in Ontario. It uses various scanning technologies and, for example, a satellite medical network.

References

AIC (American Institute for Conservation of Historic and Artistic Works). 1994a. 'Commentaries to the Guidelines for Practice: Commentary 18; Interpretation', *Code of Ethics*. Accessed 31 July 2019. https://www.culturalheritage.org/about-conservation/code-of-ethics.

AIC (American Institute for Conservation of Historic and Artistic Works). 1994b. 'Code of Ethics and Guidelines for Practice: Code of Ethics; III'. *Code of Ethics*. Accessed 31 July 2019. https://www.nps.gov/training/tel/Guides/HPS1022_AIC_Code_of_Ethics.pdf.

CAC (Canadian Association for the Conservation of Cultural Property) and CAPC (Canadian Association of Professional Conservators). 2000. *Code of Ethics and Guidance for Practice*, 3rd ed. Accessed 31 July 2019. https://capc-acrp.ca/files/Code-of-Ethics-and-Guidance-for-Practice.pdf.

Clavir, Miriam, Johnson, Elizabeth and Shane, Audrey. 1988. 'A Discussion on the Use of Museum Artifacts by their Original Owners'. In *Symposium 86: The care and preservation of ethnological materials; Proceedings*, edited by Robert L. Barclay, Mark R. Gilberg, J. Clifford McCawley and Thomas G. Stone, 80–9. Ottawa: Canadian Conservation Institute.

Cranmer Webster, Gloria. 1988. 'Conservation and Cultural Centres: U'mista Cultural Centre, Alert Bay, Canada'. In *Symposium 86: The care and preservation of ethnological materials; Proceedings*, edited by Robert L. Barclay, Mark R. Gilberg, J. Clifford McCawley and Thomas G. Stone, 77–9. Ottawa: Canadian Conservation Institute.

de Varine, Hugues. 2008. 'The Museum as a Social Agent of Development', *ICOM News* 1, 5.

Dignard, Carole, Helwig, Kate, Mason, Janet, Nanowin, Kathy and Stone, Thomas, eds. 2008. 'Preserving Aboriginal Heritage, Technical and Traditional Approaches: Proceedings of a conference symposium 2007'. Ottawa: Canadian Conservation Institute.

Everett-Green, Robert. 2014. 'Celebrated Son of Igloolik Creates Cultural Internet for his People' (includes an interview with Norman Cohn). *Globe and Mail*, 18 January 2014, 1, 4.

Fiori, Patricia. 1999. 'Standards for First Nation Collections'. In ICOM-CC Ethnographic Conservation Newsletter 19. Accessed 31 July 2019. http://www.icom-cc.org/54/document/ethnographic-conservation-newsletter-19-april-1999/?id=918.

IIC (International Institute for Conservation of Historic and Artistic Works). 1968. *The Murray Pease Report: Code of ethics for art conservators*. Accessed 31 July 2019. http://www.conservation-us.org/docs/default-source/governance/murray_pease_report.pdf?sfvrsn=2.

Keefe, Patrick R. 2007. 'The Idol Thief', *New Yorker*, 7 May 2007, 58–67.

Knowledge Network. 2014. 'Talk to Me'. *Emergency Room: Life and death at VGH*, television programme aired 28 January 2014. Burnaby, BC, Canada.

Kreps, Christina F. 1998. 'Introduction: Indigenous curation', *Museum Anthropology* 22 (1: March): 3–4.

Kreps, Christina F. 2008. 'Appropriate Museology in Theory and Practice', *Museum Management and Curatorship* 23 (1: March): 23–41.

McCue, Duncan. 2018. 'Reporting In Indigenous Communities'. Accessed 7 January 2018. http://riic.ca.

Messinger, Ruth W. 2014. *Reframing the Sh'ma to Repair the World*. Accessed 31 July 2019. https://olamtogether.org/853-2/.

Organizing Committee. 1988. 'Symposium 86'. In *Symposium 86: The care and reservation of ethnological materials; Proceedings*, edited by Robert L. Barclay, Mark R. Gilberg, J. Clifford McCawley and Thomas G. Stone, 1. Ottawa: Canadian Conservation Institute.

Phillips, Ruth B. 2011. 'Museum Pieces: Toward the Indigenization of Canadian museums'. Montreal: McGill-Queen's University Press.

Robson, James P., Sinclair, Andrew J., Davidson-Hunt, Iain J. and Diduck, Alan P. 2013. 'What's in a Name: The search for common ground in Kenora, Northwestern Ontario', *Journal of Public Deliberation* 9 (2), article 7 (October): 1–22.

Russell, Roslyn and Winkworth, Kylie. 2009. *Significance 2.0: A guide to assessing the significance of collections*. Adelaide: Collections Council of Australia. Accessed 31 July 2019. http://arts.gov.au/resources-publications/industry-reports/significance-20.

Stone, Tom. 2009. 'Listening to the Voices: Preserving Aboriginal heritage "then" and "now"; A comparison of two symposia'. In *Sharing Cultures 2009: International conference on intangible heritage*, edited by Sérgio Lira, Rogério Amoêda, Cristina Pinheiro, João Pinheiro and Fernando Oliveira, 373–81. Barcelos: Green Lines Institute for Sustainable Development.

Stoner, Joyce Hill. 2009. 'Connecting to the World's Connections: Making the case for conservation and preservation of our cultural heritage; A partnership project of the Salzburg Global Seminar and the Institute of Museum and Library Services'. *Salzburg Global Seminar 466 Report*, October–November 2009. Accessed 31 July 2019. http://www.salzburgglobal.org/fileadmin/user_upload/Documents/2000-2009/2009/466/SessionReportPrint466.pdf.

3

The role of conservation education in reconciliation: the example of the Iraqi Institute for the Conservation of Antiquities and Heritage

Jessica S. Johnson, Kim Cullen Cobb and
Brian Michael Lione

Introduction

World-class cultural property, including museum collections and arch-aeological and historic sites, is dispersed through every province in Iraq, but the knowledge necessary to preserve and administer these resources safely and effectively – particularly in times of armed conflict – is not. Cultural heritage is part of what defines a people's identity (Bouchenaki 2003). In times of uncertainty, people with the skills and desire needed to preserve cultural heritage are vital to ensure that a community's history and culture are safe for all to share, study and enjoy.

As part of 'soft diplomacy' and 'peace-building' activities after conflict, some Western governments and transnational entities are funding more cultural heritage projects that support educational programmes and practical projects across the Middle East (e.g. World Bank 2001; Odegaard et al. 2014; JICA 2017; Stein 2016; British Museum 2017). This chapter describes the development of one of these projects, the Iraqi Institute for the Conservation of Antiquities and Heritage (abbreviated as the Iraqi Institute, IICAH or simply the Institute).[1] It explores some of the ways in which conservators and other foreign cultural heritage experts supporting the effort have evolved and adapted their approaches, through collaboration with Iraqi cultural heritage professionals participating in the endeavour.

The Iraqi Institute in context

Conservation and other cultural heritage-based academic and professional communities (such as archaeology, historic preservation and architecture) have been examining the role of collaboration and working with others who have an interest in material culture for some time. Whether obliged to collaborate through new legal requirements, such as the United States' Native American Graves Protection and Repatriation Act (McManamon 2000, or through a desire to do their work 'differently' (e.g. Johnson et al. 2005; Little and Shackel 2014; Court and Wijesuriya 2015; Onciul et al. 2017; Chitty 2017), individuals and institutions have been changing attitudes and practices to work more collaboratively with stakeholders outside the traditional cultural heritage fields. At this point, however, while the responsibility of cultural heritage professionals to consider other stakeholders in a project is generally accepted, in practice the application of these ideas to a real-life project is widely variable in success and application (McManamon et al. 2008; Waterton and Watson 2013; Emerick 2017).

In post-conflict countries, there is even more need for foreign practitioners in heritage conservation to consider critically how their attitudes and methodologies may or may not work. Some examination of how this can best be done has taken place (Stanley-Price 2007), but there is a need for more research and reflection on what constitutes a successful project for heritage and for the community in the long term. Barakat (2007) clearly delineates deficiencies in international policy and practice that limit the effectiveness of postwar reconstruction programmes and illustrates how these gaps limit recovery of cultural heritage.

There is also need for the cultural heritage community in general, and for those who desire to work in these situations in particular, to explore academic and practitioners' knowledge in the relief and development community. In so doing they can draw on their longer and deeper experience with capacity-building, redevelopment and reconciliation after conflict. The approaches, experiences and successes and failures of this community have yet to be clearly examined by much of the cultural heritage community.

This chapter illustrates some of the difficulties and pitfalls of working in a post-conflict situation that is politicised, insecure and rapidly changing. This project has required constant adaptation of programmes to ensure that real change and improvement, both for individuals and for the professional heritage community, could occur. This chapter, based on a paper originally presented in 2014, has been updated to incorporate information on programmes that have taken place since the conference. Attempts to give sustainability to the project continue.

The Iraqi Institute

Since 2009 the Iraqi Institute has been helping to rebuild the community of heritage professionals tasked with caring for and protecting the ancient heritage of Iraq (Cassman et al. 2011). The Iraqi Institute is located in the city of Erbil, Iraq, in the northern Kurdistan Autonomous Region. It was conceived as a partnership between communities speaking three different languages – English, Arabic and Kurdish – who understand and value ancient and historic heritage. Funded primarily by the US Government, the Iraqi Federal Government and the Kurdistan Regional Government (KRG), along with foundations and private donors, the people involved in building the Iraqi Institute are working to overcome the impact of decades of war, genocide, economic sanctions, terrorism and political turmoil. The Iraqi Institute brings together those who believe that the preservation of heritage helps people to come together in the present time. In so doing it demonstrates how preservation of cultural heritage such as museum artefacts, archaeological sites and historic buildings, combined with safe access and clear interpretation, can promote reconciliation and inclusiveness within and between communities.[2]

The importance of the Iraqi Institute is immeasurable. The graduates of its programmes, who come from all 18 provinces of Iraq, are an expanding core of heritage professionals; they work in governmental and academic institutions specifically responsible for preservation of the country's cultural heritage. The need for such skilled people is acute. In June 2014 the invasion of Mosul and the Nineveh Province in Iraq by the Islamic State in Iraq and Syria (ISIS; also called the 'Islamic State') caused hundreds of thousands of Iraqis – including cultural heritage professionals from the Mosul Museum and the provincial offices of the State Board of Antiquities and Heritage (SBAH; the government entity with legal responsibility for ancient heritage in Iraq) – to flee. Between 2014 and 2017 ISIS activities destroyed much of Iraq's ancient and irreplaceable cultural heritage in occupied areas. Social media – together with local and international press reports and numerous projects using satellite imagery over those years – documented that in Iraq ISIS continued its tradition (clearly documented in Syria) of systematically destroying monuments, sites and objects deemed 'idolatrous'; they also sold artefacts from museum collections and archeological sites to fund their activities (see, for example, Danti et al. 2015; Drennan 2014; Kohn 2014; Barnard 2015). Alumni and future students of the Iraqi Institute will be at the forefront of documenting this damage and helping the country to recover in the future.

The ideas behind the Iraqi Institute

In 2008, when the US Government provided seed money for the Iraqi Institute, the city of Erbil, in the centre north of Iraq inside the Kurdistan Region of Iraq, was chosen as a safe location; here people could come from throughout the country to learn about heritage preservation. Kurdistan is often referred to in the media and in tourist literature as 'the other Iraq' because of its comparative safety and security. Most of the Kurdistan region is located in the Zagros Mountains, with foothills and plains lying just below. The city of Erbil is built around an ancient citadel, first mentioned in cuneiform sources in 2300 BC (MacGinnis 2014; Lawler 2014). It is touted as being up to '8,000' years old, and excavations are now taking place on the citadel that may eventually define its true age. The Erbil Citadel was inscribed on the UNESCO World Heritage list in June 2014.

The Iraqi Institute building has been renovated with funds provided by the KRG. It includes classrooms, laboratories, dormitories, a dining hall, library and all the facilities needed to support heritage professionals from throughout Iraq who work and live together as they study heritage preservation. The building is located close to the Erbil Citadel and surrounding historic neighbourhoods, including a market dating from the Ottoman period. Appointed in 2010, a Board of five Iraqis manages the Institute. Three of them work for the Iraqi Ministry of Culture's State Board of Antiquities and Heritage (SBAH) and the other two, including the Director, Dr Abdullah Khorsheed, work for the KRG at Salahaddin University. An Advisory Council of leading Iraqi and international cultural heritage professionals assist the Board; they bring decades of experience from careers with the Federal Government of Iraq and the KRG and from the academic, management and education sectors of the international heritage conservation field. Charged with overseeing development of the academic programmes, these advisors, interested colleagues and Iraqi Institute staff designed courses to address three basic areas of conservation education. These courses have been taught at the Institute since 2009 (Johnson et al. 2014).[3]

Students in Iraqi Institute classes all have a BA or higher qualification and a position in the heritage preservation field. Many work for the central SBAH in Baghdad, the KRG's Directorate-General of Antiquities or regional offices in one of Iraq's 18 provinces. Other students work for university departments of archaeology and engineering or for other government ministries. Almost 45 per cent of the students have been female. The ethnic and religious diversity of the students reflect that of Iraq: Kurd, Arab, Turkman, Christian, Muslim (Sunna and Shia) and others. They range in age from students in their mid-20s at the beginning of their careers to older professionals in their 50s, with decades of experience. After completing course work at the Institute, most students return to their original jobs. They need to adapt and apply their new skills immediately to improve preservation and access to the cultural resources in their care.

Educational programmes 2009–14

Visiting instructors who are experts in their fields teach all courses. They have been recruited from countries across the world including the US, Australia, Czech Republic, India, Iraq, Italy, Jordan, Sweden, Turkey and the UK. Cumulatively they have decades of experience working in other countries and providing education in the modern, internationally defined profession of heritage conservation. Because English is the language of international heritage preservation, daily English language instruction forms part of most programmes. All courses are taught in English, accompanied by both Arabic and Kurdish translation. Generally visiting instructors teach blocks of one to four weeks in length, with each 'module' of a longer course lasting eight to 10 weeks.

The Collections Care and Conservation Program (CCC) focuses on the care of artefacts in museums. The 30-week course consists of both introductory and advanced levels, so students may benefit from up to 60 weeks of education. The course has a focus on preventive conservation for the materials and collections found in museums in Iraq, concentrating particularly on archaeological collections.

Year 1 (Introductory): Preventive Conservation for Archaeology and Museums

The first-year course in conservation of moveable heritage provides a basic introduction to the theoretical and practical aspects of preservation of artefacts and collections. The 30-week course is divided into three modules, each requiring eight weeks for classroom instruction at the Iraqi Institute and two weeks for a practical project that individual students undertake at home.

At the end of the Year 1 Conservation Course, students are expected to have the skills to:

- understand the concepts of preventive conservation
- understand how to use a variety of tools and methods for environmental monitoring
- understand how to improve collections care in storage and on display
- know how to work safely in a laboratory
- know how to identify artefact materials and techniques found in Iraqi museums
- know how to produce photographic and written documentation
- know safe cleaning techniques for museum artefacts
- understand how to present information to become advocates for conservation
- demonstrate a greatly improved facility in English

Year 2 (Advanced): Laboratory Conservation for Archaeology and Museums

The second-year course in conservation of moveable heritage continues education in the theoretical and practical aspects of conservation of artefacts and collections. Students of the advanced level must be nominated from the Year 1 course. The programme is designed to build and reinforce technical skills set within a broader understanding of the academic field of conservation and its international community. The 30-week course is divided into three modules, each involving eight weeks of classroom instruction at the Iraqi Institute and two weeks for a practicum that individual students carry out at home. Work is carried out on objects from local museums, excavations and private individuals.

At the end of the Year 2 (Advanced) Conservation Course, students are expected to have the skills to:

- carry out a conservation project with full documentation
- understand the scientific method and how to use it to make conservation treatment decisions
- know how to carry out basic treatments for textiles, metals, ceramics, stone, ivory and other materials as available
- develop and carry out an environmental monitoring plan over a full year
- know how to create basic mounts to exhibit artefacts safely
- understand how to pack artifacts for transport safely
- understand and use information about conservation through published literature and the internet

- present themselves as advocates for conservation after they leave the Iraqi Institute
- carry out a discussion about conservation in English

The Architectural Site Conservation Course (ASC) provides a basic introduction to the theoretical and practical aspects of preserving built heritage. The 20-week course is delivered in two modules, each involving eight weeks of classroom instruction at the Iraqi Institute and four weeks for a practicum that individual students undertake at home. Students also practise technical skills on historic buildings in and around Erbil as part of the course.

At the end of the ASC Course, students are expected to have the skills to:

- understand the legal and policy frameworks of international conservation
- utilise standard terminology for architectural conservation projects
- identify and evaluate the significance of a historic building appropriately
- document historic buildings using measured drawings and photographs
- understand the basic materials and systems of historic buildings
- identify causes of deterioration and decay in historic buildings
- recommend basic emergency stabilisation procedures for historic buildings
- recommend the initial steps required in planning for future evaluations and treatments of historic buildings and sites
- communicate with greater proficiency in written and spoken English

The Archaeological Site Preservation Program (ASP) began in 2013 as a 10-week, single module course; it was taught three times throughout 2013 and 2014. The course has classroom and field components to ensure an equal balance of theoretical and practical elements. Fieldwork took place at archaeological sites around Erbil.

At the end of the ASP, students are expected to have the skills to:

- understand the theory behind, and types of, archaeological survey
- understand identification / evaluation techniques
- understand basic concepts and applications of remote sensing
- understand basic GPS and GIS techniques, and employ them in support of fieldwork
- understand the types of threats to archaeological sites

- understand approaches and techniques physically to protect / preserve archaeological sites
- identify, classify and prioritise threats to archaeological sites
- organise and present the data on site preservation priorities to support decision-making processes

Didactic method

The mission of the Iraqi Institute is 'to preserve the legacy of humanity contained in the unique cultural heritage of Iraq. It accomplishes this through educating people in conservation and preservation and by inviting professionals from around the world to share expertise'.

The most important word in its mission statement is EDUCATING – chosen very specifically in contrast to TRAINING. The authors' experiences in Iraq, since 2009, have shown that training (defined as short courses in the country or abroad) often fails to give people from crisis and conflict areas the skills, information and experience they need to effect meaningful change and improvement.

Since the beginning, programmes at the Iraqi Institute have utilised a reflective, recursive, educational approach to ensure that courses continuously evolve to meet students' needs. As conservators work more and more as educators in countries recovering from conflict or disaster, it is important to consider carefully what is taught and how this is undertaken, as well as to reflect on successes and failures to share with colleagues (e.g. Hamdan et al. 2008; Roby et al. 2008; Kurin 2011; Tandon 2011). The methodologies used to teach in traditional conservation university programmes, and the techniques of interaction that conservators are comfortable using, may not be the best way to share ideas in countries with different educational traditions and a recent history of trauma and crises. Developing an appropriate approach to education takes time and constant re-evaluation.

From the first classes in 2009 onwards, all visiting instructors were asked to provide a final report using a simple standard format (Fig. 3.1). This enabled comparable information to be collected from all teachers. These reports have been useful in several ways. First, they provide subsequent teachers in each course with real information on what the students had just been taught and issues that they might have to address further. The reports also make it easier to evaluate individual student improvement – particularly important when there is not a single teacher in the classroom at all times. As individual students respond differently

1. Introduction – include dates in Erbil and general impressions of program

2. Outline of topics covered and suggestions for improvement of curriculum

3. Review of strengths and weaknesses of students

4. List of suggested equipment, supplies, books and other resources for Iraq Institute to acquire.

5. Other suggestions for improving training and University of Delaware program in general

6. Appendices:

   - Copy of Syllabus **as taught**,

   - List of any other resources provided to the Institute (handouts, PowerPoint presentations, electronic documents, etc.);

   - List of equipment purchased and delivered to the Institute (copies of invoices will suffice).

Fig. 3.1 Outline for the Final Report for Visiting Instructors in the University of Delaware Conservation Programs at the Iraqi Institute for the Conservation and Preservation of Antiquities and Heritage. Courtesy of Iraqi Institute for the Conservation and Preservation of Antiquities and Heritage.

to different teaching styles, a student who appeared weaker in one class might shine in another. The teachers' reports provide valuable help in tracking such variation.

Visiting instructors' suggestions for improving the programme have also helped to evolve the design of programmes in later versions. For example, an instructor might note a gap in knowledge that most international instructors would assume were basic shared skills (for example measurement, public presentation or an understanding of atoms and molecules). These reports ensure that multiple instructors work on these same skills multiple times later in the courses.

Students also evaluate visiting instructors using a standard teacher evaluation form at the end of each teaching block. Translated, scanned and sent to teachers, these reviews allow instructors to adjust their subsequent teaching based on the students' input.

Formal curriculum review

In December 2011, following the completion of four courses of the Collections Care and Conservation programme, the academic director held a meeting/conference call with all of the 2011 instructors at the Walters Art Gallery in Baltimore, Maryland. Most of the teachers had taught two or more times at the Institute. This meeting was an opportunity to identify challenges in teaching the Iraqi Institute students, share ideas on successful techniques and brainstorm about the broad teaching concepts and content needed to further the programme.

Instructors expressed a general lack of clarity about the teaching goals of the programme and concern whether it was really making a difference. They observed that students lacked understanding of how the knowledge and skills introduced by the curriculum were relevant to their individual institutions. Instructors discussed methods to provide students with a broader perspective on the roles a museum can play and the ways in which ideas can be conveyed through curatorial context and display content. Many of their concerns served time and again to highlight some of the basic educational voids apparent across the student population. Prominent among these were the inability to think critically about the material presented, the seeming reluctance to become independent learners and the lack of basic manual skills.

This initial review developed the following guidelines and suggestions for instructors in the 2012 and 2013 teaching blocks:

1. Preventive conservation is the most effective method of preservation and will be stressed throughout the training
2. Focus will be placed on improving students' skills at creating condition reports, treatment proposals and treatment reports. Instructors who teach specific materials will do an oral condition report in class to help students understand the process of examining and documenting condition
3. Include topics that will help students think more broadly about museums and the role they play in society. Establish a mini-museum at IICAH that can be used repeatedly by all instructors to aid students' understanding of the wider world of museums through exhibits they create

4. Encourage students to create brief oral presentations to strengthen communication skills taught through the year
5. Provide object handling scenarios for discussion and to stimulate critical thinking skills
6. Students will develop a list of tools, supplies and equipment that is added to at the end of each block so that they have this document when they leave. Instructors and staff will help identify Iraqi and international suppliers of conservation materials

Two years later, at the end of 2013, a second curriculum review was compiled by author Kim Cullen Cobb. This review included input from the final reports of visiting instructors from the Architecture and Archaeology programmes as well as the Conservation programme – enabling us to look at issues across the three programmes and to share successful teaching techniques (Cobb 2013).

The review revealed that the Iraqis' inconsistent background education in science and computer skills and in critical thinking abilities, combined with their limited practical experience in conservation and preservation, is the main challenge encountered by instructors across all three programmes. The necessary remediation slows down the teaching process. This issue underlies other concerns, such as the often-repeated recommendation to extend the length of the teaching modules in order to teach the course topics coherently. In addition the lack of available translated teaching material and professional literature (in Arabic or Kurdish) to augment instruction seriously undermines a student's ability to start thinking critically about the information provided.

Terry Drayman-Weisser (visiting instructor for ivory conservation and Advisory Board member) has proposed a possible solution to the problems encountered by Iraqi Institute instructors.

> Being able to require pre-requisites, such as chemistry, archaeology, etc. would allow teaching to be more directed at meeting our goals [expressed as skills listed in the course description] and would create more space in the teaching schedule. Right now, so much is remedial teaching.

During the 2013 review Paul Hepworth (visiting instructor for textile conservation) contributed one important suggestion. He noted that instructors must help students to identify the key concepts that they are expected to understand, as well as what details they need to record but do not need to memorise. The overarching approach is to encourage critical thinking by separating taught information into three levels of importance:

- Key concepts: These are the main theoretical and technical ideas that the student must understand to carry out their job going forward better and to apply the problem-solving and critical thinking skills they have learned.
- Important ideas: These are specific topics or methods that add deeper meaning to the broad topics.
- Interesting details: These are very specific technical details that change based on the specific project.

As part of this 2013 review, past students from the programmes received a brief questionnaire asking for input on how their education at the Institute had affected their work. The questionnaire was an attempt to understand whether the courses were in fact changing the practice of heritage preservation in Iraq. Students were asked to respond to the following questions:

- What you do in your job now?
- What parts of your educational experience at the IICAH are you finding most useful in your job?
- Has your job changed since you left the IICAH?
- If your job has changed, in what ways has it changed?
- Has being able to use English helped you in your work?
- Have you maintained contact with the Institute and your colleagues in conservation?
- Are there additional subjects you would like the Institute to teach?
- Is there anything else you would like the Institute to know?

Eighteen students responded out of a possible 93 who had attended one or more courses between 2009 and 2013 – a response rate of 19 per cent. Flaws in translation and the poor response rate limit the usefulness of the information. However, this questionnaire and other contact in the future will help to follow the graduates as their careers develop. In the future these deficiencies will be addressed by conducting interviews, encouraging students to provide anecdotal responses to augment comments.

However, the following information was distilled from the information collected through the questionnaire:

- Several museums in Iraq have set up or renovated conservation labs and departments as a result of the students' new knowledge
- Most students listed specific topics (ceramics, GIS, etc.) that were useful, but a few also mentioned planning and developing alternative solutions as skills they learned at the Iraqi Institute

- Of those who had English classes, many noted that a better understanding of English made continuing their education and reading 'foreign' sources possible

Almost all students said they are still in contact with the Iraqi Institute, indicating a growing network of alumni. Information about the Iraqi Institute is shared with this network through the Institute Facebook page, through contact with members of the Board of Directors and informally through the students' contacts with one another.

Developing the heritage preservation community in Iraq

A total of 162 students attended US-sponsored classes at the Iraqi Institute between 2011–14. These students have come from all 18 Iraqi provinces, with many coming from Baghdad as employees of the central SBAH. Erbil has the largest contingent since these students are able to live at home and attend classes. Often the dormitory space in the Institute building is the limiting factor in determining the size and number of programmes that can be held.

Beyond learning about heritage preservation and archaeology, students at the Iraqi Institute develop a network of personal and professional relationships with colleagues from diverse geographic, cultural and religious backgrounds. Friendships, teamwork and a sense of community develop through shared experiences and interests. Through a wide variety of activities, students learn more about their country's heritage and build strong bonds with others, who will then return to positions throughout Iraq. This alumni network is helping to rebuild the strong national community of archaeologists and preservation professionals that Iraq needs to research and preserve the country's heritage.

As part of the overall strategy of long-term education and sustainability of the Iraq Institute, a number of Iraqis – designated master trainers – serve as teaching assistants or entry-level instructors. Asked to return and assist with teaching and classroom support, these top graduates work for both the SBAH and the KRG, but are assigned to the Institute. They assist visiting instructors with laboratory and classroom preparation and instruction, and work with the students on a one-to-one basis. Over time they will take over the management of the programmes and some of the teaching. International expertise will remain a major part of the Institute's educational programmes for the foreseeable future, however, as this idea is built into the Institute's mission.

The facilities of the Iraqi Institute have also been used by other teaching and research programmes from a number of different countries (see Table 3.1). Through these programmes about 150 more students have taken courses at the Institute, with a basic fee charged to outside programmes for the use of classrooms, laboratories and dormitories. These programmes bring more people to the Institute, expanding the experiences and interactions of all students and master trainers.

Meetings at the Institute have invited the provincial directors-general of antiquities and university professors – the supervisors and educators of heritage preservation professionals – to ensure they have a complete understanding of the education that Institute students receive. These meetings have been critical in ensuring supervisors and other managers are knowledgeable about the Institute and in helping students to effect change after returning to their home institutions. It also helps to ensure that appropriate students are recommended to participate in the programmes.

In addition to the community of students, teachers and managers, a broader support network has been established and expanded through regular Advisory Council/Directory Board meetings, in Erbil.

Table 3.1 Other institutions that have used Iraqi Institute facilities for research and education programmes. Source: the authors.

Organisation	Project description	Year
International Commission on Missing Persons (ICMP)	Training programmes	2011
Superior Institute for Conservation and Restoration, Italy	Conservation training programmes	2011–13
University of Athens, Greece	Archaeological research	2011
Adam Mickiewicz University of Poznán and Warsaw University, Poland	Archaeological field school	2012
Technical University of Berlin, Germany	Preservation of Erbil Kayseri (Ottoman market)	2012
Leipzig and Leiden Universities	Archaeological research	2013
World Monuments Fund (WMF)	Archaeological site management training	2013, 2014
Boston University	Archaeological training programmes	2013, 2014
University of Arizona	Archaeological repositories training	2014

Such encounters bring international advisors into the country to witness the real constraints and the real possibilities of teaching heritage preservation in Iraq. The meetings have been instrumental in keeping all stakeholders engaged with the process of developing the teaching methodology and the curriculum.

Education and reconciliation

After the fragmentation of conflict, people and communities have to find ways to come back together again. The ancient heritage of Iraq is one of the things that individuals with different backgrounds (religious, ethnic, gender, language) perceive to be important and can identify with. At the Iraqi Institute the following key facts support reconciliation and development of a larger shared community:

- Students selected to attend courses are already working in heritage preservation in governmental or academic institutions
- Selection of students always includes choosing individuals from across the country
- Students live together in the Iraqi Institute dormitory at the same site as classrooms and laboratories; they share in communal tea time and lunch time meals prepared at the Institute
- Class projects are designed to develop teamwork and public presentation skills to share new knowledge more broadly
- Students tour a variety of local sites and institutions that showcase local ethnic communities as well as shared ancient heritage[4]
- Students improve computer skills and more become fluent in social media through Facebook
- Courses have a high percentage of practical projects, allowing students to share skills and knowledge informally
- Top students are invited to return as master trainers
- Iraqi Institute web presence (Facebook, blogs) keeps graduates abreast of current happenings

2014–16

In August 2014 – soon after the original paper, 'The social impact of cross-disciplinary conservation', was presented at the conference – ISIS advanced close to Erbil. They were said to be within shelling distance of the international airport, a development that forced the cancellation of a course and the evacuation of lecturers and students. However, the security situation improved later that same year and into 2015 as the KRG kept ISIS from gaining a foothold in the Kurdistan Region of Iraq. Planning for new educational programmes began in early 2015, though the focus and approach of the Institute changed from one of capacity-building for long-term skills development to one supporting more immediate needs of disaster preparedness and emergency response. In May 2015 a coalition of organisations, including the University of Pennsylvania, the Smithsonian Institution, the Prins Claus Fund and the International Centre for the Study of the Preservation and Restoration of Cultural Property (ICCROM), offered a short course to 18 Iraqi heritage professionals. They used the 'First Aid to Cultural Heritage in Times of Crisis' (FAC) methodology pioneered by ICCROM (Tandon et al. 2014).

The success of the initial 'First Aid' course led the Smithsonian to seek additional funding to expand the Institute's emergency course offerings. In early 2016 the Smithsonian began its first course in 'Fundamentals of Heritage Conservation', attended by 18 students. In a departure from previous long-form, specialised courses, the new version sought to teach the basic skills that all Iraqi heritage professionals would need to manage antiquities and heritage threatened or affected by conflict. The course included much of the ICCROM FAC method-ology of documentation, stabilisation, recovery and protection; it also expanded on it by including disaster risk management strategies for protecting endangered heritage. As part of this preventative approach, the participants were encouraged to coordinate and work with those not traditionally affiliated with heritage management in Iraq (where heritage is predominantly state-run), such as local citizens, municipal-ities, security and military forces and religious communities. In so doing the students were able to encourage peace-building and reconciliation through a shared interest in the past.

Nimrud Rescue Project, 2017

Near the close of the first 'Fundamentals' course, Iraqi and coalition forces intensified their offensive against ISIS in and around Mosul. By mid-November 2016 ISIS had been pushed out of Nimrud, the ancient Assyrian site located 30 km (20 miles) southeast of Mosul. More than a year earlier ISIS had publicly detonated several reliefs and sculptures at the site. They used bulldozers to destroy the remains of a ziggurat, pushing sculptural pieces into large piles and wrecking all site support facilities (Danti et al. 2015).

Early in 2017 representatives of the Smithsonian met with Mr Qais Rashid, Deputy Minister of Culture and head of the SBAH. In this meeting the Smithsonian offered their support to continue to focus their successful efforts of 2015 and 2016, this time working on an actual site with a dedicated team of SBAH employees. Deputy Minister Rashid indicated his willingness to accept the Smithsonian's assistance. He suggested that Nimrud – once a popular destination for heritage tourism and a site of long-term archaeological investigation – should be the first site considered in a new effort. The rescue of Nimrud would be an important first step in showing the people of Iraq and the wider world how highly Iraq continues to value its cultural heritage – and how terrorism fails to change those national values. Within a few months, with funding from the US Government and the Smithsonian secured, the Nimrud Rescue Project began in earnest. Working on it were a team of 24 Iraqis, including eight master trainers from the Iraqi Institute, plus several experts from the Smithsonian and partners (Couzin-Frankel 2017).

The Nimrud Rescue Project represents a continued evolution of collaboration between the Iraqi heritage establishment and international heritage organisations. The Project focuses on devising and implementing a recovery plan for Nimrud while simultaneously defining a transferrable process and protocol to use on other affected sites. Continuing an Institute tradition, local Erbil sites are used for practical exercises.

Conclusion and thoughts

The success of the Iraqi Institute for the Conservation of Antiquities and Heritage is fundamentally the result of the people, from student to visiting expert, who come together to share new ideas and approaches. There can be no significant preservation of the wealth of ancient and historic material culture in Iraq without people who are educated in current theoretical approaches and skilled in practical application of those theories. Nor can there be any long-term, significant support of foreign and local research without people who understand how that research is organised and framed. The creation of a long-term political strategy for saving heritage, in the face of development and lack of interest in the past, is not possible without educated people – those who have the skill and knowledge to take and adapt international ideas and strategies that have worked elsewhere and to frame them for the needs and difficulties in Iraq. Aslan (2014) also noted the need for this kind of capacity-building across the region.

At a graduation ceremony in 2013, one of the students called the Institute a 'little Iraq'. The friendships that are made there, and the community of students, teachers and supporters that is developing, will go a long way to rebuild and restore the expertise required to protect and re-establish Iraq's heritage. The need now is to build new museums and parks able to educate all Iraqi people about their heritage and to share it with the rest of the world. Iraqi people again face horrendous challenges in surviving the latest conflict and rebuilding their lives and communities. The Iraqi Institute will continue to be part of this rebuilding, assisting local heritage professionals to save the unparalleled remnants of some of the earliest civilisations in the world. These dedicated Iraqi citizens are working together to save, restore and share their heritage – and to rejoin the international community of professionals, scholars and experts doing the same things all over the world.

Acknowledgements

Funding for the sustainable development of the Iraqi Institute of Antiquities and Heritage has been provided by the US Embassy in Baghdad, the US Department of State's Cultural Heritage Center, the KRG, the Erbil Governor's office, the Iraqi SBAH, the Mellon Foundation, the Getty Foundation, Bank of America, Tru Vue, the J.M. Kaplan Fund, the Prins Claus Fund and numerous private individuals.

We thank all our colleagues in the SBAH and the KRG who have supported the Iraqi Institute and its development since 2008. We would also particularly like to thank the many partners who have dedicated countless hours to sustaining the dream of a safe place for people to come and work together to learn about saving heritage, in particular Vicki Cassman, Catherine Foster, Rebecca George, Katharyn Hanson, Lisa Huber, Debra Hess Norris, Nancy Odegaard, Lois Olcott Price, John Russell and Terry Drayman-Weisser. In addition to the Board of Directors and the Advisory Council, support for the authors and their work comes from the current director of the Iraqi Institute, Abdullah Khorsheed and many people in Iraq, including Aram Mohammed Amin Ahmed, Nihayet Abdullah, Sana Hurmiz, Karokh Ismael, Yassir Mahdi, Sebastian Meyer, David Michelmore, Vian Rasheed, Shukran Salih, Gouhar Shemdin and Dara Yacoubi, as well as many staff members of the Iraqi Institute and the US Consulate in Erbil.

Notes

1. The name 'Iraqi Institute for the Conservation of Antiquities and Heritage' has been shortened both to 'Iraq Institute' (in colloquial English and in Arabic and Kurdish) and to 'IICAH' (usually by US agencies). In this chapter the more widely used 'Iraqi Institute' will be used as the shortened form, unless the name is copied from another document.
2. A list of media reports about the Iraqi Institute collected since 2010 can be found at https://www.artcons.udel.edu/outreach/global-engagement/iraqi-institute. Accessed 31 July 2019.
3. A current list of the Iraqi Institute Board of Directors and Advisory Council can be found at https://www.artcons.udel.edu/outreach/global-engagement/iraqi-institute/governance. Accessed 31 July 2019.
4. These include the Kurdish Textile Museum (http://www.kurdishtextilemuseum.com/); the Syriac Heritage Museum, Shanidar Cave and sites related to the Assyrian King Sennacherib and his capital at Nineveh. Accessed 31 July 2019.

References

Aslan, Zaki. 2014. 'Education and Professionalization for Heritage Conservation in the Arab Region: Review of current status and strategic directions', *Conservation and Management of Archaeological Sites* 16 (2): 117–30.

Barakat, Sultan. 2007. 'Postwar Reconstruction and the Recovery of Cultural Heritage: Critical lessons from the last fifteen years'. In *Cultural Heritage in Postwar Recovery*, edited by N. Stanley-Price. Papers from the ICCROM Forum, 4–6 October 2005. ICCROM Conservation Studies 6, Rome: ICCROM.

Barnard, Anne. 2015. 'Race in Iraq and Syria to Record and Shield Art Falling to ISIS'. *New York Times*, 8 March 2015. Accessed 31 July 2019. http://www.nytimes.com/2015/03/09/world/middleeast/race-in-iraq-and-syria-to-record-and-shield-art-falling-to-isis.html.

British Museum. 2017. The Iraqi Scheme website. Accessed 31 July 2019. http://www.britishmuseum.org/about_us/museum_activity/middle_east/iraq_scheme.aspx.

Bouchenaki, Mounir. 2003. 'The Interdependency of the Tangible and the Intangible Cultural Heritage'. Keynote address, 14th ICOMOS General Assembly and International Symposium. *Place, Memory, Meaning: Preserving intangible values in monuments and sites*. Accessed 31 July 2019. http://openarchive.icomos.org/468/.

Cassman, Vicki, Johnson, Jessica S. and Odegaard, Nancy. 2011. 'Building a Museum Conservation Community in Iraq'. In *Plying the Trades: Pulling together in the 21st Century*. Oaxaca, Mexico: 8th North American Textile Conservation Conference, 8–12 November 2011.

Chitty, Gill. 2017. *Heritage, Conservation and Communities: Engagement, participation and capacity building*. London; New York: Routledge.

Cobb, Kim Cullen. 2013. 'Iraqi Institute for the Conservation of Antiquities and Heritage Review of Program Curricula 2009–2013'. Unpublished report.

Court, Sarah and Wijesuriya, Gamini. 2015. *People-Centred Approaches to the Conservation of Cultural Heritage: Living heritage*. Rome: International Centre for the Study of the Preservation and Restoration of Cultural Property.

Couzin-Frankel, Jennifer. 2017. 'Mission Aims to Salvage What's Left of Nimrud', *Science* 357 (6358): 1340–1. https://doi: 10.1126/science.357.6358.1340.

Danti, Michael, Branting, Scott, Paulette, Tate and Cuneo, Allison, eds. 2015. *Report on the Destruction of the Northwest Palace at Nimrud (ASOR Cultural Heritage Initiatives)*. Accessed 8 January 2018. http://www.asor-syrianheritage.org/report-on-the-destruction-of-the-northwest-palace-at-nimrud/.

Drennan, Justine. 2014. 'The Black-Market Battleground'. *Foreign Policy*, 17 October 2014. Accessed 31 July 2019. http://www.foreignpolicy.com/articles/2014/10/17/the_black_market_battleground_syria_iraq_isis.

Emerick, Keith. 2017. 'The Language Changes but Practice Stays the Same: Does the same have to be true for community conservation?' In *Heritage, Conservation, and Communities: Engagement, participation, and capacity building*, edited by G. Chitty. London; New York: Routledge.

Hamdan, Osama, Shaaban, Tagrid and Benelli, Carla. 2008. 'Experiences in Mosaic Conservation Training in the Middle East'. In *Lessons Learned: Reflecting on the theory and practice of*

mosaic conservation, edited by Aïcha Ben Abed and Thomas Roby. Los Angeles, CA: Getty
Conservation Institute.

Japanese International Cooperation Agency (JICA). 2017. *The Project for the Conservation Center in
the Grand Egyptian Museum*. Accessed 31 July 2019. https://www.jica.go.jp/project/english/
egypt/0702247/index.html.

Johnson, Jessica S., Heald, Susan, McHugh, Kelly, Brown, Elizabeth and Kaminitz, Marian. 2005.
'Practical Aspects of Consultation with Communities', *Journal of the American Institute for
Conservation* 44: 203–15. Accessed 31 July 2019. http://cool.conservation-us.org/jaic/art-
icles/jaic32-03-004_indx.html.

Johnson, Jessica S., Lione, Brian Michael, Hess Norris, Debra, Olcott Price, Lois, Salih, Shukran,
Shemdin, Gouhar and Drayman-Weisser, Terry, eds. 2014. 'Collaboration, Sustainability,
and Reconciliation: Teaching cultural heritage preservation and management in Iraq'. In
ICOM-CC 17th Triennial Conference Preprints, Melbourne, 15–19 September 2014, edited by
J. Bridgeland, art. 0305, 8 pp. Paris: International Council of Museums.

Kohn, D. 2014. 'Isis's Looting Campaign'. *The New Yorker*, 14 October 2014. Accessed 31 July 2019.
http://www.newyorker.com/tech/elements/isis-looting-campaign-iraq-syria.

Kurin, Richard. 2011. *Saving Haiti's Heritage: Cultural recovery after the earthquake*. Washington,
DC: Smithsonian Institution.

Lawler, Andrew. 2014. 'Erbil Revealed', *Archaeology* (Sept/October 2014). Accessed 31 July 2019.
https://www.archaeology.org/issues/145-1409/features/2419-kurdistan-erbil-excavations.

Little, Barbara J. and Shackel, Paul A. 2014. *Archaeology, Heritage, and Civic Engagement: Working
toward the public good*. Walnut Creek, CA: Left Coast Press.

MacGinnis, John. 2014. *A City in the Dawn of History: Erbil from the cuneiform sources*.
Oxford: Oxbow Books.

McManamon, Francis P. 2000. 'Native American Graves Protection and Repatriation Act (NAGPRA)'.
In *Archaeological Method and Theory: An encyclopedia*, edited by L. Ellis. New York: Garland
Publishing, Inc.

McManamon, Francis P., Stour, Andrew and Barnes, Jodi A., eds. 2008. *Managing Archaeological
Resources: Global context, national programs, local actions*. Walnut Creek, CA: Left Coast Press.

Odegaard, Nancy, Bott, Suzanne, Hamraz, Muzghan, Jeffery, R. Brooks and Rawan, Atifa. 2014.
'Professional Education for Afghan Cultural Heritage Faculty'. In *ICOM-CC 17th Triennial
Conference Preprints, Melbourne, 15–19 September 2014*, edited by J. Bridgland, art. 0307,
8 pp. Paris: International Council of Museums.

Onciul, Bryony, Stefano, Michelle L. and Hawke, Stephanie. 2017. *Engaging Heritage, Engaging
Communities*. Woodbridge: The Boydell Press.

Roby, Thomas, Alberti, Livia, Bourguignon, Elsa and Ben Abed, Aïcha. 2008. 'Training of Technicians
for the Maintenance of in Situ Mosaics: An assessment of the Tunisian initiative after three
years'. In *Lessons Learned: Reflecting on the theory and practice of mosaic conservation*, edited by
Aïcha Ben Abed and Thomas Roby. Los Angeles, CA: Getty Conservation Institute.

Stanley-Price, Nicholas, ed. 2007. 'Cultural Heritage in Postwar Recovery'. Paper from the ICCROM
Forum held on 4–6 October 2005. ICCROM Conservation Studies 6, Rome: ICCROM.

Stein, Gil J. 2016. 'The Oriental Institute Partnership with the National Museum of Afghanistan'.
In *Oriental Institute 2015–2016 Annual Report*, edited by G.J. Stein, 130–5. Chicago, IL:
University of Chicago Press.

Tandon, Aparna. 2011. 'First Aid for Haiti's Cultural Heritage', *Museum International* 62 (4): 72.

Tandon, Aparna, Rouhani, Bijan, Dal Maso, Anna and Hamid Salah, Abdel. 2014. 'Culture Cannot
Wait: International and national courses on first aid for cultural heritage in times of conflict'.
In *ICOM-CC 17th Triennial Conference Preprints, Melbourne, 15–19 September 2014*, edited by
J. Bridgland, art. 0309, 8 pp. Paris: International Council of Museums.

Waterton, Emma and Watson, Steve. 2013. 'Heritage and Community Engagement: Collaboration
or contestation?' A reproduction of the *International Journal of Heritage Studies* 16, 1–2.
New York; London: Routledge.

World Bank. 2001. *Cultural Heritage and Development: A framework for action in the Middle East and
North Africa*. Washington, DC: World Bank.

4

Community involvement in built heritage conservation: the case study of the Birzeit Historic Centre Project, Palestine

Anna Teresa Ronchi

Introduction

In recent decades, international discourse on heritage conservation has solicited a closer relationship between cultural, social and economic issues and those related to sustainable development. This has given rise to an interest in the use of natural resources and cultural capital as bearers of evolutionary potential for human societies. Moreover this concept has been asserted, for example, in the UNESCO Universal Declaration on Cultural Diversity, which states that 'cultural diversity is one of the roots of development' (UNESCO 2001). In considering the analogy between the role of cultural diversity for social development and biodiversity for the evolution of natural ecosystems, one can conclude that conservation and the transformation of cultural heritage may be considered an ethical duty, pursuant to the principles of intergenerational and intragenerational equity.

This chapter focuses on the conservation of a particular category of cultural heritage, namely historical districts, which can be defined as 'the result of a historic layering of cultural and natural values and attributes' (UNESCO 2011). This category includes the built environment, social and cultural practices and values, economic processes and the intangible dimensions of heritage. The potential of historical districts to be used for sustainable development has been investigated by drawing on research concerning territorial development, in which *territorial capital* is defined as:

the stock of assets which form the basis for endogenous development in each city and region, as well as to the institutions, modes of decision-making and professional skills to make best use of those assets. (OECD 2001)

Such resources produce collective benefits in local areas, as they cannot be found elsewhere with the same qualities. Built cultural heritage, inherently local and immovable, is accordingly part of this capital. Through conservation activities and promotion of these activities, built heritage can become a strategic resource for local development.

Built environment and local communities are linked in a process of co-evolution, in which heritage is preserved and transformed according to the evolution of people's values and needs. At the same time communities benefit through processes of self-identification and enhancement. For example, built heritage can act as an attraction for tourism. Conservation of that built heritage also offers an opportunity: the practice of conservation, in and of itself, can be a resource for development. In this sense two crucial needs emerge:

- to clarify the relationship between conservation practice and social development – assuming that, in order to become a catalyst, conservation should be able to increase local resources for long-term development such as knowledge capital, social capital and organisational capacity
- to ensure that any conservation work undertaken will be culturally, socially and economically sustainable over time

The following discussion builds on the assumption that community engagement can help to fulfil these aims.

Social dynamics in local development and the role of heritage conservation

Studies on territorial development have argued that strategic resources which are part of territorial capital (for example, built heritage) can only be mobilised through a collective and coordinated action taken by local actors (Dematteis and Governa 2005). Theories on collective action, however, have shown that these processes may encounter significant difficulties, even in cases where there is a strong shared interest, since coordination of individuals involve huge costs, not necessarily financial ones (Olson 1965). In other words, social dynamics may affect development.

This topic has been investigated since the 1980s through studies in the field of economics, for instance research on development processes observed in Italian 'industrial districts'.[1] The term 'industrial districts' refers to regions defined by social and geographic borders in which people's livelihoods are based on small businesses. It was shown that the industrial districts had great capacity to innovate in times of economic crisis. Sociological studies showed that success was due to the ability of local people to act collectively and to adapt their activities to external pressures. Although these dynamics appeared spontaneous in character, success of local businesses was attributed to specific political and economic strategies designed to reinforce local networks of relations. Moreover, a strong cultural and political identification contributed to strengthening trust between people, reducing coordination costs and facilitating economic negotiations (Bagnasco 1999). The experience of the industrial districts has therefore shown that, in order to promote development, it is important to invest in reinforcing cooperative networks among local individuals, to enable local people to access and share resources and to increase what various authors have referred to as social capital.[2]

Bringing these considerations into the heritage domain, it can be argued that conservation processes could act as a 'catalyst for networking' (Della Torre 2010), encouraging social dynamism and supporting the organisational capacity of local actors. In recognising this capacity, scholars in cultural economy have introduced the concept of a cultural district (Santagata 2005), in which cultural capital and heritage serve as a 'social platform for capacity creation' (Sacco 2009).

An exemplary project in which conservation of built heritage was promoted as an opportunity for territorial development was introduced in the 1990s in the south of Sweden by the Regional Museum of Halland. In the face of a recession, institutions in this region managed to create new jobs by offering specialised training to local people then hiring the trained workers for local building restoration projects. The need for long-term employment opportunities for the region was also considered: jobs were created to support cultural activities in the restored buildings, thereby encouraging tourism. However, while the collaborative network made up of government, regional institutions and the building industry proved successful in this specific context, reliance on inter-institutional partnerships and public funding proved to be a weakness when this model was applied in regions with different political, cultural and economic circumstances (Gustafsson 2009).

The model of the evolved cultural district was introduced to overcome these limitations (Canziani 2006). In this framework a single institution plays the role of coordinator for the district, with heritage projects emerging from local communities and private investors. Success would therefore depend on the will and cooperation of the population who own, use, preserve and transform the built heritage. In 2006, based on this model, the Lombardy Region of Italy launched pilot heritage revival projects with the support of a local banking foundation. Financial resources were directed mainly towards works on listed buildings and training for skilled professionals. However, the public was largely unaware that these projects were taking place. A shift in awareness could have been promoted by investing resources in activities directed to local communities. This, in turn, would promote social commitment towards heritage conservation and the increase of the demand for related services.

Benefits of community involvement on the sustainability of conservation

Community involvement has been increasingly employed in projects concerning the conservation of built heritage carried out in developing contexts. In order to foster sustainable local development of jobs and other business opportunities, however, conservation projects need to act as catalysts for further activity. Given these goals, three main issues have to be considered:

1. Developing a localised, qualified practice for conservation of built heritage directly depends on the availability of skilled, local construction workers. Community involvement must also foster a desire for shared learning of relevant knowledge and skills between local workers and conservators
2. In order that conservation can be implemented sustainably over time, it is necessary to foster transition from a *praxis* based on 'one-off' comprehensive restoration work to a system of regular maintenance, based on preventive care. In fact, while maintenance of buildings is frequently poor or non-existent, regular implementation would permit a reduction in the costs of intervention (Forster and Kayan 2009), prevent the loss of historical material and lessen the need for new building elements. To this end community involvement should focus on increasing awareness of the importance of ongoing care
3. So that conservation-led, local development can be sustainable from a social and economic viewpoint, local built heritage has to remain meaningful to local communities. Thus community development projects should set out to identify and define how the built heritage reflects the needs and interests of various local stakeholders

The assumption is that community involvement can help to fulfil these aims because it can promote the learning of high-standard conservation practice, acting at the level of both the individual and the community. As for individuals, studies on experiential learning have shown that immersion in a concrete experience enables deeper learning, leading to changes in the learners' patterns and actions (Myers, et al. 2010). However, heritage conservation involves multiple actors and, in order to increase the quality of the common *praxis*, the development of dynamic learning as a collective practice is also required.

Studies on collective and organisational learning highlight a mutually beneficial relationship between the intellectual capital of organisations, intended as 'the knowledge and knowing capability of a social collectivity' (Nahapiet and Ghoshal 2008), and their social capital. This topic has also been addressed by research on communities of practice (CoP), defined as 'groups of people who share a concern, a set of problems, or a passion about a topic, and who deepen their knowledge and expertise in this area by interacting on an on-going basis' (Wenger et al. 2002). According to the CoP approach, within a community the learning process is enabled by a shared repertory of knowledge, largely tacit, which supports the ability to learn new behaviours and to innovate. Some authors argue that both normative elements and world-views (which include values) would play a key role in these processes (Bawden 2010). Moreover, direct engagement in an activity developed within a community, whose social contextual conditions support individual feelings of competence, autonomy and relatedness, has proved to foster the development of intrinsic motivation towards the activity itself (Ryan and Deci 2000).

To summarise, the integration of participatory strategies in projects concerning the conservation of built heritage can help to increase social capital, key for collective learning processes, and can also support the development of both specialised skills and motivation to undertake conservation, laying the groundwork for further implementation.

State of the practice of community involvement in built heritage conservation

In recent years the role of local communities in the preservation of cultural heritage has been brought to the attention of the public by many international organisations. For instance, Australia ICOMOS stated in the Burra Charter (1999) that 'conservation, interpretation and management of a place should provide for the participation of people for whom the place has special associations and meanings, or who have social, spiritual or other cultural responsibilities for the place'. Similarly, in the Framework Convention on the Value of Cultural Heritage for Society (2005), the Council of Europe has recalled the importance of sharing responsibilities between authorities and civil society in the management of cultural heritage, experiencing innovative 'legal, financial and professional frameworks which make possible joint action' in order to promote social cohesion and prevent conflicts.

UNESCO has gone further in the Vienna Memorandum (2005). In this it has stressed the importance of a comprehensive public consultation in the development and implementation of the Management Plans for historic urban landscapes, and has recognised 'common' built heritage as a relevant asset for local communities. These statements were also referred to in the UNESCO Recommendation on Historic Urban Landscape (2011), which recommended community engagement as a tool for education, empowerment, visioning and consensus building. Community engagement has also been considered a bolster for local governance, as it can prove very useful for resolving conflicts of interest with regard to reuse of buildings.

Additionally, we must consider the role that local communities play 'in the production, safeguarding, maintenance and re-creation of the intangible cultural heritage' (UNESCO 2003). Considering that the built environment is continually transformed by intangible cultural processes, the intimate relationship between tangible and intangible dimensions of heritage is irrefutable. This issue was addressed in the ICOMOS Québec Declaration on the Preservation of the Spirit of Place (2008), which states that 'it is through interactive communication and the participation of the concerned communities that the spirit of place is most efficiently safeguarded, used and enhanced'.

Despite the growing interest in community involvement in conservation practice – as well as the fact that the topic has been addressed through many research and field projects – international declarations have not yet demanded implementation. In 1998, for example, the Getty Conservation Institute (GCI) launched a project to investigate strategies for involving communities in identifying projects and drawing up management plans for cultural heritage sites. Having observed that conservation professionals generally do not possess skills essential to manage participation processes, GCI subsequently designed the 'Heritage Values, Stakeholders and Consensus Building' project, with the aim of developing and testing professional training materials to help to fill this gap. As a further example in 2008, building on several case studies, UNESCO and UN-HABITAT edited a manual directed at city professionals. The manual described a set of strategies and tools for community engagement in the rehabilitation of historic districts, in order to promote their integration within local practices.

Even though such publications on techniques for engaging community participation exist, including some not strictly created for heritage conservation professionals, the form of engagement inevitably depends on the specific context of intervention. Common factors of success can be identified. These include an efficient organisational structure among actors and a flexible and multilevel design of the participatory process. What follows is an overview of participatory strategies which could be used at different stages of processes of heritage conservation:

- provision for ways to relay information and provide regular communication throughout the process
- awareness-raising campaigns
- participatory activities which result in the identification and definition of heritage values
- participatory activities to identify community needs and priorities related to heritage (for example, scenario assessment)
- direct engagement in conservation practice through professional training and volunteering
- direct engagement in preventive maintenance and periodic monitoring
- campaigns of dissemination of information about good (and bad) conservation practice
- participation in resource raising

In order to evaluate the impact of community participation on local development projects properly, assessments need to be undertaken for some time after the end of a project. Yet funding programmes seldom include resources for these follow-up assessments. This chapter aims to fill that gap, however, by presenting and evaluating the diverse physical and societal impacts engendered by a conservation project which set out to foster community involvement within a region of political instability.

Birzeit, Palestine: a case study and evaluation

The project concerns the rehabilitation of the historic centre of Birzeit, a village 10 km north of Ramallah, Palestine (Fig. 4.1). The project began

Fig. 4.1   Aerial view of the historic centre of Birzeit. © Digitalglobe 2014.

in 2007 and was coordinated by Riwaq, a Ramallah-based NGO dedicated to the preservation of the Palestinian architectural heritage in the West Bank and Gaza.

Riwaq initiated work on rural areas by carrying out documentary and architectural surveys of 420 villages from 1994 to 2007. This research, published as *Register of Historic Buildings*, revealed that 50 per cent of the historic buildings were located in just 50 villages. In 2007 Riwaq therefore launched the '50 Villages Project' with the aim of protecting this heritage through rehabilitation and revitalisation. Based on this extensive study, Birzeit was selected as a pilot development project.

Several factors affected this decision, in addition to the village's rich architectural and environmental heritage. Collaborative prospects looked promising: Riwaq had previously collaborated with Birzeit Municipality and the council had shown political goodwill towards the proposed regeneration programme. Birzeit also had its own university, the presence of which appeared to provide fertile ground for collaboration. Similarly local civic societies, such as the Rozana Cultural Association, were on hand to facilitate implementation of the project. Overall it was hoped that the project to revive Birzeit's built heritage, combined with extensive community involvement in the project, would drive the establishment of new businesses related to tourism and allow Riwaq to refine a method for regeneration that could be applied elsewhere.

Birzeit therefore represents an excellent opportunity to study the relationship between community involvement and heritage conservation. Indeed, one of the most important features of the project was that community participation was considered to be not only important as a goal, but also as a means for socio-economic development. To this end, several evaluations of different parts of the project had already been carried out by different entities (de Cesari 2010; Riwaq 2010, 2011, 2012, 2013; Tannerfeldt and Rosenberg 2011; Lamprakos 2013). These studies provided quantitative data and qualitative information that readily supported meta-evaluation of the project, further informed and supported by a member of Riwaq's team who had participated in the project from the beginning.[3]

Description of the case study

The historic centre of Birzeit occupies an area of approximately 4.6 hectares. The buildings form a fairly homogeneous group of which 108 are of historic interest (according to Riwaq's *Register of Historic Buildings*). The buildings consist of one- or two-storey stone structures dating back to the late nineteenth and early twentieth centuries. The majority of them are privately owned but, prior to the launch of the project, most were disused (Fig. 4.2). The 1980s saw rapid change in village life with the introduction of Birzeit University's campus outside the historic centre, an event that fostered urban sprawl and accelerated the abandonment of the historic centre by its inhabitants.

The 'Rehabilitation of the Birzeit Historic Centre Project' was launched by Riwaq in partnership with the municipality (the project's owner), the Rozana Cultural Association and the Department of Architecture at Birzeit University. It spanned the period from 2007 to 2011, came at a total cost of US$ 1.45 million and was mostly funded by Riwaq's major donor, the Swedish International Development Cooperation Agency (SIDA).[4] The project's goal was both to protect heritage values and to revitalise the historic centre with social and economic infrastructure development. These societally systemic aims demanded a review of local planning regulations, in lieu of national heritage protection laws. This work in turn identified the restoration and adaptive reuse of historic buildings as fundamental to the fulfilment of the project's aims.

Riwaq integrated the local community from the outset of the project with the establishment of a specific Community Outreach working unit, its formation predicated on the assumption that 'in order for local communities to start valuing and protecting heritage, they should start feeling the benefit of reusing this heritage' (Muhawi 2011). The local community was immediately engaged in a participative mapping project in order to identify landmarks and places of interest from a local perspective. As they did so a multidisciplinary team of professionals, supported by students, carried out analyses of the built heritage and its social, economic and regulatory environment.

The next step involved organising a community planning workshop which sought to identify the community's aspirations in relation to the project. After several meetings involving participation of major stakeholders – institutions, civic organisations, residents and property owners – a shared vision for the future of the village began to emerge. This was to create a mixed-use area which would contain both residential and commercial spaces, with a particular focus on creating affordable housing. Provision was also made to develop some of the buildings for educational and cultural purposes in order to attract people back to the historic centre and so to provide a further catalyst for rehabilitation.

Results of the multidisciplinary studies and community workshop allowed a strategic plan for the centre to be drawn up. The plan provided detailed instructions and a work plan relating to both urban planning and restoration of the buildings. In 2010 the strategic plan was ratified by the Municipal Council, which also established an architect-led special unit to lead the rehabilitation.

During the planning phase, Riwaq implemented rehabilitation projects which combined full-scale conservation of selected buildings as well as widespread preventive measures. These projects were linked to the Job Creation Through Conservation (JCTC) programme, supported by SIDA and aimed at lowering the local unemployment rate. The JCTC programme requires most of the workers and site supervisors to be hired from the local community. In addition, the use of labour-intensive methods and local materials are required by the tender documents. What is more, the programme empowers the community to approve the choice of the contractor and monitor the quality of the work.

The first phase of full-scale conservation work transformed two buildings, both strategically located on the main street of the village. One was converted into a guest house and the other into a restaurant. In 2011 adaptive reuse of two more buildings began; these now host the Birzeit University guest house and the Palestinian Circus School respectively.

In order to maximise dissemination of the project's benefits, Riwaq prioritised preventive conservation work over interventive work. Preventive work predominantly consisted of small interventions aimed at prolonging the life of the buildings, such as shoring up foundations, consolidating walls, insulating roofs and undertaking small removals or integration work. Between 2008 and 2011 four campaigns of preventive work were carried out, the last directly promoted by the local municipality. Riwaq also defined activities for which each building could be used, in order to show the inhabitants their potential. This plan was motivated by the belief that 'reusing abandoned historic buildings is probably the most efficient and successful way to protect them' because 'it ensures their on-going maintenance' (Muhawi 2011).

In order to draw attention to the heritage buildings a communication campaign was carried out, directed at different targets. Campaign activity included public meetings, guided tours, summer camps for children and 'volunteer days', during which people were invited to help out with conservation work. In addition, in order to focus attention on the value of the built heritage, two annual awards were established: a drawing competition for students and an award for best intervention. Moreover, in 2009, Riwaq created the Riwaq's Think Net – an international and interdisciplinary network of researchers aimed at increasing the international visibility of the Birzeit Project and its approach to rehabilitation. Furthermore, between 2009 and 2012 Riwaq participated in the Mutual Heritage Project.[5] Through this the project was able to access funds for the production of heritage guides and maps and to gain the support of the creation of tourist paths between sites of architectural interest within the West Bank.

Fig. 4.2   View of El Etem courtyard, Al Ein Road. © Mutual Heritage 2009.

Fig. 4.3   Intervention of street paving. © Mutual Heritage 2009.

Six years after the start of the rehabilitation process the Birzeit Project was awarded the 2013 Aga Khan Award for Architecture, in recognition of its impact on the area's social, economic and political development.

Evaluation

This study aims to clarify and evaluate the relationship between community involvement and local development within the Birzeit Project's approach to rehabilitation. At the same time it seeks to identify success factors in relation to the participatory process, which might offer transferable insights applicable to historic districts in other geographical contexts. Existing evaluations have already stressed the value of community involvement in processes implemented in Birzeit. For instance, the Aga Khan Development Network's Jury (2014) stated that 'the Revitalisation of Birzeit Historic Centre is a dynamic project in which the NGO of Riwaq succeeds in mobilising stakeholders and local craftsmen into a process of healing that is not merely physical but that is social, economic and political'. However, while descriptions of the actions implemented for community involvement do now exist, a comprehensive account of their effects has not so far been provided.

The appraisal, or meta-evaluation, given below is based largely on the data and findings provided by previous studies. The data has been collected and re-organised in order to draft a comprehensive investigation into the effectiveness, efficiency, relevance and impact of the project,[6] with a focus on understanding the effects of community involvement.

Effectiveness

The overall objective of the Birzeit Project was twofold: to preserve (through conservation) and to revitalise (through socio-economic development) the historic centre. Through conservation, buildings that were substantially rebuilt covered 2010 m^2, while preventive work was applied to 6191 m^2. Conservation intervention also affected 2784 m^2 of open space. In addition, 1183 m^2 of open space was enhanced by the installation of infrastructure and street tiling (Fig. 4.3) (Riwaq 2012). These interventions as a whole affected approximately 25 per cent of the overall historic centre, equivalent to around 70 per cent of the built area. The quantitative data, therefore, suggests that the project was successful in increasing the overall state of conservation of the centre. Other evaluation reports highlighted the quality of conservation works, observing that they were conducted without harming architectural coherence and by using affordable traditional techniques and local materials (Lamprakos 2013).

From a socio-economic perspective, the effectiveness of the project can be evaluated, first of all, in terms of the job opportunities it generated. Between 2008 and 2011 Riwaq's conservation of the historic buildings generated 10,382 direct work days, of which about 30 per cent concerned preventive conservation (Tannerfeldt and Rosenberg 2011; Riwaq 2012). Additional employment opportunities were generated off-site, thanks to the involvement of administrative personnel, truck drivers and artisans who supplied the materials. According to Riwaq's method for estimation, indirect work days count for around the 50 per cent of the direct ones. Consequently, within the Birzeit Project, 5,191 indirect work days were generated.

In relation to socio-economic development purposes, however, the effectiveness of the project should be evaluated through consideration of both the number of short-term job opportunities and the long-term socio-economic benefits enabled by conservation works. Impact over time can be measured, for instance, by considering the number of new businesses that opened in the restored buildings, able to attract both local and non-local customers as well as the related number of users. While it is possible to indicate the number of businesses which opened between 2008 and

2011 (a restaurant, two guest houses and a circus school), it is difficult to measure the number of people who benefited.

Efficiency

Comparison of the data referred to total cost and number of direct work days for complete and preventive conservation works carried out between 2008 and 2011 (Tannerfeldt and Rosenberg 2011; Riwaq 2012), shows that the cost per work day for preventive conservation came out as 30 per cent lower than for complete conservation. The choice to implement preventive conservation measures on buildings proved significantly efficient, as the spread of low-cost interventions resulted in highly beneficial community and heritage impacts. Moreover, preventive conservation work is labour intensive: based on Riwaq's experience, 80 per cent of the budget, on average, is allocated for labour, in the face of 65 per cent for complete conservation (Muhawi 2011). Investments in preventive conservation are thus better suited for contributing to the creation of employment over the medium term. Additionally, from a long-term perspective, the practice of preventive conservation as ongoing building maintenance reduces the probability of the community incurring significant future costs for major restoration.

Relevance

A comprehensive process of community involvement ensured that the project met the needs of the beneficiaries. The local municipality was involved from the start. This helped to build political commitment and to promote capacity building; it also helped to generate interest in the project from the inhabitants and building owners. As a member of Riwaq's team stated:

> Municipalities always helped us to gain people's trust, because most of the time and until we prove the contrary, people may suspect our intentions and treat us as outsiders. (Arch. S. Safi. personal communication, 11 March 2011)

Indeed, although Riwaq's team was locally rooted, it continued to remain something of an outside force – a position that allowed it to act as a mediator among stakeholders in the elaboration of the village's strategic plan.

Impact

The Birzeit Project impacted the village in diverse ways. It raised the level of political commitment and interest in heritage conservation by the local municipality. This interest was tangible in that a specific heritage conservation unit was created within the municipality, with a budget allocation in 2011 of 200,000 NIS (approximately 50.000 USD, Riwaq 2011), for continuing rehabilitation work in the historic centre. The Birzeit Project also increased the level of specific conservation skills in the community and raised the skill capacity of contractors, workers and craftspeople. This increase in the quality and quantity of the skill base allowed the community to host educational and social functions in the historic centre. Social use of the restored buildings was consequently able to continue to raise awareness of the role of heritage preservation in society.

Although it is difficult to give an exact measure of the overall socio-economic impact of the project on the local community, it can be observed that, in the wake of the reuse of the buildings restored by Riwaq, seven new businesses opened in the centre as a result of local, non-government initiatives by 2012 (Riwaq 2012). Some new businesses were located in the conserved buildings themselves; other works inspired work on further buildings, the work carried out autonomously by local residents. For example, between 2011 and 2013 an old house was rehabilitated through the initiative of the family who owned it and the Jerusalemite AlNayzak organisation, in collaboration with Birzeit Municipality and Riwaq. Today this building hosts an interactive centre for Science and Technology (Fig. 4.4).

Additionally, improvements to associated infrastructure and open space allowed provision of basic services for tourists. It was possible to organise revenue-generating cultural events, such as the annual heritage week coordinated by Rozana Cultural Association, which came to attract up to 40,000 visitors per year; the ninth edition, held in July 2017, attracted 30,000 visitors (Rozana n.d.). What is more, the project had improved the skill set of Riwaq's team itself. In fact, after the Birzeit pilot project, similar projects were started in six more villages.[7] Processes of intervention were gradually refined, becoming even better able to serve the specific needs of local communities and offer assistance to local entrepreneurs.

Critical issues
There are some critical issues, however, which somewhat dampened the positive impacts of the project.

Instability of political support for conservation by the local municipality has threatened future implementation of conservation works. The establishment of a special heritage unit had seemed to embed

Fig. 4.4 Saadeh House, rehabilitated in 2011–13, hosts an interactive centre for Science and Technology. © Anna Teresa Ronchi 2016.

conservation practice securely within local politics. However, after two years of service the heritage unit was closed due to the turn of political events and changes in economic priorities. Furthermore, while the local communities had been directly involved in preventive conservation work through the JCTC programme, thereby generating job opportunities and interventions in a large number of buildings, in hindsight more effective actions could have been implemented. For example, in addition to the complete intervention on some buildings and the preventive conservation of most of them, strategies for future maintenance could have been identified. As reported by SIDA, in reference to the JCTC project they funded:

> the contractor is responsible for repair and certain maintenance of the building during the first year after handing over … [and] … all users are (according to agreement) expected to take care of the continued maintenance … [but] … some partners have limited resources and even cheap repairs are delayed or neglected. (Tannerfeldt and Rosenberg 2011)

A mechanism to ensure that this did not happen in the Birzeit Project would have been desirable. A site visit held in 2016 allowed us to verify that some of the buildings restored or treated by preventive conservation were suffering from degradation due to lack of maintenance, such as deterioration of roof renderings and growth of vegetation, which may cause water infiltration leading to further damage.

The lack of long-term economic sustainability has also proved to be a major weakness of the project. The rehabilitation of the centre was funded mainly by international donors and, in order to carry the process forward, it would be necessary to identify adequate opportunities for public–private partnership aimed at sustaining local conservation activities. This would require the municipality to assume a leadership role and provide incentives or subsidies for maintenance works in order to encourage investment by private owners or leaseholders. At the same time, the fees collected from leasing public properties could be allocated to further conservation works.

In addition to economic resources, work plans for regular maintenance would also require specific organisational skills and capacities. To this end, the JCTC programme could have been conceived as an opportunity not only for creating short-term job opportunities, but also for establishing a company that could operate inside and outside the village. Such an idea, however, would have required not only on-site training, but also the reinforcement of managerial and administrative skills.

In other words, in order to promote further development by way of conservation, the project would have required the creation and implementation of additional administrative and financial mechanisms, as well as diverse training schemes.

Despite the shortcomings of the local council, however, Riwaq did manage to set up an effective organisational structure. By promoting cooperative strategies, Riwaq successfully coordinated a network involving local authorities, private owners, residents and other NGOs. The multidisciplinary team possessed both technical and social skills; it was able to coordinate conservation issues and social needs through community engagement. This contributed to an environment conducive to learning, inducing motivation towards conservation – as shown by the growing interest and level of initiative manifested by the local municipality and by private investors.

Notes

1. In Italy, studies on industrial districts were mostly promoted by the economist Giacomo Becattini and his research group. They built on the theories of Alfred Marshall, which described the model in the late nineteenth century.
2. Among the rich literature on this topic we mention just two key references: Coleman (1988) and Fukuyama (2000).

3. Arch. S. Safi, project coordinator and at the time also part of the Community Outreach Unit, contributed by direct interviews (2011, 2016), exchange of emails (2011, 2013) and the provision of access to unpublished documents.
4. Other funders were Birzeit Municipality; Birzeit Pharmaceutical Company; Institute for Walloon Heritage (IPW) in Belgium; Wallonie-Bruxelles International (WBI); Belgian Government; The Representative Office of the Netherlands in Ramallah.
5. The aim of the project, funded by the European Union in the framework of the Euromed Heritage IV Program, was the identification, documentation and promotion of the built heritage of the nineteenth and twentieth centuries, in order to encourage its integration within current economical and social contexts. The Mutual Heritage Consortium was led by Laboratoire CITERES (Université François-Rabelais, Tours, France).
6. The following OECD (2002) definitions are applicable here. Effectiveness: the extent to which the development intervention's objectives were achieved, or are expected to be achieved, taking into account their relative importance. Efficiency: a measure of how economically resources/inputs (funds, expertise, time, etc.) are converted to results. Relevance: the extent to which the objectives of a development intervention are consistent with beneficiaries' requirements, country needs, global priorities and partners' and donors' policies. Impact: positive and negative, primary and secondary long-term effects produced by a development intervention, directly or indirectly, intended or unintended.
7. In 2012 similar projects were launched in Hajjeh, Jamma'in, 'Abwein, Adh Dahiriya, Beit Iksa, Deir Ghassana. Riwaq, Annual Report 2012, 7.

References

Aga Khan Development Network. 2014. 'Aga Khan Award for Architecture: Revitalisation of Birzeit Historic Centre'. Accessed 31 July 2019. https://www.akdn.org/architecture/project/revitalisation-birzeit-historic-centre.
Australia ICOMOS. 2000. *The Burra Charter: The Australia ICOMOS Charter for Places of Cultural Significance 1999*. Burra: Australia ICOMOS.
Bagnasco, Arnaldo. 1999. *Tracce di Comunità: Temi Derivati da un Concetto Ingombrante*. Bologna: Il Mulino.
Bawden, Richard. 2010. 'The Community Challenge: The learning response'. In *Social Learning Systems and Communities of Practice*, edited by Chris Blackmore, 39–56. London: Springer.
Canziani, Andrea. 2006. 'Beni Culturali e Governance: Il Modello dei Distretti Culturali.' PhD thesis. Milan: Politecnico di Milano.
Coleman, Samuel James. 1988. 'Social Capital in the Creation of Human Capital', *American Journal of Sociology* 94. Supplement: Organisations and Institutions: Sociological and economic approaches to the analysis of social structure: 95–120.
Council of Europe. 2005. *Council of Europe Framework Convention on the Value of Cultural Heritage for Society (The Faro Convention)*. Strasbourg: Council of Europe.
de Cesari, Chiara. 2010. 'Creative Heritage: Palestinian heritage NGOs and defiant arts of government', *American Anthropologist* 112 (4): 625–37.
Della Torre, Stefano. 2010. 'Conservazione Programmata: I Risvolti Economici di un Cambio di Paradigma', *Il Capitale Culturale: Studies on the value of cultural heritage* 1: 47–55.
Dematteis, Giuseppe and Governa, Francesca, eds. 2005. *Territorialità, Sviluppo Locale, Sostenibilità: Il Modello SLoT*. Milan: Franco Angeli.
Forster, Alan M. and Kayan, Brit. 2009. 'Maintenance for Historic Buildings: A current perspective', *Structural Survey* 27 (3): 210–29.
Fukuyama, Francis. 2000. 'Social Capital and Civic Society', *IMF Working Paper* no 00/74. Washington, DC: IMF Institute.
Gustaffson, Christer. 2009. 'Modelling Experiences from Regional Development and Learning Districts using Built Cultural Heritage and Collaborative Management Research'. In *Learning Districts: Patrimonio Culturale, Conoscenza e Sviluppo Locale*, edited by Francesca Putignano, 79–95. Rimini: Maggioli Editore.
ICOMOS – International Council on Monuments and Sites. 2008. *Québec Declaration on the Preservation of the Spirit of Place*. Québec: ICOMOS.

Lamprakos, Michele. 2013. 'Revitalisation of Birzeit Historic Centre: Birzeit, Palestine. 2013 on site review report.' Accessed 31 July 2019. https://archnet.org/publications/2570.

Muhawi, Farhat Y. 2011. 'Cultural heritage: An integrated approach to development; Towards a decentralized system of regeneration of architectural heritage in the Occupied Palestinian Territories'. In *Consciences Patrimoniales – Heritage Awareness*, Vol.3, edited by Emilie Destaing, 53–73. Bologna: Bononia University Press.

Myers, David, Smith, Stacie Nicole and Shaer, May. 2010. *A Didactic Case Study of Jarash Archaeological Site, Jordan: Stakeholders and heritage values in site management*. Los Angeles, CA: Getty Conservation Institute.

Nahapiet, Janine and Ghoshal, Sumantra. 2008. 'Social Capital, Intellectual Capital, and the Organisational Advantage', *The Academy of Management Review* 23 (2): 242–66.

OECD – Organisation for Economic Co-operation and Development. 2001. *OECD Territorial Outlook: Territorial economy*. Paris: OECD.

OECD – Organisation for Economic Co-operation and Development. 2002. *Glossary of Key Terms in Evaluation and Results Based Management*. Paris: OECD.

Olson, Mancur. 1965. *The Logic of Collective Action: Public goods and the theory of groups*. Cambridge, MA: Harvard University Press.

Riwaq. 2010. *Annual Report 2010*. Ramallah: Riwaq. Accessed 29 December 2017. http://www.riwaq.org/sites/default/files/annual%20report%202010.pdf.

Riwaq. 2011. *Annual Report 2011*. Ramallah: Riwaq. Accessed 29 December 2017. http://www.riwaq.org/sites/default/files/Annual%20Report%202011.pdf.

Riwaq. 2012. *Birzeit Project Portfolio*. Unpublished document.

Riwaq. 2013. *Annual Report 2013*. Ramallah: Riwaq. Accessed 29 December 2017. http://www.riwaq.org/sites/default/files/Annual%20Report%202013.pdf.

Rozana. n.d. 'Rozana Association'. Accessed 29 December 2017. http://rozana.ps/.

Ryan, Richard M. and Deci, Edward L. 2000. 'Intrinsic and Extrinsic Motivations: Classic definitions and new directions', *Contemporary Educational Psychology* 25: 54–67.

Sacco, Pier Luigi. 2009. 'Lo Sviluppo Locale Come Shock Culturale'. In *Learning Districts: Patrimonio Culturale, Conoscenza e Sviluppo Locale*, edited by Francesca Putignano, 47–54. Rimini: Maggioli Editore.

Santagata, Walter. 2005. 'I Distretti Culturali nei Paesi Avanzati e Nelle Economie Emergenti', *Economia della Cultura* XV (2): 141–52.

Tannerfeldt, Göran and Rosenberg, Göran. 2011. *Facts on the Ground: A review of Sida's support to historic environment preservation in the Occupied Palestinian Territories*. Stockholm: SIDA.

UNESCO – United Nations Educational, Scientific and Cultural Organization. 2001. *Universal Declaration on Cultural Diversity*. Paris: UNESCO.

UNESCO – United Nations Educational, Scientific and Cultural Organization. 2003. *Convention for the Safeguarding of the Intangible Cultural Heritage*. Paris: UNESCO.

UNESCO – United Nations Educational, Scientific and Cultural Organization. 2008. *Historic Districts for All: A social and human approach for sustainable revitalization*. Paris: UNESCO.

UNESCO – United Nations Educational, Scientific and Cultural Organization. 2011. *Recommendation on the Historic Urban Landscape*. Paris: UNESCO.

UNESCO World Heritage Committee. 2005. *Vienna Memorandum on 'World Heritage and Contemporary Architecture – Managing the historic urban landscape'*. Paris: UNESCO.

Wenger, Etienne, McDermott, Richard A. and Snyder, William M. 2002. *Cultivating Communities of Practice: A guide to managing knowledge*. Boston, MA: Harvard Business Review Press.

5
Putting sustainability into practice: the use of locally available materials in conservation

Flavia Ravaioli

Introduction

While international conventions from the 1962 Venice Charter onwards have cast stewardship towards world heritage as a shared responsibility at a global level, this has come hand in hand with a growing recognition of the cultural losses resulting from the globalisation of the heritage field. The tension between the local and the global nature of heritage is mirrored by the universal/specific duality within the debate on conservation principles (Graham et al. 2000; Cleere 2001).

The development of codes of ethics and practice for conservators came as a response to the progressive internationalisation of the field and was key to gaining professional recognition. Recently the tenets on which these codes are based have been critiqued, as the focus of preservation efforts moves away from the physical fabric to incorporate social values (Clavir 2002; Jones and Holden 2008). Practitioners are now called to confront broader issues that surround the care and interpretation of heritage, and to engage in decision-making regarding social, economic and environmental sustainability (Avrami 2009; Cassar 2009; de Silva and Henderson 2011). Conservation and other heritage practices are being described as cultural constructs that are grounded in specific geographic, socio-political and historical contexts (Kreps 2003; Colwell-Chanthaphonh 2009).

Sustainability is increasingly being proposed as a guiding principle for heritage management (for example English Heritage 1997; ICOMOS 2001) and has spurred the rethinking of standards in collections care

(Davies and Wilkinson 2008). In preventive conservation the focus is shifting from prescribing solutions to promoting agreed methods for arriving at a solution that fits the individual context (Michalski 2011). Institutional response has come in the form of Triple Bottom Line accounting, which requires museums and heritage organisations to report on the impact of their actions on *People, Planet and Profit* (Lithgow et al. 2008; Lithgow 2011).

International standards are strongly biased in favour of the European contexts in which they were elaborated. As a consequence, the attempt to apply them elsewhere may disempower local heritage practitioners. The contradictions deriving from the application of international standards in low-income countries became apparent in the course of the Prevention in Museums in Africa (PREMA) initiative. Run by the International Centre for the Study of the Preservation and Restoration of Cultural Property (ICCROM) in the 1990s, PREMA provided training opportunities for museum professionals from sub-Saharan Africa. The organisers described the challenge of teaching compliance with conservation ethics while taking into account the paucity of local resources. A key concern was that participants would experience frustration and disheartenment upon return to their home institutions due to the wide gap between learning and practical applications (Barclay and Antomarchi 1994, 63). Twenty-five years on, international standards are still impracticable in most of the world.

Following years of budget cuts to heritage institutions across Europe and elsewhere, there is widespread need for tools that help to put sustainability into practice. This chapter explores the use of methodologies as frameworks for elaborating individual solutions in collections care. The author proposes a method for selecting locally accessible storage materials in challenging contexts, where resources are limited and specialised materials unavailable. Although this research stemmed from the author's experience of attempting to source conservation materials while working on archaeological sites, accessing specialised materials is a challenge faced by conservators in many different contexts. Reasons for this range from the lack of sufficient funds to strict customs regulations, remoteness of the location and absence of suppliers in the region.

An example of such challenges comes from the author's own experience. In spring 2013 and 2014 a team from University College London began to excavate the two multi-period tell sites of Gurga Ciya and Tepe Marani, located in the Suleymaniya region of Iraqi Kurdistan, close to the Iranian border (Fig. 5.1). When faced with the task of setting up a basic conservation laboratory for the newly excavated sites, importing

Fig. 5.1 The multi-period tell site of Gurga Ciya, in the Sharizor Plain, Iraqi Kurdistan. © the author 2014.

specialised materials was not an option. Security threats discouraged travelling to the major cities, and materials that were usually imported from Baghdad were not available at that time (this applied to several solvents, for instance, including acetone). A range of materials was eventually purchased by the author in the nearby city of Suleymaniya, thanks to the guidance of colleagues working in the region. Locally available materials included a few laboratory grade solvents (but not acetone), foam and packaging materials of various types, as well as a collection of tools, glass and plastic containers, crates and boxes.

Standards in preventive conservation

The development of standards is considered essential to the establishment of conservation as an independent profession in its own right, rather than an auxiliary to archaeology and museum curatorship. When the first published standards of practice were presented in 1963, Dr A. van Schendel – then president of the International Institute of Conservation of Historic and Artistic Works (IIC) – was quoted as saying that their adoption marked the transition in conservation between the craft phase and the professional phase (Murray Pease Committee 1964, 116). In the following decades the need to ground the newly emerging discipline in an accepted corpus of principles and methods resulted in a burgeoning of codes of ethics with accompanying guidelines for practice (reviewed by Bell 1997). These included the American Alliance of Museums (AAM) 1991, amended 2000; American Institute for Conservation of Historic and Artistic Works (AIC) 1967, last revision 1994; United Kingdom Institute for Conservation of Historic and Artistic Works (UKIC), now Institute of Conservation (ICON) 1982, last revision 1996; European Confederation of Conservator-Restorers' Organisations (ECCO) 2002. Prescriptive documents for preventive measures followed shortly afterwards and by the 1990s had been published all over the world (reviewed by Alcántara 2002).

Standardisation is expected to bring a range of benefits, from facilitating decision-making to providing legitimacy to funding requests. The results of research have become more comparable and communication between institutions is made easier by the use of a common terminology (Alessandrini and Tabasso 1999). Yet the limits of standards have been increasingly highlighted, particularly within the long-standing debate on museum climate specifications. For example, it has become apparent that the enshrined values of 50 per cent relative humidity and 18°C are simply not attainable in non-temperate climates and are not sustainable in other locations (see Michalski 2007; Ashley-Smith et al. 2013). In 2014 a joint IIC and ICOM-CC declaration on environmental guidelines stressed the importance of setting sustainable goals. It stated that 'guidelines for environmental conditions for permanent display and storage should be achievable for the local climate' (ICOM-CC and IIC 2014).

The requirement that only conservation grade materials be employed is less frequently challenged, despite the fact that such materials represent a considerable expense for small institutions and are not available in most of the world. Materials are referred to as 'conservation grade' or 'archival quality' when they are widely believed to be safe for prolonged contact with cultural property; they are required to have demonstrated chemical stability and 'superior ageing properties', through accelerated ageing tests or from their long history of use (Appelbaum 2007, 315). Common knowledge may not reflect reality, however, as manufacturers can alter products' composition without notice, thus rendering previous test results obsolete.

Part of the problem lies in the difficulty of in-house material testing. Despite its long career, the Oddy test[1] for accelerated ageing is not a feasible solution in most contexts. It requires an oven to be kept running for 28 days, for example, which poses a considerable health and safety risk. Some scientists have questioned its reliability, noting that a comprehensive evaluation of its results on the basis of materials' long-term performance is yet to be undertaken (Green and Thickett 1993; Tsukada et al. 2012).

The need to find alternatives to the Oddy test has resulted in several publications that present quicker, simpler methods (Daniels and Ward 1982; Thickett and Lee 2004; Odegaard et al. 2005; Strlič et al. 2010). Though many of these require costly chemicals and a well-equipped laboratory, some tests can be adapted for use in more basic settings. Selected tests were reviewed by the author on the basis of their practicability in challenging contexts.[2]

Responding to local needs: appropriate solutions for conservation

When international standards elaborated in high-income countries prescribe the use of specific materials and techniques, this results in what development scholars call an 'inappropriate technology transfer'. Schumacher (1973) first observed that importing solutions from developed to developing areas of the world was not only ineffective, but also caused the loss of traditional technologies and ways of life. He proposed the use of technologies which would be simple, easy to maintain and suitable for the specific context in which they are to be employed. 'Appropriate technologies' must be intensive in the use of abundant resources and economical in the use of scarce ones; they must also be low-cost and accessible to low-income persons (Thormann 1979). Materials, like technologies, can only be considered appropriate when they match both user and need in complexity and scale (Hazeltine and Bull 1999, 3). Imported materials seldom have these characteristics and many present problems of cost and availability in the long term.

Several scholars have claimed the concept's relevance to the heritage field (Kreps 2008; Staniforth 2010). In 1979 the United Nations Educational, Scientific and Cultural Organization (UNESCO) commissioned a study on the use of traditional techniques and development strategies adapted to local socio-economic realities in relation to preservation. This resulted in a brief publication, '"Appropriate technologies" in the conservation of cultural property' (UNESCO 1981), which brings together the contributions of various heritage practitioners on the subject since then. The concept has been explored more recently by Jigyasu's research on the role of local knowledge in disaster mitigation and post-disaster heritage reconstruction in low-income countries (2002).

Planning models for sustainability

In the past two decades, heritage professionals have put forth a range of methodologies that provide flexible structures for dealing with the complexity of cultural heritage management.

1. Values-based planning processes seek to reconcile the need for individualised solutions with the effort to maintain objectivity in elaborating general policies for sites and collections (Pearson and Sullivan 1995; Mason and Avrami 2002; de la Torre et al. 2005, among others).
2. Models based on a risk-management approach aim for the most cost-effective reduction of threats to the collection or site by comparing risks linked to each decision with all other predicted risks (Ashley-Smith 1999; Waller and Michalski 2005). Blades and colleagues have applied a risk-management approach specifically to pollution control in museum environments (2000; see also Tétrault 2003).
3. Re-Org: In 2007 UNESCO and ICCROM began the three-year joint project *Preventive Conservation of Endangered Museum Collections in Developing Countries*. One of the results of the project was Re-Org (www.re-org.info) – a methodology for reorganising storage spaces with few resources. This has since been tested all over the world (Lambert 2011). Part of its success depends on the fact that it makes storage reorganisation accessible worldwide to institutions with very different budgets.

Standards in the real world: the use of non-specific conservation materials

Professional literature almost invariably offers accounts of instances in which standards for preventive care were met or surpassed. The use of non-specific materials in museums and stores is rarely acknowledged in published reports, although the cost and scarce availability of conservation grade items suggests that alternatives are often employed. This was certainly true in the author's experience of fieldwork on archaeological sites. However, a literature review found little published information on the practicalities of selecting materials in challenging contexts or on suppliers in low- and middle-income countries (some exceptions are Severson 1999; Kariya and Peachey 1999).

It is probable that professionals are reluctant to write about practices that are not endorsed by the scientific conservation community. This is not surprising given that the scientific approach has characterised the profession for most of its brief history (Clavir 1998). Only recently have concerns for sustainability and inclusivity gained more weight in shaping heritage management choices, reflecting what has been described as a paradigm shift from a materials-based, objectivity-driven discipline to one with a more people-centred approach (Avrami et al. 2000; Muñoz Viñas 2005). Implicit values are resistant to change, however, and for many practitioners the principle of scientific conservation remains essential to the profession.

The lack of information in professional literature on the use of non-specific conservation materials led the author to carry out a small-scale survey in 2013[3] among heritage professionals who work in challenging contexts. Available only in English, the survey solely reflects fieldwork practice; its respondents work in challenging contexts occasionally, but are based in larger institutions. Language and access to the internet limited the survey's reach.

The vast majority of respondents reported difficulties in sourcing materials and purchased at least part of their supplies locally (Fig. 5.2). However, this seemed to be determined by necessity rather than choice, as local availability was rated among the least sought characteristics in packaging materials. Effectiveness in protecting objects from mechanical damage, ageing properties and chemical stability were primary considerations (Fig. 5.3). Although many respondents expressed concern over the possible emission of pollutant gases, most acknowledged that materials were not tested directly by them or by their colleagues. It is interesting to note that materials with poor ageing properties were considered more of a threat to collections than dust accumulation, identified by several studies as a major cause of deterioration (Lithgow et al. 2005; Brimblecombe et al. 2009). Ensuring protection against dust was considered important by less than one-third of practitioners.

A great variety of contexts appear to pose challenges in terms of material availability. Participants referred to experiences of fieldwork in 22 different countries, including European states and the USA, on archaeological sites as well as religious sites, museums and libraries. While almost all respondents seemed aware of the risks resulting from inappropriate storage, some commented that deterioration was more likely to

Sourcing conservation materials in current fieldwork practice

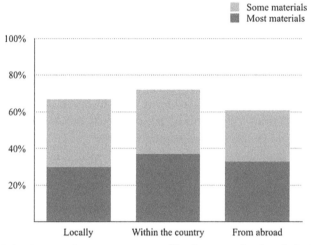

Fig. 5.2 Respondents to a survey of heritage professionals in 2013 were split almost equally into three groups: those who bought most or some materials locally, those who shop within the country and those who look abroad. 'Locally' was defined as 'within one hour's drive from the workplace'. © the author 2014.

Relevance of various characteristics

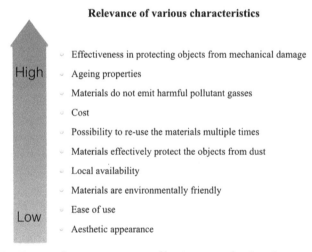

Fig. 5.3 Respondents to a survey of heritage professionals were asked to rate the importance of different characteristics of packaging materials. © the author 2014.

occur as a consequence of other issues such as unsecure storage areas, pests, lack of insulation, poor handling and access policies.

Some respondents commented that they had stopped using local materials due to their poor ageing properties – a problem also encountered by the author during fieldwork in Egypt, at the archaeological site of Tell al-Amarna. Materials employed for packaging were mostly brought from the UK by team members or purchased in Cairo. Items available in the nearby town of Mallawi, such as bubble wrap and plastic sheeting, became brittle and disintegrated in the course of a few years (Julie Dawson, pers. comm. 2013). When a range of packaging materials were purchased locally by the author and brought to the UK for extensive testing, all but one were found to be poly-vinyl chlorides, which age badly and emit harmful pollutant gases.

To sum up, employing some local materials that are not conservation grade appears to be common practice on heritage sites around the world, although this is not reflected in the literature. Local expertise and common use in the local area do not appear to be determining elements in the selection of materials, nor is local availability a major consideration. Providing protection against mechanical damage is rightly considered an important function of packaging materials, yet the threat posed by dust accumulation is underestimated.

Developing a methodology for selecting locally accessible storage materials

Appropriate packaging can be a highly cost-effective way of protecting objects, as it acts against several key agents of deterioration[4] at the same time. Packaging can reduce the risk of mechanical damage during handling, prevent the deposition of airborne particles and shield an artefact from light. Impermeable containers offer protection from water and pests, as well as creating microclimates that buffer rapid environmental fluctuations (Larkin et al. 1998). Together with a good labelling system, packaging can increase accessibility and reduce the risk of artefacts becoming disassociated and lost.

As storage materials are likely to be needed in large quantities, it is particularly important that they are sourced locally. A methodology for selecting appropriate materials in challenging contexts is proposed here and summarised in the following diagram.

The selection process occurs in three phases: collection of information, assessment, response and review. The ideal premise is a general storage policy grounded on a comprehensive appraisal of the collection's preservation requirements. ICOM's reference manual for museum practice presents a straightforward system for identifying possible risks and assessing them using rank order scales (Michalski 2004). This type of evaluation can be carried out by a small team and is mostly based on common sense. Similarly the Re-Org method guides practitioners through elementary surveying and appraisal in order to establish preservation priorities.

On this basis a list of the types of storage materials needed is compiled. Information can then be collected on the range of materials

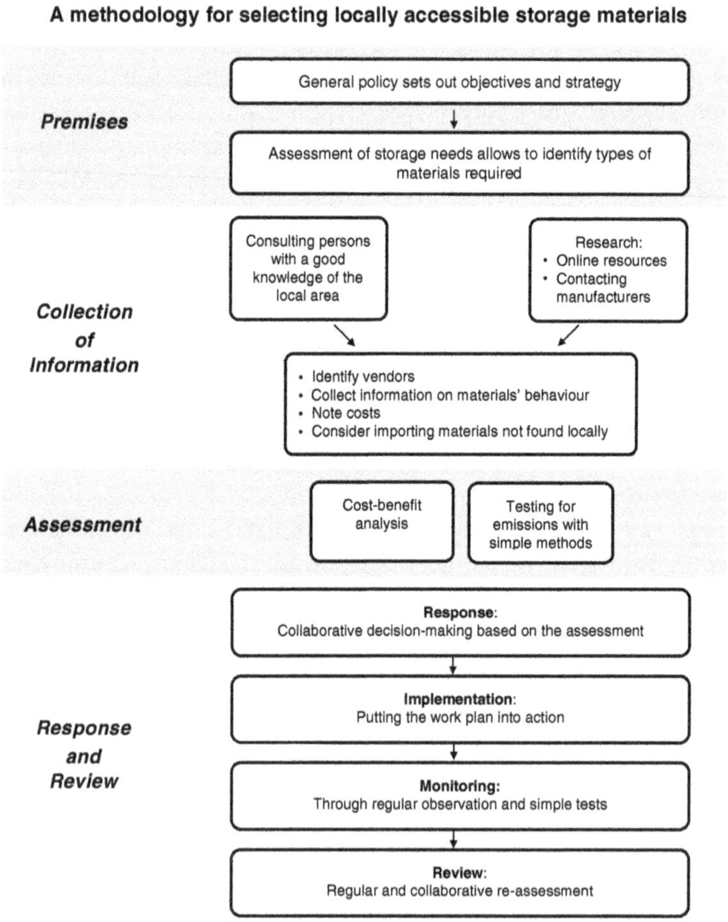

A methodology for selecting locally accessible storage materials

Fig. 5.4 Diagram summarising the proposed methodology.
© the author 2014.

available locally and their characteristics, potential vendors and costs. If essential items are not available, the costs and time requirements of importing are considered and available options assessed through cost-benefit analysis and material testing.

Cost-benefit analysis

Various cost-benefit appraisal methods have been elaborated for collections care (see Staniforth 1990; Cassar 1998 among others). A simplified version of this tool can be applied to the selection of appropriate storage materials (Fig. 5.5). Six categories for assessment are proposed here, each of which can be weighted according to perceived importance for the project at stake. This is best done as a team in order to reflect a multiplicity of views. A relative weight expressed as a percentage can be attributed to each aspect with the exclusion of cost; this will be considered at a later stage. As well as helping to think through problems, matrices such as these provide a record of the decision-making process, making explicit the options that were considered and the reasons behind the final choice (Michalski and Rossi-Doria 2011).

Criteria	Relative weight (%)	Score from 1 to 4 for Option 1	Weighted score	Score from 1 to 4 for Option 2	Weighted score	Total of weighted scores
Ease of use						
Possibility of re-use						
Mechanical properties						
Local availability						
Chemical interaction with the artefacts						
Ageing properties						
Totals	100	-	-	-	-	400

Fig. 5.5 A model matrix for comparing the benefits of various options in the selection of locally available storage materials (after Cassar 1998, 43). © the author 2014.

Re-evaluating testing techniques

The survey suggested that the difficulty of testing materials with limited resources is likely to be one of the major obstacles to the adoption of local alternatives. There is consequently an important need to identify simple techniques to test for harmful emissions. The effects of pollutants[5] can be described as accelerated ageing and include metals corrosion, embrittlement of organics and salt formation on stone and ceramics. The emission of harmful gases from display and storage materials has been discussed extensively by Blades and co-workers (2000), Hatchfield (2002), Tétreault (2003) and Grzywacz (2006), as well as by Schieweck and colleagues (2009). An assessment of simple test methods carried out by the author (Ravaioli 2013) was based on the following criteria:

- material availability
- complexity of the procedure
- reliability
- cost
- health and safety

Test methods that rated very poorly in any single criterion were excluded. The remaining ones were tried out on non-specific storage materials collected in the vicinities of two archaeological sites in Iraqi Kurdistan and Egypt. Results were then compared with those obtained through Oddy testing. Cost and availability were assessed through online research into distributors and shipping provisions, while an evaluation of Health and Safety was carried out by examining Material Safety Data Sheets for each substance employed and the potential hazards involved in the procedure. A summary of the evaluated tests appears at the end of this chapter as note 2.

The results were encouraging, with at least one suitable test being found for most types of materials commonly used in storage. The methods assessed enable the detection of chlorides, sulphides and organic acids. A major drawback is the fact that a practicable test for the detection of aldehydes could not be identified. The tests proved particularly valid for evaluating the suitability of paper products; testing for pH, alum and lignin is straightforward and can be carried out in most contexts. However, several of the chemicals employed in tests for other classes of materials are hazardous and research on safer alternatives would be of great value. An assessment of long-term emissions can be complemented with surface pH measurements using universal indicator paper and with an assessment of the short-term emission of gases using *Image Permanence Institute 'A–D Strips'* (Garside and Hanson 2011).

Whatever the procedure employed, the results of material testing should always be interpreted with caution. The processes by which materials produce harmful emissions are complex and determined by multiple factors. Manufacturers can change product composition without notice, while even identifying manufacturers may be a challenge in itself. When the author collected packaging materials for testing in Egypt and Iraqi Kurdistan, a major problem was that most bore no indication of their manufacturer or composition. The language barrier was a further obstacle. As a result, any test could be considered valid only for the specific batch of material that had been purchased. Items that did have a brand name came from larger supermarkets; these included cling film, plastic bags for freezing and food containers.

Response and review

Decision-making based on the results of assessment is best done collaboratively and by keeping the key principle of sustainability in mind. Regular monitoring of stored collections is an essential review process that allows for the identification of possible deterioration mechanisms. A simple way of checking the indoor environment is by placing silver, copper and lead coupons with a freshly cleaned surface close to stored artefacts. The coupons will be more reactive than the objects and corrode if significant levels of pollutants are present (Thickett and Lee 2004, 27). Packaging and storage materials should be examined periodically and any change in appearance noted and investigated.

Keeping things in perspective

When considering the risks involved in the use of potentially unstable materials, it is important to keep things in perspective. The 2005 Heritage Health Index showed that, at the time, only 11 per cent of heritage institutions in the USA had adequate storage facilities (Heritage Preservation website). In 2011 a UNESCO and ICCROM international survey revealed that 60 per cent of the world's stored collections are in such poor conditions that they cannot be used for any type of museum activity (ICCROM 2011). Twenty-one different types of problems were identified as 'major' or 'drastic' by more than one in five museums in the

Fig. 5.6 Packaging materials at the Suleymaniya market. © the author 2014.

world, ranging from lack of space and absence of trained staff to active pest infestation and unsecured doors.

For many heritage institutions the priority is to cover the 'ten basic collection preservation strategies' recommended by Michalski. These include having a reliable roof, walls and windows, as well as reasonable order in storage (Michalski 2004, 58). The priority worldwide is to promote training in preventive conservation and encourage good general management of storage areas using available resources.

The alarming results of the 2011 survey were recalled a few years ago by ICOM in a document, *Reconnecting with Collections in Storage: Recommendations* (ICOM 2017), which was presented as a resolution at the general conference in Kyoto in 2019 (Resolution No. 4 'Measures to safeguard and enhance collections in storage throughout the world'). All concerned bodies and individuals are urged 'to take all measures and make use of all the available tools and developed methodologies at their disposal' to improve the state of stored collections throughout the world.

Conclusions

Appropriate preventive conservation strategies should be encouraged in all heritage contexts. However, they are particularly advisable when resources are very limited as they have the highest cost/benefits ratio (La Rocca and Nardi 1994); adopting local technologies and materials can increase this ratio further. The lack of published information on the use of local alternatives to conservation grade materials is a key obstacle to their wider adoption in practice, and also to their safe use. The author certainly found this to be an issue in her experience of working on archaeological sites. Practitioners around the world would benefit greatly from regional lists of suppliers.

In the absence of reliable information on the long-term behaviour of available materials, the best approach is an assessment based on the results of simple testing. A greater number of low-cost and low-tech test methods are needed, particularly for detecting aldehydes. Online databases would allow the sharing of test results for non-specific materials that may be employed in conservation. This would benefit the state of collections worldwide and allow heritage institutions to make better use of scarce resources.

Although specialised materials are costly and unavailable in many parts of the world, this need not prevent the implementation of appropriate collections care. The risks of employing alternative materials should be assessed in the context of other possible risks to the collection: they are likely to be low compared to those resulting from poor general management. Potential threats can be reduced using a simple selection process such as the one described in this chapter. Regular monitoring will enable conservators readily to detect adverse reactions in artefacts.

Methodologies that focus on the process of conservation may prove more effective in encouraging good practice than international standards, giving agency to those directly involved in the care of their heritage. Techniques and materials should never be transferred unquestioningly by the 'experts'. They should rather be chosen according to local needs as part of an inclusive process of decision-making.

Acknowledgements

This research was part of a dissertation for a Master of Science in Conservation for Archaeology and Museums at UCL, supervised by Dr Renata Peters. Fieldwork on the site of Gurga Ciya, Iraqi Kurdistan, carried out as part of this project, was funded by The British Institute for the Study of Iraq. Many colleagues generously offered their advice and support: Sandra Bond (UCL), Julie Dawson (Fitzwilliam Museum), James Hales (UCL), Anjali Jain (UCL), Jennifer Marchant (Fitzwilliam Museum), Jessica Johnson (Smithsonian Museum Conservation Institute), Hemn Nuri (Suleymaniya Museum), Sophie Rowe (Scott Polar Research Institute), Christina Rozeik (Scott Polar Research Institute), Professor David Wengrow (UCL). Their expertise has saved me from many errors; those that inevitably remain are entirely my own responsibility.

Notes

1. The Oddy test consists of enclosing test materials in a vessel with silver, copper and lead metal coupons, in conditions of elevated temperature and humidity that accelerate corrosion rates (Oddy 1973, 1975). The test is now employed widely in the revised '3 in 1' procedure developed by Robinet and Thickett (2003).
2. The tests evaluated include:
   Aluminon test for the detection of alum (Barrow 1969; Thickett and Lee 2004, 23; Odegaard et al. 2005, 34). This colorimetric test detects the presence of aluminon ions (Al^{+3}) in paper or board.
   Beilstein test for the detection of chlorine (Vogel 1966; Thickett and Lee 2004, 18; Odegaard et al. 2005, 109). Chlorine and chlorides containing materials can degrade to produce hydrochloric acid. This will harm many materials, including copper, iron and silver (Tétreault 2003, 109).
   Glycerol and pH test (Tétreault 1992; Odegaard et al. 2005, 184). This test determines the presence of volatile organic acids.
   Lead acetate and pyrolysis test (Feigl and Anger 1972; Odegaard et al. 2005, 146–9). This test determines whether materials such as rubber, ebonite, wool and some protein-based materials contain sulphur. Burning the sample causes sulphide formation, which will react with lead acetate paper to produce a brown lead sulphide. Two variations of the test are described by Odegaard et al. (2005, 146–9). One is more suitable for rubber or ebonite. The second variation will indicate the presence of organic bound sulphur in wool.
   pH and Silver nitrate test for chlorines (Odegaard et al. 2005, 111). This test is useful for detecting chlorines in materials (such as poly-vinyl chloride and chlorinated rubber) through pyrolysis.
   Phloroglucinol test (Thickett and Lee 2004, 22; Odegaard et al. 2005, 156). A colorimetric spot test for the detection of lignin containing fibres.
3. The survey was sent out via SurveyMonkey, the Conservation Dist List (COOL website) and a conservation blog (CCCH website). In the course of one month 38 heritage professionals

from 12 countries participated. Over half of respondents defined themselves as conservators/ restorers, one-third were archaeologists and the remainder were museum professionals, heritage managers, students or academics.

4. The 10 key agents of deterioration as listed by the Canadian Conservation Institute (CCI) are the following: 1. direct physical forces; 2. thieves and vandals; 3. fire; 4. water; 5. pests; 6. contaminants or pollutants; 7. radiation (light, ultraviolet and infrared); 8. incorrect temperature; 9. incorrect relative humidity; 10. dissociation or custodial neglect (Waller 1995).

5. In this context pollutants are defined as gaseous, solid or liquid particles that are known to deteriorate cultural property through chemical reactions with components of the object (Tétreault 2003, 142).

References

Alcántara, Rebeca. 2002. *Standards in Preventive Conservation: meanings and applications*. Rome: ICCROM.

Alessandrini, Giovanna and Tabasso, Marisa Laurenzi. 1999. 'Conservation of Cultural Property in Italy: The UNI-NORMAL Committee for the Definition of Technical Standards'. In *The Use of and Need for Preservation Standards in Architectural Conservation*, edited by Lauren B. Sickels-Taves, 24–32. West Conshohocken: American Society for Testing and Materials (ASTM).

AAM – American Alliance of Museums. *Code of Ethics for Museums*, adopted 1991; amended 2000. Accessed 21 September 2020. https://www.aam-us.org/programs/ethics-standards-and-professional-practices/code-of-ethics-for-museums/.

AIC – American Institute for Conservation of Historic and Artistic Works. *Code of Ethics and Guideline for Practice*, published 1967; revised 1994. Accessed 21 September 2020. https://www.culturalheritage.org/about-conservation/code-of-ethics.

Appelbaum, Barbara. 2007. *Conservation Treatment Methodology*. Oxford: Elsevier.

Ashley-Smith, Jonathan. 1999. *Risk Assessment for Object Conservation*. Oxford: Butterworth-Heinemann.

Ashley-Smith, Jonathan, Burmester, Andreas and Eibl, Melanie, eds. 2013. *Climate for Collections: Standards and uncertainties. Postprints of the Munich Climate Conference 7 to 9 November 2012*. Munich: Archetype in association with Doerner Institute.

Avrami, Erica. 2009. 'Heritage Values and Sustainability'. In *Conservation: Principles, dilemmas and uncomfortable truths*, edited by A. Richmond and A. Bracker, 177–83. Oxford: Butterworth-Heinemann, in association with the Victoria and Albert Museum.

Avrami, Erica, Mason, Randall and de la Torre, Marta, eds. 2000. *Values and Heritage Conservation. Research report*. Los Angeles, CA: Getty Conservation Institute.

Barclay, Robert L. and Antomarchi, Catherine. 1994. 'PREMA: A conservation strategy for African collections'. In *Preventive Conservation: Practice, theory and research. Preprints of the contributions to the Ottawa Congress,* 12–16 September 1994, edited by Ashok Roy and Perry Smith, 61–4. London: The International Institute for Conservation of Historic and Artistic Works.

Barrow, William J. 1969. *Permanence/Durability of the Book VI. Spot tests for unstable book and record papers*. Richmond, VA: Dietz Press.

Bell, D. 1997. *Guide to International Conservation Charters, Technical Advice Note 8*. Edinburgh: Historic Scotland.

Blades, Nigel, Oreszczyn, Tadj, Bordass, Bill and Cassar, May, eds. 2000. *Guidelines on Pollution Control in Heritage Buildings*. London: Re:Source and The Council for Museums, Archives and Libraries.

Brimblecombe, Peter, Thickett, David and Yoon, Young Hun. 2009. 'The Cementation of Coarse Dust to Indoor Surfaces', *Journal of Cultural Heritage* 10 (3): 410–14.

Cassar, May. 1998. *Cost/Benefits Appraisals for Collection Care: A practical guide*. London: Museum & Galleries Commission.

Cassar, May. 2009. 'Sustainable Heritage: Challenges and strategies for the twenty-first century', *APT Bulletin: Journal of Preservation Technology* 40 (1): 3–11.

CCCH – Conversations on Conservation of Cultural Heritage. Accessed 21 September 2020. http://uclconversationsonconservation.blogspot.co.uk/.

Clavir, Miriam. 1998. 'The Social and Historic Construction of Professional Values', *Studies in Conservation* 43 (1): 1–8.

Clavir, Miriam. 2002. *Preserving What is Valued: Museums, conservation and First Nations*. Vancouver; Toronto: UBC Press.

Cleere, Henry. 2001. 'The Uneasy Bedfellows: Universality and cultural heritage'. In *Destruction and Conservation of Cultural Property*, edited by Robert Layton, Peter G. Stone and Julian Thomas, 22–9. London: Routledge.

Colwell-Chanthaphonh, Chip. 2009. 'The Archaeologist as a World Citizen: On the morals of heritage preservation and destruction'. In *Cosmopolitan Archaeologies*, edited by Lynn Meskell, 140–65. Durham, NC; London: Duke University Press.

COOL – Conservation OnLine. 'Conservation DistList'. Accessed 21 September 2020. https://cool.culturalheritage.org.

Daniels, Vincent and Ward, Susan. 1982. 'A Rapid Test for the Detection of Substances Which Will Tarnish Silver', *Studies in Conservation* 27 (2); 58–60.

Davies, Maurice and Wilkinson, Helen. 2008. *Sustainability and Museums: Your chance to make a difference*. London: Museums Association.

de la Torre, Marta, MacLean, Margaret G.H., Mason, Randall and Myers, David. 2005. *Heritage Values in Site Management: Four case studies*, edited by Marta de la Torre. Los Angeles, CA: Getty Conservation Institute.

de Silva, Megan and Henderson, Jane. 2011. 'Sustainability in Conservation Practice', *Journal of the Institute of Conservation* 34 (1): 5–15.

Demas, Martha. 2002. 'Planning for Conservation and Management of Archaeological Sites: A values-based approach'. In *Management Planning for Archaeological Sites: An international workshop organized by the Getty Conservation Institute and Loyola Marymount University, 19–22 May 2000, Corinth, Greece*, edited by Jeanne-Marie Teutonico and Gaetano Palumbo, 27–54. Los Angeles, CA: Getty Conservation Institute.

English Heritage. 1997. *Sustaining the Historic Environment: New perspectives on the future. An English Heritage discussion document*. London: English Heritage.

ECCO – European Confederation of Conservator-Restorers' Organisations. 2002. *Professional Guidelines of the European Confederation of Conservator-Restorers' Organisations*. Accessed 21 September 2020. www.ecco-eu.org/fileadmin/user_upload/ECCO_professional_guidelines_II.pdf.

Feigl, Fritz and Anger, Vinzez. 1972. *Spot tests in inorganic analysis*, 6th English ed. New York: Elsevier.

Garside, Paul and Hanson, Lesley. 2011. 'A Systematic Approach to Selecting Inexpensive Conservation Storage Solutions', *Journal of Conservation and Museum Studies* 9 (4–10). Accessed 21 September 2020. www.jcms-journal.com/article/view/25.

Graham, Brian, Ashworth, Greg J. and Tunbridge, John E. 2000. *A Geography of Heritage: Power, culture & economy*. London: Hodder Arnold.

Green, Lorna R. and Thickett, David. 1993. 'Interlaboratory Comparison of the Oddy Test'. In *Conservation Science in the U.K.*, edited by Norman H. Tennent, 111–16. London: James & James.

Grzywacz, Cecily M. 2006. *Monitoring for Gaseous Pollutants in Museum Environments*. Los Angeles, CA: Getty Conservation Institute.

Hatchfield, Pamela B. 2002. *Pollutants in the Museum Environment: Practical strategies for problem solving in design, exhibition and storage*. London: Archetype.

Hazeltine, Barrett and Bull, Christopher. 1999. *Appropriate Technology: Tools, choices, and implications*. San Diego; London: Academic Press.

Heritage Preservation. http://www.heritagepreservation.org/HHI/ (page discontinued).

ICCROM – International Centre for the Study of the Preservation and Restoration of Cultural Property. 2011. *The International Storage Survey*. Accessed 21 September 2020. www.iiconservation.org/archive/www.iiconservation.org/news/indexdc83.html?p=1268.

ICOM – International Council of Museums. 2017. 'Reconnecting with Collections in Storage: Recommendations', *On Board. News and Reports from the Directory Board* 14 (2): 14–15.

ICOM-CC – International Council of Museums Committee for Conservation and IIC – International Institute for Conservation. 2014. *Environmental Guidelines. ICOM-CC and IIC Declaration*. Accessed 21 September 2020. www.icom-cc.org/332/-icom-cc-documents/declaration-on-environmental-guidelines/#.WlaHAvHc7OR.

ICOMOS – US International Council on Monuments and Sites. 2001. *Thematic Statement of ICOMOS International Conference, Philadelphia, April 2000*. www.usicomos.org/past-symposia/2001-usicomos-international-symposium/.

Jigyasu, Rohit. 2002. 'Reducing Disaster Vulnerability Through Local Knowledge and Capacity: The case of earthquake-prone rural communities in India and Nepal'. PhD thesis. Norwegian University of Science and Technology.

Jones, Samuel and Holden, John. 2008. *It's a Material World: Caring for the public realm*. London: Demos.

Kariya, Hiroko and Peachey, Claire. 1999. 'On-site Storage of Excavated Materials', *Field Notes: Practical guides for archaeological conservation and site preservation 9*. Turkey: Japanese Institute for Anatolian Archaeology.

Kreps, Christina F. 2003. *Liberating Culture: Cross-cultural perspectives on museums, curation and heritage preservation*. London; New York: Routledge.

Kreps, Christina F. 2008. 'Appropriate Museology in Theory and Practice', *Museum Management and Curatorship* 23 (1); 23–41.

La Rocca, Eugenio and Nardi, Roberto. 1994. 'Preventive Conservation and Restoration: A matter of costs'. In *Preventive Conservation: Practice, theory and research; Preprints of the contributions to the Ottawa Congress, 12–16 September 1994*, edited by Ashok Roy and Perry Smith, 24–7. London: The International Institute for Conservation of Historic and Artistic Works.

Lambert, Simon. 2011. 'RE-ORG: A methodology for reorganizing museum storage developed by ICCROM and UNESCO'. In 'Réinventer les Methodologies', edited by Muriel Verbeeck-Boutin. *CeROArt* 6. Accessed 21 September 2020. ceroart.revues.org/2112.

Larkin, Nigel R., Makridou, Elena and Comerford, Gill. 1998. 'Plastic Storage Containers: A comparison', *The Conservator* 22 (1): 81–7.

Lithgow, Katy. 2011. 'Sustainable Decision Making – Change in National Trust Collections Conservation', *Journal of the Institute of Conservation* 34 (1).

Lithgow, Katy, Lloyd, Helen, Brimblecombe, Peter, Yoon, Young Hun and Thickett, David. 2005. 'Managing Dust in Historic Houses: A visitor conservator interface'. In *ICOM Committee for Conservation, 14th Triennial Meeting, The Hague Preprints, 12–16 September 2005*, edited by Isabelle Verger, Vol. II, 662–9. London: James & James.

Lithgow, Katy, Staniforth, Sarah and Etheridge, Paul. 2008. 'Prioritizing Access in the Conservation of National Trust Collections', *Studies in Conservation* 53, supp. 1. Contributions to the London Congress, 15–19 September 2008: 178–85.

Mason, Randall and Avrami, Erica. 2002. 'Heritage Values and Challenges of Conservation Planning'. In *Management Planning for Archaeological Sites: An international workshop organized by the Getty Conservation Institute and Loyola Marymount University, 19–22 May 2000, Corinth, Greece*, edited by Jeanne-Marie Teutonico and Gaetano Palumbo, 13–26. Los Angeles, CA: Getty Conservation Institute.

Michalski, Stefan. 2004. 'Care and Preservation of Collections'. In *Running a Museum: A practical handbook*, edited by Patrick J. Boylan, 51–89. Paris: ICOM. Accessed 21 September 2020. https://unesdoc.unesco.org/images/0014/001410/141067e.pdf.

Michalski, Stefan. 2007. 'The Ideal Climate, Risk Management, the ASHRAE Chapter, Proofed Fluctuations, and Toward a Full Risk Analysis Model'. In *Contribution to the Experts' Roundtable on Sustainable Climate Management Strategies, Tenerife, Spain, April 2007*. Los Angeles, CA: Getty Conservation Institute. Accessed 21 September 2020. www.getty.edu/conservation/our_projects/science/climate/paper_michalski.pdf.

Michalski, Stefan. 2011. 'Museum Climate and Global Climate: Doing the right thing for both'. In *Reflections on Conservation. CCI Newsletter*. Ottawa: CCI, 9–11.

Michalski, Stefan and Rossi-Doria, Matteo. 2011. 'Using Decision-Diagrams to Explore, Document and Teach Treatment Decisions, with an Example of Their Application to a Difficult Painting Consolidation Treatment'. In *ICOM Committee for Conservation, ICOM-CC, 16th Triennial Conference, Lisbon, 19–23 September 2011*, edited by J. Bridgland, 1–8. Almada: ICOM-CC.

Muñoz Viñas, Salvador. 2005. *Contemporary Theory of Conservation*. Oxford: Elsevier Butterworth-Heinemann.

Murray Pease Committee. 1964. 'The Murray Pease Report', *Studies in Conservation* 9 (3): 116–21.

Oddy, William A. 1973. 'An Unsuspected Danger in Display', *Museums Journal* 73 (1): 27–8.

Oddy, William A. 1975. 'The Corrosion of Metals on Display'. In *Conservation in Archaeology and the Applied Arts*, edited by Norman S. Brommelle and Perry Smith, 235–7. London: International Institute for Conservation of Historic and Artistic Works.

Odegaard, Nancy, Carroll, Scott and Zimmt, Werner S. 2005. *Material Characterization Tests for Objects of Art and Archaeology*, 2nd ed. London: Archetype.

Pearson, Michael and Sullivan, Sharon. 1995. *Looking After Heritage Places: The basics of heritage planning for managers, landowners and administrators.* Melbourne: Melbourne University Press.

Ravaioli, Flavia. 2013. 'Selecting Locally Accessible Materials for Use in Preventive Conservation'. Master of Science thesis, University College London.

Re-Org. n.d. Accessed 21 September 2020. https://www.iccrom.org/section/preventive-conservation/re-org.

Robinet, Laurianne and Thickett, David. 2003. 'A New Methodology for Accelerated Corrosion Testing', *Studies in Conservation* 48 (4): 263–8.

Schieweck, Alexandra, Salthammer, Tunga and Watts, Simon F. 2009. 'Indoor Pollutants in the Museum Environment'. In *Organic Indoor Air Pollutants: Occurrence, measurement, evaluation*, 2nd ed., edited by Tunga Salthammer and Erik Uhde, 273–300. Weinheim: Wiley-VCH Verlag GmbH & Co. KGaA.

Schumacher, Fritz E. 1973. *Small is Beautiful: Economics as if people mattered.* New York: Harper & Row.

Severson, Kent. 1999. 'Conservation and Related Materials: Suppliers and shopping in Turkey', *Field Notes: Practical guides for archaeological conservation and site preservation* 3. Turkey: Japanese Institute for Anatolian Archaeology.

Staniforth, Sarah. 1990. 'Benefits Versus Costs in Environmental Control'. In *Managing Conservation: Papers given at a conference held jointly by the United Kingdom Institute for Conservation and the Museum of London, October 1990*, edited by Suzanne Keene, 28–31. London: UKIC.

Staniforth, Sarah. 2010. 'Slow Conservation', *Studies in Conservation* 55 (2): 74–80.

Strlič, Matija, Kralj Cigić, Irena, Možir, Alenka, Thickett, David, de Bruin, Gerrit, Kolar, Jana and Cassar, May. 2010. 'Test for Compatibility with Organic Heritage Materials: A proposed procedure', *e-Preservation Science* 7: 78–86.

SurveyMonkey. www.surveymonkey.com. Accessed 29 July 2020.

Tétreault, Jean. 1992. 'Measuring the Acidity of Volatile Products', *Journal of the International Institute for Conservation – Canadian Group*, 17: 17–25.

Tétreault, Jean. 2003. *Airborne Pollutants in Museums, Galleries, and Archives: Risk assessment, control strategies, and preservation management.* Ottowa: Canadian Conservation Institute.

Thickett, David and Lee, Robert. 2004. *Selection of Materials for the Storage or Display of Museum Objects.* British Museum Occasional Paper 111. London: British Museum Press.

Thormann, Peter. 1979. 'Proposal for a Programme on Appropriate Technology Prepared by the United States Agency for International Development'. In *Appropriate Technologies for Third World Development: Proceedings of a conference held by the International Economic Association at Teheran, Iran*, edited by Austin Robinson, 278–402. London: Palgrave Macmillan.

Tsukada, Masahiko, Rizzo, Adriana and Granzotto, Clara. 2012. 'A New Strategy for Assessing Off-Gassing from Museum Materials: Air sampling in Oddy test vessels', *AIC news* 37 (1): 1, 3–7.

UKIC – United Kingdom Institute for Conservation of Historic and Artistic Works, now Institute of Conservation (ICON). 1996. *Code of Ethics and Rules of Practice of the United Kingdom Institute for Conservation of Historic and Artistic Works.* London: UKIC. Accessed 21 September 2020. www.nigelcopsey.com/reports/training/training_ukic_ethics.pdf.

UNESCO – United Nations Educational, Scientific and Cultural Organization. 1981. *'Appropriate Technologies' in the Conservation of Cultural Property.* Geneva: UNESCO Press.

Vogel, Arthur Israel. 1966. *Elementary Practical Organic Chemistry*, 2nd ed. London: Longman.

Waller, Robert. 1995. 'Risk Management Applied to Preventive Conservation'. In *Storage of Natural History Collections: A preventive conservation approach*, edited by Carolyn L. Rose, Catharine A. Hawks and Hugh H. Genoways, 21–7. Iowa City, IA: Society for the Preservation of Natural History Collections.

Waller, Robert and Michalski, Stefan. 2005. 'A Paradigm Shift for Preventive Conservation, and a Software Tool to Facilitate the Transition'. In *ICOM Committee for Conservation, Preprints of the 14th Triennial Meeting, The Hague, 12–16 September 2005*, edited by J. Bridgland, 733–8. London: James & James.

6

The 'Open Lab Project': addressing the skills deficit of volunteer community archaeologists in Lincolnshire, UK

Craig Spence

Introduction

This chapter explores an area of concern related to volunteer-led community archaeology projects – and the archaeological assemblages that they sometimes generate – through a critical review of a project designed to strengthen and advance community skills capacity in this area. The possession and processing of assemblages of archaeological finds can present community archaeology groups with opportunities to widen their public engagement and participation levels. Such materials also present a range of issues and problems for such groups, however, particularly in association with the structured transition between post-excavation activity and archival deposition. These problems – often associated with a deficit of particular skills – can, in extreme cases, critically undermine the value of the archaeological activity undertaken. In reviewing a project developed within a university context, this chapter demonstrates not only a method of resolution for such issues but also considers further, sometimes unforeseen benefits that were realised, both for the archaeological process and the participants themselves.

Across the UK, volunteer community archaeologists engage actively and with great enthusiasm in archaeological projects. Many of these comprise an element of archaeological intervention (for a definitional discussion of 'community archaeology' in the UK see Thomas 2017). Such interventions, where they involve excavation or field-walking, can generate substantial quantities of archaeological materials and artefacts. For professional and academic archaeologists it is self-evident that such assemblages require appropriate processing, conservation, cataloguing, research and archiving. Volunteer community archaeologists, although often knowledgeable within the limits of their projects and clearly dedicated to their success, frequently lack higher level archaeological skills; they thus have a limited conceptual understanding and procedural capability with regard to post-excavation activity. Such a lacuna in archaeological capacity may in the worst cases expose archaeological records and artefacts to damage, dispersal and permanent loss.

Yet these negative outcomes are rarely, if ever, the result of a deliberately cavalier attitude among the project participants. Most often they arise through a genuine lack of knowledge and understanding of the necessary post-excavation processes. A failure to appreciate either the significance or fragility of recovered archaeological material may exacerbate the situation. In addition volunteer archaeologists may lack awareness of wider responsibilities to the finite cultural heritage that should, in fact, direct archaeological project design. In particular, the responsibility and resources needed to engage adequately with professional practitioners and ensure appropriate public archival deposition cannot be met. (For a discussion of this relationship see Isherwood 2011.)

A national survey of community archaeology groups and their activities was undertaken by the Council for British Archaeology (CBA) (Thomas 2010). The survey found that community archaeology and heritage groups facilitated a wide range of relevant activities supported by very high numbers of volunteers. Of more than 2,000 active groups, around 450 identified themselves as participating in archaeological fieldwork and related activities. Within this number, some 200 engaged in activities focused upon a form of archaeological intervention (Thomas 2010, 24–7).

Such interventions can involve excavation on a variety of scales with the concomitant generation of assemblages of finds. In most cases it is likely that appropriate project design, often a pre-requisite to the securing of adequate funding, will support a suitable level of post-excavation activity. On the other hand, inadequate project design or poor budgeting can result in post-excavation steps being shortened or even curtailed on those community projects driven by excavation as the primary participatory activity. A similar scenario can be found in poorly resourced field-walking projects: enthusiasm for the fieldwork activity is often not matched by that for participation in the post-excavation process. In both cases the rationale for deposition of material in publicly accessible archaeological archives is frequently poorly understood. As a consequence that stage of project design and delivery is routinely under-resourced.

While the above figures from the CBA show that 43 per cent of those UK groups that undertook some form of practical archaeological activity engaged in fieldwork interventions, only 31 per cent indicated that they worked with archaeological finds in a post-excavation or archival context. These figures suggest a disparity between the generation of assemblages of finds and their appropriate processing and archival deposition, producing a 'failure' rate of around 10 intervention projects per year between 2004 and 2009. Given that some of the indicated 'finds' activities are likely to have been associated with work on material previously deposited in archives (see, for example, Cooper 2011), this figure is undoubtedly an underestimate. Such a model of project completion failure is not unique to community-led projects; professional/commercial interventions can also encounter similar issues. In those cases, however, the incomplete work is more often understood and characterised as a 'backlog'; future completion remains an inherent assumption within subsequent operational planning. For community groups such assumptions often fail to become established for a variety of reasons, for example resource shortages, inadequate skills capacity, a lack of appropriate professional support or organisational weakness.

Where finds assemblages are generated, even when initial post-excavation processing has taken place, a lack of specific skills and resources can hinder further progress. In particular, without appropriate knowledge or guidance finds tend to be catalogued at only a rudimentary level. More significantly, storage is frequently inadequate in terms of meeting even basic conservation and environmental standards. The dynamic nature of community archaeology groups means that – in a way similar to commercial archaeological contractors, but for different reasons – they are always looking for the next project. Fieldwork activities are often seen as the primary means to attract and maintain a membership that is both interested and active. This can mean that the material results of previous projects become overlooked as resources expire and enthusiasm wains. The resulting finds assemblages become 'orphaned'. While fieldwork records are, to varying degrees, written up and/or reported, the finds can become either forgotten or, at best, disassociated with the records. The space requirements of such 'orphaned' finds, without post-excavation completion and consequently no possibility of archival deposition, means that they are often haphazardly relocated out of sight in the various garages, sheds and attics of the membership.

The Project

In response to such issues, a team of academics and professional archaeologists at Bishop Grosseteste University (BGU-UK), Lincoln took a decision to develop a programme of practical support for post-excavation projects among local community archaeology groups. The resulting project proposal was successful in gaining support from the Heritage Lottery Fund (HLF). The Fund recognised the potential to enhance protection for the moveable heritage in the possession of such groups as well as the opportunities for targeted capacity-building among participant volunteers (for a review of the HLF's 'outcomes framework' see Maeer 2017, 45–7). Known as the 'Open Lab and Road Show Project', its key aims were as follows:

- to train and support volunteers in archaeological artefact cataloguing, basic conservation and analysis
- to engage with both established community heritage groups and the wider public through the open lab and road show events
- to establish a group of skilled volunteers who could develop future community participation projects based on the holdings of the Lincolnshire Archaeological Archives
- to deliver a related outreach and schools education programme of activities

Scheduled to run over a two-year period between 2012 and 2014, the project was staffed by Zoë Tomlinson, a professional community archaeologist, supported during the first year by a professional finds specialist; funding limitations meant that both positions were structured as part-time employment. Overall management of the project fell to the author as a member of the academic team at the host university.

Organisation

While in its initiation the project can be defined most clearly as 'top-down', it was always intended that a significant level of project direction and management should be placed in the participants' hands. It is widely recognised that the most successful outcomes are achieved by community archaeology projects that engage volunteers and professionals in a dynamic collaborative structure (for a good example see Rowe et al. 2014). Bearing this in mind, and in order to engage more directly with – and empower the leadership of – the various community groups that were to be beneficiaries of the activity, a Project Steering Group was formed.

The Steering Group comprised a representative from each group, usually the current chair of the group, together with staff of the university, the City of Lincoln Council city archaeologist, the county's finds liaison officer for the Portable Antiquities Scheme and the collections access officer representing the Lincolnshire Archaeological Archive, run by Lincolnshire County Council (LCC). The composition of the Steering Group thus provided a very effective mix of academic, professional and voluntary archaeological interests. It met on a regular basis, both to channel information back to the groups' membership and to air views and concerns arising from the groups. The meetings also provided recurrent opportunities to receive critical feedback on specific activities as the project progressed.

Initially a pyramidal structure was conceived for formal communication between the project staff and the participants. Each group chair was asked to nominate a 'volunteer co-ordinator' and an 'outreach co-ordinator' from among their membership. These individuals were to act as points of contact between the community archaeologist and the groups' wider memberships. In most cases this worked well, with information and messages, mainly email based, being relayed effectively via these individuals. With some groups, however, communications came to be channelled more frequently and directly through the chair of the group. This situation arose when no suitable volunteer could be found or as a result of changes in the composition of the group's active members over the course of the project.

The project successfully engaged five local groups. Six were initially invited to participate, but one formally declined to take part, citing a lack of suitable post-excavation material to work on. Nonetheless individual members of that group became involved in the project at a more general level and through participation in the skills development workshops. Groups came from across the extensive rural county of Lincolnshire, although the more active participants were inevitably those geographically closest to Lincoln and the university campus. One group, which had a base over 48 km (30 miles) and about an hour's drive away, attended sessions on the university campus during the project's early phases. As their levels of skill and understanding developed, however, most of this group's members chose to meet separately at a more convenient location. Such an approach inevitably limited the level of support that could be given to the group, in particular denying them the full use of the university's facilities.

Support from the university

Making effective use of the archaeological facilities and resources of the university was a major driver for the project. Such facilities, while used for teaching and research activity during term-time and weekdays, were far less likely to be used in such an intensive way during holiday periods, evenings and weekends. One of the university's strategic aims is to engage with the local community on a mutually beneficial basis, and the 'Open Lab and Road Show Project' could be located firmly within such a policy. Indeed, an important factor in gaining the support of the Heritage Lottery Fund was the significant in-kind support that the university was able to gift to the project. Such support included the free use of teaching rooms and lab space, as noted above – principally at times when such space would otherwise be underused – and access to the university's library on a reader-only basis. In addition, a small amount of academic staff input was offered, as was specific support from both the university's IT and reprographics services.

The range of equipment and resources needed to support a suitably 'professional' approach to post-excavation activities was not in most cases readily available to the participating community groups. It was assessed, however, that the archaeological equipment resources of the university had sufficient spare capacity to accommodate a controlled level of community group usage. Such lab-based resources included microscopes of low and high power, studio photographic equipment and general finds quantification and processing equipment: callipers, electronic scales and the like. In addition, the HLF grant supported the provision of a range of basic finds-related consumables that were, significantly, of an appropriate conservation and archival standard. Among the resources most in demand were polythene bags and boxes, silica gel, acid-free tissue paper, Tyvek labels, humidity indicator strips and acid-free archival boxes of standard dimensions.

There were further benefits in utilising BGU-UK's archaeology facilities. The university provided a suitably flexible yet neutral space for the participating groups to attend. Here they were able to avoid the politics of inter-group rivalries which might have arisen had a group-specific location been chosen as a meeting place. In addition, all the participant groups appreciated the university's generosity in opening its doors to them. Using the institution's premises also encouraged individual participants to adopt a positive approach to personal learning and skills development in a psychological echo of BGU-UK's primary function.

Delivering the project

The project ran for just over the scheduled two years. It principally consisted of regular, lab-based, finds processing sessions that took place on a weekly basis (Fig. 6.1). Finds sessions occurred most frequently on Wednesday afternoons, a regular time at which no teaching was delivered. To enhance accessibility, additional sessions were hosted on evenings and weekends. Each session took place over a period of generally three to four hours with generous breaks for tea and biscuits. While two of the groups preferred evening attendance, the greatest and most regular participation occurred during the weekday sessions. It soon became clear, however, that the additional weekend sessions attracted only a very small number of different participants when compared to the well-attended weekday sessions. As a consequence, during the second year almost all meetings for processing, cataloguing and research were held on weekdays, supported by just one weekend meeting per month.

The skills development workshops were organised differently (Fig. 6.2). These were publicised in advance as one-off events, timetabled on a weekday evening and made open to the general public. Lasting between two and three hours, each workshop was led by a subject-relevant

Fig. 6.1 Volunteers take part in a typical 'Open Lab' session to process and catalogue their finds. © the author 2013.

Fig. 6.2 Participants in a skills workshop take a closer look at some examples of Roman ceramics. © the author 2013.

professional or academic archaeologist. Sessions covered topics such as basic finds conservation, animal osteology, Roman and medieval ceramics, site and finds photography, and environmental sampling and processing. In each case, practical workshop activities enhanced what was often an introductory talk or lecture. Those delivering the sessions were asked to focus on what could be achieved realistically by volunteers, while also drawing attention to those aspects of each topic that remained firmly within the professional or specialist's purview. As well as providing an introduction to identification, sampling, processing and analysis, significant emphasis was placed on the ultimate goal of archival deposition.

An early element of the project involved volunteers in the construction of a group of portable display boxes. These were designed to demonstrate the range and scope of archaeological finds that might be encountered across the East Midlands. This activity was formulated to introduce project participants to the appropriate methods of handling, managing and interpreting finds. The boxes formed the core of the archaeological 'Road Show', the ostensible purpose of which was to engage the wider public with various concepts of archaeology by focusing on finds-related activities. The 'Road Show' presented objects of differing types, materials and periods through the use of a mixture of genuine archaeological artefacts and replicas, some of which were specially commissioned. The process of constructing the boxes and learning to present their contents to the public introduced the volunteers to a number of useful skills. In particular, enhanced knowledge and practical skills related to the demands of object- and material-specific conservation were key objectives.

Over the two years of the project the volunteers, and the groups they represented, made significant progress in the cataloguing, stabilisation (which included very basic conservation measures), packaging and analysis of their respective finds assemblages. A number of key skills were developed and all participants gained valuable additional knowledge and confidence in the post-excavation process. Through that process a range of project outcomes were achieved that were clearly associated with the original project aims. However, a number of unforeseen archaeological outcomes and personal developments can also be associated with the project.

Foreseen outcomes

It is clear that with reference to the aims of the project, as stated in the preceding section, all were achieved to a greater or lesser extent. Individual volunteer community archaeologists were engaged in a learning and practice exercise in relation to the post-excavation processing, cataloguing, analysis and archiving of pre-existing artefact collections previously identified as 'orphaned' finds assemblages. They engaged with the project not directly as individuals, but either as current members of one of the participant groups or by joining a relevant local group before taking part in 'Open Lab' activities. Through this process they came to develop an enhanced degree of ownership and hence responsibility for the finds on which they were working. This also had the added benefit for the groups of increasing their membership; as a result the project strengthened group membership. It was seen as a critical factor for the sustainability of the project, both generally and with regard to the specific 'orphaned' finds assemblages that individuals developed a close association with the material on which they were working. This not only encouraged a personal sense of responsibility among the participants; it also, most significantly, instilled a desire to ensure that the finds would eventually reach the archive.

Processing, cataloguing and packaging

The project staff directly supported the local groups in processing and cataloguing their various assemblages of archaeological materials. In particular, steps were taken to review the packaging and hence archival stability of differing classes of artefact and materials. This stage of the project made direct reference to meeting the required conservation demands of the finds, with groups being invited to bring their assemblages for temporary deposition at the university's archaeology lab. The project was able to purchase secure, dedicated storage cabinets within which the material could be housed; it could also be accessed easily by volunteers during lab sessions. On arrival the material was assessed by the project staff and a plan of action agreed with each community group.

The majority of the finds were found to be inappropriately packaged using a wide variety of containers. Metal tins, often of the biscuit variety, and small (non-airtight) plastic boxes, often re-used take-away food containers of random shapes and sizes, predominated. In addition, finds were stored in various bags including plastic shopping carrier bags and freezer bags; artefacts were cushioned using cotton wool and patterned kitchen paper towels. Moreover, a great variety of writing implements had been used to label the packaging with a range of outcomes; some labelling was clearly visible, but other labels were faded or illegible. Furthermore, while some groups had used acceptable terminology in labelling others had devised their own systems, which in some cases were inappropriate for coherent cataloguing.

As a consequence, volunteer training during the first few months of the project focused on repackaging and re-labelling the material and reviewing conservation conditions for each class of finds. Lincolnshire benefits from a standardised published manual for archaeological practice, but this was principally written with commercial projects in mind. Although available freely online, it is framed in a way that most community-based archaeologists found inaccessible (LCC 2012). Because of its significance for archival deposition, the project staff adhered closely to this guidance. They worked to extract and simplify relevant information to ensure the participants not only followed best practice, but understood it in an appropriately contextualised way.

It is with reference to this first phase of the project's activity where perhaps the greatest – although apparently most mundane – success was to be found: the instillation of a professional approach among the volunteers regarding the correct packaging and labelling of archaeological finds. Following relevant conservation standards and guidelines, all the material was systematically assessed, repackaged and labelled consistently. In particular, use was made of the *First Aid for Finds* publication to provide an easily accessible yet authoritative source of basic conservation information for the volunteers (Watkinson and Neal 1998).

The first stage in the repackaging process was to make use of new polythene bags of an appropriate standard, with 'write-on' strips, to repackage most of the finds. Such finds consisted primarily of ceramics, building material and animal bones. In a number of instances it was agreed that additional cleaning was required as part of this process. This step was followed by ensuring that labels were only written using permanent marker pens, either directly on packaging or on Tyvek labels. Ensuring the consistent use of such indelible markers by the volunteers had to be repeatedly enforced; some individuals were on occasion discovered to still be using ballpoint pens and similar non-permanent inks for labelling. The retention of some examples of the discarded packaging as a demonstration aid, replete with faded and illegible labels, proved particularly beneficial in changing such behaviours.

Overcoming challenges

Two other areas of success with regard to appropriate packaging can also be highlighted. A significant number of iron finds in an advanced state of corrosion were presented during the initial project deposition phase. This situation was aggravated by such objects having been stored in a mixed collection with finds of other materials. An early training activity ensured that volunteers understood the relevant use of absorbent agents, such as silica gel, in the packaging of metals in order to create an airtight 'drybox' environment. Conversely, a small number of organic finds had been allowed to dry out and so to decay. In neither case were the finds presented of great individual significance; for example, the iron objects were mainly fragments of nails or similar. In this case, however – in contrast to the somewhat reluctant attitude expressed by some to the use of indelible markers – the volunteers readily engaged with the concept of appropriate packaging. It appears that they were genuinely unaware that such object decay might be retarded relatively easily, and could therefore identify immediate and positive benefits of changing their behaviour in this area.

A further revelation with regard to packaging for the volunteers, and especially the chairs of the groups, was the knowledge that the County's Archaeological Archive had approved conservation standards and dimensions for storage boxes. Both direct instruction in the archival deposition process by the staff of the archive and a project visit to the archive itself provided significant benefits. The volunteers were able to appreciate at first hand the importance of the space efficiency requirements of archival storage, as well as the associated need for standardised labelling of bags and boxes. While most volunteers had expressed enthusiasm for the pleasing aesthetic of using standardised sizes of packaging, they had not appreciated the critical utility that such an approach bestows on the efficient management of a long-term archive. The visit to the Archaeological Archive thus proved to be one of the highlights of the project. The timing of the visit to fall during the second year of the project was also beneficial. By that stage the volunteers involved were well-versed in – and engaging with – the basic principles of finds processing, packaging and labelling.

Once repackaged and stabilised, the activity of the project participants shifted to the systematic cataloguing and recording of finds for 'assessment' purposes. This element of the project was directed by the project staff, actively supported by a range of specialists. In particular, the ceramic specialists were able to guide the process to collate materials and generate information and records in a form that the specialists could more easily work with. This both empowered the volunteers by taking them further than simply *washing the pot* and helped them also to form a more practical and detailed understanding of the subsequent steps of ceramic identification and quantification. Wherever possible, the specialists made appointments to go through the assemblages during a scheduled 'Open Lab' session. At such meetings they would demonstrate to the volunteers the stages of laying out, sorting and approaches for initial identification.

A further important – and planned – outcome of this process was to open the volunteers' eyes to the advanced skill set possessed by the specialists, emphasising its professional complexity and, conversely, the limitations of the volunteers' own abilities in these areas. The necessary cost of professional, specialist, post-excavation analysis was outlined, demonstrated and justified. As a result subsequent funding bids by at least two of the groups were far better informed in the area of budgeting for specialist support than might otherwise have been the case.

Some additional areas of cataloguing and recording were also undertaken enthusiastically by the participants. Particularly favoured activities included the recording and identification of coins and animal bones. The work with coins required an advance in the participants' skills with regard to studio photographic techniques. The positive outcome of this training was readily seen, with a move from out-of-focus photographs of various digital resolutions to higher quality images in standard formats acceptable for archiving. Initial coin identification was undertaken and some volunteers developed particular knowledge in this area. Identifications were verified during a scheduled visit by a numismatist; further analysis was left for professional consultation at a later date. A similar approach was taken to the cataloguing of animal bone, with particular volunteers gaining specific skills in identification sufficient to support initial sorting. A visit by an osteoarchaeologist again helped to confirm identifications and guide further quantification. However, the final stages of the animal bone analysis and report writing remained firmly within the purview of the professional.

Sustainability of future archaeological projects

In terms of the future sustainability of community archaeology projects, the overriding aim was to equip the volunteers with the knowledge, skills and resources to undertake post-excavation work in an increasingly independent manner. A further objective was to enhance the groups' understanding of professional standards, and the obligation upon them to plan and budget accordingly were they to undertake future archaeological interventions. This approach emphasised the significance of project design, academic/administrative consultation, appropriate budgeting and the contribution of professional archaeologists to facilitate the various stages of their projects. While the groups did possess a clear understanding of their general responsibilities to the shared heritage, and with regard to community engagement, their knowledge of professional best practice once again proved limited. The project raised both the groups' leadership ability and understanding, achieving demonstrable levels of success.

As noted earlier, a series of 14 more formal skills development workshops were organised for the project. These were attended by significant numbers of the participants. However, a pattern also developed by which some groups sent representatives who would then relay their experience back to the wider group membership. This approach helped to extend the reach of the workshops, at least with regard to key information. The value of the workshops was measured through both practical outcomes and formal evaluation. Positive practical outcomes were perceived through a more efficient and systematic approach taken by participants of 'Open Lab' sessions in areas of activity covered by the workshops. When asked formally whether the workshops would help to inform future archaeological practice among the groups, 86.7 per cent responded positively. The evaluative data also indicated that in terms of attendance the most popular subject matter was medieval and Roman ceramics (attracting 78.6 and 64.3 per cent respectively), followed by numismatics (50 per cent) and then by a more practical artefact drawing workshop (42.9 per cent) (see Fig. 6.2). The last event was so well received that participants independently arranged further drawing workshops; these they self-funded outside of the structure of the project.

Evaluation

Evaluation exercises were undertaken at both the halfway point of the project and at its conclusion. Over the two years of the project some 150 'Open Lab' sessions took place, equating to roughly 750 hours of community engagement. With regard to individual participant involvement, a rough estimate of volunteer activity indicated that at least 9,000 volunteer hours were committed to the project. As noted above, five different groups took part. However, some presented more than one assemblage of material for processing. In all, 10 different projects were brought to the 'Open Lab' sessions, the majority of which reached a stage ready for archival deposition by the end of the project. A further group of projects remain as ongoing activities still being pursued by the groups – but now with a clear system of working and defined objectives that will result in archival deposition.

Thus one of the project's primary aims was achieved: that of archival deposition of finds which would otherwise probably not have found their way into the public sphere. While the staff of the archive welcomed this practical outcome, they also recognised the project's wider and ongoing benefits. As the archive's collections access officer observed:

I genuinely can't remember a project as successful as this in a long time, certainly not in terms of bridging the amateur/professional divide and forging new relationships. I think the new archaeological landscape it has created going forward is, if anything, even more important than the archives that will be deposited. (Tomlinson 2014)

One area that did not perhaps entirely meet the ambition of the original aim was that related to public outreach and educational activities. While a number of such activities and events were successfully delivered, the intensive nature of delivering training and supervising lab-based finds sessions tended to monopolise the available time of the staff. In addition the educational activities, when delivered through schools, depended upon the support and organisational accommodation of the host schools. Regrettably in many cases the demands of curriculum and formal teaching, together with other workload pressures among teachers, inhibited access to schools for the 'Road Show' activities.

On reflection, the team decided that a schools-based workshop approach was probably best located within a separate dedicated project. Further development of this activity was beyond the staffing resources of the 'Open Lab' project as currently funded. Nonetheless imaginative use of public contact opportunities when they arose allowed the team to deliver just over 300 person days of outreach activities to some 1,660 individuals – including nearly 800 children – across the two years of the project (Tomlinson 2014). It is important to note that most of these interactions were facilitated jointly between project staff and volunteer participants.

Unforeseen outcomes

While the project had clearly stated aims with expected outcomes, there were a number of other outcomes that the project team had not entirely foreseen or which proved more significant than expected. As stated earlier, by locating the 'Open Lab' sessions physically within the BGU-UK's campus, it was hoped to avoid any inter-group rivalries. In practice, however, the behaviour of the various groups in attendance was far more collaborative than might have been expected. Though focusing mainly on their own assemblages of material, the participants were constantly supportive of each other and curious about each group's finds and progress.

Indeed, an outcome aligned with this, which was to some extent particularly unexpected, was the role played by a number of the more highly skilled volunteers.

A small number of volunteers came to the project with pre-existing skills and knowledge in a variety of areas. For example, one individual turned a particular interest in photography into a shared skill resource for all the groups. After taking initial advice from project staff on the requirements of archival small finds photography, she effectively became the key point of contact and advisor for volunteers engaged in such photography. Another participant, a retired research chemist, applied his skills and knowledge to the application of the university's Raman spectrometer to the identification of various materials from the assemblages – in particular the pigments of Roman painted wall plaster. His dedication to this task was sufficient to generate two consultation visits by project staff and volunteers to experts at University College London and the British Museum. A final example is that of a volunteer whose particular knowledge of archaeological mollusc recording and identification resulted in him leading a skills workshop on the subject. He was subsequently 'contracted' by a group different to his own to produce an identification and assessment report on their mollusc samples.

The relationships between groups were greatly strengthened as volunteers explored sharing skills and knowledge collaboratively between themselves, independent of the project. This proved a significant outcome for the 'Open Lab and Road Show Project' with regard to the future sustainability of community archaeology in the county. At the same time it demonstrates the part that skilled 'citizen researchers' can play in supporting wider archaeological practice, including potential benefits for local academic and professional/commercial archaeologists.

While it had always been an aim of the project to help participants develop a coherent understanding of the role played by specialists in archaeological post-excavation processes, the project's success in this area was actually greater than expected. The participants quickly came to appreciate the role of such specialists. Yet also, even more importantly, the groups came to a clear recognition of their limitations in this regard. This was important as, when providing advice to support subsequent funding bids, there was little need to remind the groups of the importance of correct and timely engagement with the various and relevant specialists. Instead it was possible to focus such guidance more effectively on the specific requirements of each particular project.

That subsequent costing and project planning was well-structured was confirmed when two of the groups were awarded funding for further archaeological fieldwork projects. One such project involved limited open-area excavation at a known archaeological site, while the other was an extensive programme of urban test-pitting and community engagement. Both projects incorporated appropriate levels of professional support retained through funded contracts.

Improved wellbeing and related benefits

Less tangible but equally important outcomes were a range of wellbeing and health-related benefits. By the end of the project there was evidence for an increased sense of self-worth and improved physical and mental wellbeing among a number of the volunteer participants. While much of this evidence was subjective, formal project evaluation feedback and qualitative interview responses have helped to confirm this positive effect (see Simpson and Williams 2008 for a discussion of approaches to evaluation). The creation of a networking culture between the groups not only positively supported further archaeological activity through the sharing of experience and specific skills, but also strengthened social interactions and initiated new-found friendships (Tomlinson 2014; English Heritage 2014). Overall a clear sense of communal and intellectual value was established among the participants which appears in most cases to represent the foundations for longer-term commitments and actions.

It is more difficult to assess any direct economic value associated with the project, other than a crude correlation between general archaeological costs and the number of hours of 'labour' delivered by the volunteers. There is also little, if anything, in the wider literature to provide base-data against which such a measure might be evaluated. Indeed, while some attempts have been made recently to assess the economic value of heritage participation, these have defined such actions as passive – framing those who visit heritage as an 'audience' rather than as individuals actively engaged through participatory activity (see English Heritage 2014; Fujiwara et al. 2014). Clearly the type of heritage engagement described here might be more correctly aligned with the participatory activity of, say, 'playing sport' rather than more passive forms of consumption. As Melville (2014, 5) notes, with reference to Bickerton and Wheatley (2013):

> Another recent study found that visiting historic sites did have a statistically significant impact on well-being, one that was similar to attending arts events, greater than that for visiting museums, and less than that for playing sports.

In addition, if purely economic benefits are to be assessed, then the contributory nature of archaeological research conducted upon public archives – which thereby generates positive outcomes as a wider public good – should be seen as a multiplying factor (Lipe 2002; Burtenshaw 2017).

Thus although the wellbeing benefits of the 'Open Lab' project – and participation in archaeological activities more generally – can only be assessed through subjective reflection, it is clear that positive benefits certainly exist. Such benefits include greater personal confidence, enhanced intellectual motivation and improved community engagement and friendships. It is evident that participants of the current project received all these benefits; in the case of some individuals, attendance at practical sessions had more specific and positive outcomes for their personal health, both physical and mental. As a result, the project's legacy is not only an ongoing engagement with archaeology by a group of community volunteers with enhanced skills, but also a group of people whose wellbeing and quality of communal interaction has been demonstrably enhanced.

Conclusion

The 'Open Lab' project set out to tackle a problem identified by professional and academic archaeologists, although equally recognised by the volunteer participants. It concerned the failure to complete post-excavation processes and thus to deposit finds assemblages into the appropriate public archaeological archive. The project focused upon skills development as the means by which such assemblages could be translated from a precarious 'orphaned' status to publicly secure archival deposition. The raising of the participants' levels of knowledge and understanding of archaeological process were significant additional outcomes. A range of personal and social benefits also accrued to the participants. This will help to provide a strong foundation for the future sustainability of community-based archaeology projects.

The project, as noted, was initiated as a 'top-down' concept. However, through the responsive approach taken by the project staff toward the participant groups, a strong element of 'bottom-up' direction in fact ensued. While some aspects of this direction required careful management to ensure that professional standards of conservation care, analytical rigour and archival norms were maintained, the process became essentially collaborative.

The project delivered significant outcomes for the funds invested, yet the time-limited nature of project funding presents a key weakness going forward. Access to professional support and advice is essential if community-initiated projects are to be successful. The unpredictable nature of archaeological intervention, the complexities of certain forms of research and the sometimes fluctuating nature of group membership all present challenges to even the most highly skilled volunteer archaeologists. While funders are happy to provide resources on a project-by-project basis, most shy away from commitments to the provision of long-term professional staffing. Despite archaeological archives in the UK being managed by local public authorities, the current economic conditions make it highly unlikely that suitable levels of professional support can be provided from the public purse. The current project was based in a university, however, and so was able to make excellent and efficient use of the institution's resources for community benefit.

As universities, at least in the UK, move toward a more financially autonomous model and engage in rhetoric of increased 'civic' worth and contribution, the focus for such community support should perhaps be further developed within that setting. Community archaeology provides a very real way in which universities can reach out to their 'local' communities in a process of interactively popular, yet firmly scholarly, practice, and a number have successfully engaged in such activities. As noted during this project, it is also a way in which universities, through creative engagement with skilled 'citizen researchers', can advance their own archaeological research enquiries, with demonstrable levels of 'public impact' providing a clear institutional benefit. Such a model constructs university-supported community archaeology as a well-defined public good, based on a dynamic process of shared learning and knowledge exchange.

References

Bickerton, Craig and Wheatley, Daniel. 2013. *Arts, Cultural Activity, Sport and Wellbeing.* Nottingham: Nottingham Trent University.

Burtenshaw, Paul. 2017. 'Economics in Public Archaeology'. In *Key Concepts in Public Archaeology*, edited by Gabriel Moshenska, 31–42. London: UCL Press.

Cooper, Don. 2011. 'Post-Excavation Processing: A case study'. In *Community Archaeology: Themes, methods and practices*, edited by Gabriel Moshenska and Sarah Dhanjal, 35–41. Oxford: Oxbow Books.

English Heritage. 2014. *Heritage Counts 2014, England.* Swindon: English Heritage.

Fujiwara, Daniel, Kudrna, Laura and Dolan, Paul. 2014. *Quantifying and Valuing the Wellbeing Impacts of Culture and Sport.* London: Department for Culture, Media & Sport.

Isherwood, Rob. 2011. 'Community Archaeology: Conceptual and political issues'. In *Community Archaeology: Themes, methods and practices*, edited by Gabriel Moshenska and Sarah Dhanjal, 6–17. Oxford: Oxbow Books.

LCC – Lincolnshire County Council. 2012. *Lincolnshire Archaeological Handbook*. Lincoln: Lincolnshire County Council. Accessed 29 July 2019. https://www.lincolnshire. gov.uk/residents/environment-and-planning/conservation/lincolnshire-archaeological-handbook/29200.article" https://www.lincolnshire.gov.uk/residents/environment-and-planning/conservation/lincolnshire-archaeological-handbook/29200.article.

Lipe, William D. 2002. 'Public Benefits of Archaeological Research'. In *Public Benefits of Archaeology*, edited by Barbara J. Little, 20–8. Gainesville, FL: University Press of Florida.

Maeer, Gareth. 2017. 'A People-Centred Approach to Heritage: The experience of the Heritage Lottery Fund 1994–2014', *Journal of Community Archaeology & Heritage* 4 (1): 38–52.

Melville, Duncan. 2014. 'Why Do Economists Think Heritage is Worth Protecting?' *Research News* 21: 3–5. Swindon: English Heritage.

Rowe, Samantha, Stewart, Elizabeth J. and Roberts, David. 2014. 'Perspectives on Community Archaeology: exploring collaborations between Merseyside Archaeological Society and the Museum of Liverpool', *Journal of Community Archaeology & Heritage* 1 (2): 155–72.

Simpson, Faye and Williams, Howard. 2008. 'Evaluating Community Archaeology in the UK', *Public Archaeology* 7 (2): 69–90.

Thomas, Suzie. 2010. *Community Archaeology in the UK: Recent findings*. York: Council for British Archaeology.

Thomas, Suzie. 2017. 'Community Archaeology'. In *Key Concepts in Public Archaeology*, edited by Gabriel Moshenska, 14–30. London: UCL Press.

Tomlinson, Zoë. 2014. *Archaeology Open Lab and Road Show Project: End of project report*. Lincoln: Bishop Grosseteste University.

Watkinson, David and Neal, Virginia. 1998. *First Aid for Finds*, 3rd ed. London: Rescue / UKIC Archaeology Section with the Museum of London.

7
Cultural heritage conservation and public benefits: effectiveness of Kenya's legal and administrative framework

Gilbert Kituyi Wafula

Introduction

On 27 August 2010 Kenya adopted a people-centered Constitution that heralded a new beginning in the country's history. The most important ingredients in this Constitution include declaration of the sovereignty of the people, provisions for the decentralisation of power and resources to the local level, recognition of the need for improved access to basic needs for vulnerable members of society and a rich Bill of Rights that provides for fundamental rights and freedom rights of citizens. This event has resulted in a citizenry that is more politically empowered and more knowledgeable about their rights on issues of social justice.

Sustainable social development – recognised in the Constitution as a national value – is one of the major ways in which citizens' expectations of improved livelihoods can be achieved. In this kind of atmosphere archaeology and other disciplines face the challenge of how to help promote efforts towards a sustainable use of resources for social development that benefits the entire public – especially ordinary citizens, who have tended to be sidelined in previous times. Here heritage conservation is relevant because it is directly connected to the main societal concerns such as development, economy, education, health and environment. Heritage conservation projects entailing social development are duty bound to ensure ordinary citizens and local communities accrue benefits.

Success in the efforts made towards cultural heritage conservation will ultimately depend on how the interests of all stakeholders in the whole process are observed. According to de la Torre and Mason (2002, 3) value is the main reason why heritage is conserved in the first place; no society makes an effort to conserve what it does not value. They also point out that the stakeholders of social values are usually members of the public who traditionally do not participate in the work of experts and whose opinions are traditionally disregarded. In today's changing environment, however, archaeologists and other heritage experts have to take the matter of public benefit more seriously. Although preservation is important, it should be undertaken for some tangible reason and not simply for its own sake. Since ordinary people are the ones in constant interaction with this heritage, there is need for it to provide some tangible social and economic benefits for them. This would justify the reason for expecting ordinary people to contribute to long-term conservation efforts.

With this background in mind, the aim of this chapter is to assess the effectiveness of Kenya's legal and administrative policy framework on the general public's concerns over the potential benefits that can be accrued from cultural heritage. This is done by identifying obstacles in the framework that impede the potential benefits that the public can accrue from Kenya's cultural heritage resources.

Key terms and concepts

The key terms and concepts employed in this chapter are *heritage, cultural heritage* and *archaeological heritage*; they are used interchangeably depending on context. Other terms such as *the public, public interest* and *public benefits* are used with specific meaning.

Cultural heritage

Some authors distinguish between natural heritage and cultural heritage because heritage encompasses both natural and cultural elements; others subsume natural heritage under cultural heritage, arguing that nature is always perceived through culture. Due to the author's background in archaeology, the focus of this chapter is on cultural heritage – not only because of archaeology's immense contributions to this type of heritage, but also because it is the concept recognised in Kenya's legal structures. The National Museums and Heritage Act (CAP 216 of the Laws of Kenya) defines cultural heritage as:

(a) monuments; (b) architectural works, works of monumental sculpture and painting, elements or structures of an archaeological nature, inscriptions, cave dwellings and combinations of features, which are of universal value from the point of view of history, art or science; (c) groups of separate or connected buildings which, because of their architecture, their homogeneity or their place in the landscape, are of outstanding value from the point of view of history, art or science; (d) works of humanity or the combined works of nature and humanity, and areas including archaeological sites which are of outstanding value from the historical, aesthetic, ethnological or anthropological point of view; and includes objects of archaeological or paleontological interest, objects of historical interest and protected objects. (Republic of Kenya 2006, 5–6)

In this chapter a more relevant definition of cultural heritage, which recognises it as a tool for social and economic development, is that defined by the Council of Europe's Framework Convention on the Value of Cultural Heritage for Society (2005). The Convention defines cultural heritage as:

a group of resources inherited from the past which people identify, independently of ownership, as a reflection and expression of their constantly evolving values, beliefs, knowledge and traditions. It includes all aspects of the environment resulting from the interaction between people and places through time.

Some scholars apply the term cultural heritage generally, but others distinguish between the different types. These include tangible (material) and intangible (non-material) cultural heritage, moveable and immoveable cultural heritage, built heritage and archaeological heritage. Although most of these different types of heritage are closely linked, special focus here is upon archaeological heritage for the reason given above.

Archaeological heritage

In the context of this chapter, a suitable definition of archaeological heritage is that defined by the European Convention on the Protection of the Archaeological Heritage (Council of Europe 1992, Article 1). According to the Convention archaeological heritage constitutes as follows:

All remains and objects and any other traces of humankind from past times are considered to be elements of the archaeological heritage. ... [This] shall include structures, constructions, groups of buildings, developed sites, moveable objects, monuments of other kinds as well as their context, whether situated on land or under water.

The public

In archaeology this term means two main things: the state and the people (Matsuda 2004, 66). The first concept covers the state and its institutions, those structures that govern the practice of archaeology, together with their officials. Although this chapter examines state aspects such as the laws, institutions, structures and policies, the main focus is on the second meaning, that of the public – the people who, according to Merriman (2004, 1–2), are the individual members of society whose reactions form public opinion and who, in theory, should ultimately benefit from the archaeologists' research. In this conception the public constitutes 'general' or 'ordinary' members of the public. Matsuda (2004, 66) notes the distinction between 'the public' and 'the private', the latter being associated with the intimate realm of human activities, such as the family. In the context of this chapter 'the public' refers to ordinary citizens, especially unemployed people. They form the majority of the population living in poverty, represented in the Kenyan political context by the name *Wanjiku*.

Public interest

Deriving from 'the public' is the term 'public interest', or what Bozeman calls the 'common good' (Bozeman 2007, 97). According to the Dictionary. com (2018), 'public interest' means firstly the welfare or wellbeing of the general public and the commonwealth, and secondly appeal or relevance to the general public. In academic literature this concept is controversial. Many authorities dismiss it on the grounds that its intended meaning is often susceptible to manipulation by 'individual' or 'private' interests for their own advantage. The government can claim to be doing something in the public interest yet actually do the opposite, for example, such as legislating and enacting laws in support of hidden individual, group or class interest. As a solution Bozeman (2007, 12) suggests that since public interest is an ideal that is unachievable, it is more useful to measure 'public values' that have specific, identifiable content. He explains that such values:

> are those providing normative consensus about (a) the rights, benefits and prerogatives to which citizens should (and should not) be entitled; (b) the obligations of citizens to society, the state and

one another; and (c) the principles on which governments and policies should be based. (Bozeman 2007, 13)

In the context of this chapter, 'public interest' is regarded as what is for the common good of all citizens – what our laws, regulations and policies should strive to achieve without disadvantaging some segments of the population. The use of the dichotomous concepts of public interest and private interest, as applied by some archaeologists, is based on the premise that archaeological heritage is of public interest, beyond private interests, hence meriting protection (Carman 2002, 97; Merriman 2004, 1–3). Therefore 'public interests' should be distinguished from 'private interests' – the concerns of individual people, groups of people or classes who have, in the context of Kenya, been historically advantaged over ordinary citizens in society.

Public benefits

The public benefits of heritage are related to the value and significance that the public attaches to heritage. There are many different ways in which heritage benefits or values are perceived in society. The two main categories of heritage values are intrinsic values and instrumental values (Merryman 1989); how valuable or beneficial they may be depends on the stakeholder in heritage conservation. Intrinsic benefits of heritage, on the one hand, are based on the idea that the heritage has an inherent value in and of itself – not merely as a means of acquiring something else. These kinds of benefits are not directly observable in forms such as pleasure, cognitive growth or empathy. On the other hand, instrumental benefits provide tangible benefits. They offer the means of achieving broad social and economic goals, such as economic growth, enhanced social capital, improvements in learning skills, health, water, etc.

Though both types of benefits are important, instrumental benefits are the more relevant in the context of this chapter. According to Dümcke and Gnedovsky (2013, 6), many authors addressing the value of cultural heritage often complement the definition of cultural heritage applied by the Council of Europe's (2005) Framework Convention on the Value of Cultural Heritage for Society with a notion of the heritage sector constituted by specialised activities that involve heritage and are related to other social and economic sectors in two strands:

A sector of activities on its own, which provides jobs and generates growth (direct impact, mainly economic but which can include other dimensions of development as well) and spill-over social and economic effects of cultural heritage in other fields, such as agriculture, regional development, environment, science and education, tourism, technology, innovation, social cohesion, intercultural dialogue, etc.

Context

Members of the general public in Kenya, like those in many other countries in Africa, share persistent social and economic challenges including poverty, illiteracy and disease. According to a relatively recent World Bank report, Kenya faces challenges of poverty, inequality, governance, low investment and low economic productivity. These combine to limit the country's ability to achieve rapid, sustained growth rates with the power to transform the lives of ordinary citizens (World Bank 2014). More revealing information released by an earlier World Bank report entitled 'Kenya Economic Update' indicated that between 34 and 42 per cent of Kenyans live in abject poverty (Randa and Gubbins 2013). The report indicated that since the early 1990s the country's poverty had 'declined slowly (at about one percentage point per year) but absolute levels remain very high (about 42 per cent in 2009)'. It further observed that although the level of poverty in Kenya was still quite high, the country had the opportunity to eliminate extreme poverty by 2030 in line with the World Bank's global poverty target – if it managed to reduce levels by two percentage points each year.

Poverty and inequality in Kenya are bedfellows. Inequality was, in fact, one of the main factors associated with the 2007/2008 post-election violence in the country. This problem here is so big that despite Kenya being for many years the biggest economy in East Africa, the majority of its people are substantially poorer than those in neighbouring Uganda, a country with a far smaller economy. According to a report by the World Bank and the IMF (2013), Uganda's poverty rate stood at 38.01 per cent, while that of Kenya was 43.37 per cent. A World Bank press release (World Bank Press Release 2013) noted that Kenya's 'high rate of poverty reduction is only possible if growth is accompanied by reduction in inequality, to enable the poor to benefit, to a disproportionate extent'. Another recent report noted that Kenya's high rate of poverty reduction is only possible if growth is accompanied by reduction in inequality, to enable the poor to benefit, to a disproportionate extent. Another recent report by the Kenya National Bureau of Statistics (Mwangi 2013) called *Exploring Kenya's Inequality: Pulling apart or pooling together?* also raises the alarm on the challenge for Kenya posed by widening socio-economic inequality. The report warns of the concerning trend of an ever-increasing gulf in the wellbeing of individuals and communities.

Why should one be wary of inequality in our society? Inequality can result in non-income disparities in social amenities such as health and education outcomes, further undermining public investment in poverty reduction (Wilkinson and Picket 2010). The report by the Kenya National Bureau of Statistics referred to above (Mwangi 2013) identifies the main social and economic challenges of inequality in Kenya as access to employment, education, water, sanitation and housing. As a result of the country's social and economic inequality there exist two main classes in society: the rich and privileged few on the one hand and the general public, or ordinary person, on the other hand. The latter is engaged in a constant struggle to make ends meet.

Among the reasons for Kenya's widespread socio-economic inequality is the belief by those in political leadership in trickle-down economics; they hope that with an improved economy the lives of ordinary Kenyans will also improve. Another main reason is educational disparity, which necessarily advantages some few Kenyans to access resources over others. Other reasons are a bias in the allocation of public resources – the result of historical and political motivations – and a failure to develop sectors of the economy which have the economic potential to benefit the poor majority.

The irony of the dire picture given above is that Kenya possesses a wide range of resources, including archaeological heritage (and other forms of cultural heritage). These can make a potentially significant contribution in addressing the main challenge of poverty that afflicts the majority of the population. Kenya possesses a wealth of archaeological heritage which has hitherto not effectively been utilised to transform people's livelihoods.

Archaeological heritage is an important ingredient in Kenya's identity in the world; its contribution to the country's heritage goes far beyond the discipline itself. It has, for example, contributed to paleontology, boasting one of the biggest collections of prehistoric fossils. Here evidence has shown that our common human ancestor lived on the shores of Lake Victoria and once wandered the plains of the Great Rift Valley. Many of the country's fossils, preserved by the National Museums of Kenya (NMK), show that the earliest human beings came from this country before migrating to other continents – hence the claim of Kenya and eastern Africa to be the 'cradle of humankind'. Archaeology has also contributed significantly to history, providing a good picture of the migration and settlement of the immediate ancestors of today's peoples and the formation of Africa's main ethnic nations. Kenya also possesses many other cultural sites that depict historic architecture and cultural landscapes, including those on the World Heritage List (UNESCO 2015).

One of the challenges that the above sites encounter is the danger of destruction, both from natural forces and human actions. The latter include pressure for infrastructural development and urban growth by government (both national and county) and private interests (mostly those of the rich). Another major concern is the fact that members of local communities inhabiting the neighbourhoods of such sites pose a threat to their conservation. Given that the majority of these people have no alternative sources of livelihood they contribute, consciously or unconsciously, in their destruction – for example, by re-using artefacts and features as sources of income in order to meet their daily needs. This calls for heritage conservation efforts that consider the interests of local people to help ensure that development projects and other uses of heritage do indeed provide social and economic benefits to local communities.

Theory and method

Theoretical framework

This chapter is premised on the New Development Paradigm developed by Stigliz in the late 1990s (Stigliz 1998). The main features of this paradigm are the equitable and sustainable wellbeing of human beings and the rest of nature, people-centred development and active participation in research activities. An example of ensuring that people participation in social development is achieved is to involve the views of ordinary people and local communities before embarking on any development project that might impact them. This paradigm promotes transformational leadership, which recognises that citizens are the ones who ultimately make decisions.

The chapter is also influenced by the public interest theory advocated by Bozeman (2007), which was directed at the theory of economic individualism prevalent in the West. In a society such as Kenya's where high inequality exists, with wide gaps between the living standards of rich and poor, this theory is relevant. The work is also influenced by the critical theory of postmodernism, which requires researchers and scholars to examine the status quos of the societies in which they live. Marxist theory is also relevant, as it advocates for the inclusion of the proletariat's interests; in Kenya's case, such inclusion relates to research activities and development initiatives instead of merely serving the interests of elites.

Data collection

Using official documents and academic papers including journal papers and book chapters, this chapter examines instruments including the national Constitution, national laws, national policies and international protocols to seek information on the general public's concerns in human rights, ethics, justice, opportunities for sustainable development and social wellbeing.

For human rights and ethical concerns, there is a need to know whether the fundamental human rights and freedoms are provided for and whether moral obligations are motivated – for instance, the morality of using people's cultural heritage resources without giving them due compensation, and hence leading to an unequal society in which a few people live in luxury while most lead miserable lives. For justice, there arises the issue of the unfairness of having an unequal and unfair society. Do the laws protect weak and vulnerable members of society? How practical are these laws? For instance, a country may have a good constitution, but fail to put it into practice.

For sustainable development, given that people have sovereign power, other issues arise. Do local communities and lay people, for example, have an opportunity to participate in development projects? Are there opportunities for different stakeholders to engage and venture into the heritage business sector? On the issue of social wellbeing, are there modalities to promote development projects that put in place social amenities such as health services, water and the like, which can benefit ordinary people?

The data

The Constitution of Kenya 2010

The Constitution of Kenya 2010 (Republic of Kenya 2010), published in May 2010 and promulgated on 27 August of the same year, is the supreme law in Kenya. It replaced the 1963 independence constitution, overhauled because of a belief that it was outdated and no longer in tune with the changing times.

Some of the new Constitution's most significant features in regard to how the public can benefit from cultural heritage and conservation include:

- Article 1 on sovereignty of the people and supremacy of the constitution, which provides for people empowerment
- Article 6 addresses regional inequality by providing for 'devolution', or rather decentralisation
- Article 10 identifies sustainable development as a national value
- Article 11 recognises culture as the foundation of the nation with Section 3 (a) protecting local communities. Such communities should accordingly be compensated by royalties for the use of their cultures and cultural heritage
- A rich Bill of Rights (see Chapter 4 of Kenya's Constitution, inaugurated in 2010) providing for fundamental rights and freedoms and recognising the socio-economic rights of ordinary citizens

Environment Management and Coordination Act (EMCA) 1999

The EMCA (Republic of Kenya 1999) is an Act of Parliament establishing a legal and institutional framework for the management of the environment. It provides for Environmental Impact Assessment (EIA), requiring a 'systematic analysis of projects, policies, plans or programs to determine their potential environmental impacts' and 'the significance of such impacts and to propose measures to mitigate the negative ones'.

According to Oloo and Namunaba (2010), the major weakness of the EMCA is that it primarily focuses on natural environment issues, touching only rarely on cultural heritage. Where cultural heritage is mentioned in the Act, it seldom receives the attention it deserves.

The significance of this Act to archaeologists' interests is that a project can be solely based on it; private developers may then proceed to ignore archaeological heritage and get away with it. The danger to the general public and local communities, unfamiliar with archaeological heritage materials, is that these can be destroyed without their knowledge, which would be an injustice to public and communities alike.

The National Museums and Heritage Act, Cap 6 of 2006

The National Museums and Heritage Act (Republic of Kenya 2006) is the most comprehensive legal and administrative structure on issues of cultural heritage that Kenya has ever possessed. It is also currently the most important and powerful legal basis that safeguards cultural resources in Kenya. The Act arose from the need to address staff restructuring and physical infrastructure for the National Museums of Kenya (NMK), which is included in the final document. For the first time ever it can be seen in the text that, as the name implies, protection of heritage was made to stand out. This emphasis is demonstrated in instances such as the inclusion of heritage concepts in the law and the appointment of heritage wardens.

The Museums and Heritage Act consists of 81 different sections plus subsidiary legislation. These are grouped into 12 parts, with the significant ones including the preliminary, establishment, functions and powers of the NMK, financial provisions of the NMK, heritage declarations, searches and discoveries, protected areas, monuments, antiquities and protected objects, export and powers of enforcement.

The Act provides for establishment, control, management and development of the NMK. The NMK's functions include identification, protection, conservation and transmission of the cultural and natural heritage of Kenya. As legal custodian, the Act allows the NMK to conduct Environmental Impact Assessments (EIA) for proposed development projects.

The NMK represents an administrative structure. It is the legal custodian of natural and cultural heritage, for example archaeological finds, submarine settlements and shipwrecks, and historical monuments.

The National Museums and Heritage Act, Cap 6 of 2006 has various weaknesses that may have significant impact on the public interest in benefiting from heritage. These include

- A lack of incentives for communities and individuals to invest in income-generating cultural resource conservation programmes. This impedes efforts in sustainable development and the social wellbeing of locals
- Vague guidance on procedures of involving other stakeholders in use of cultural resources
- As a stakeholder (albeit a major one), the interests of the Act can clash with those of potential rivals, such as private museums
- The Act does not clearly spell out measures to ensure benefits are shared with the affected communities. This leaves local people and communities at its mercy, which raises moral concerns
- Although the NMK is empowered to do Environment Impact Assessments, as noted above, this role is shared with another authority, NEMA. Based on the Environment Management and Coordination Act, however, NEMA can also ignore the NMK. There is therefore no single law or body solely in charge of cultural impact assessments, which is a danger to the country's heritage

These are major gaps and weaknesses that impede the potential benefits ordinary people and communities can accrue from their heritage resources.

International protocols and conventions

Kenya is a signatory to many regional and global protocols and conventions. These include:

- The International Covenant on Economic, Social and Cultural Rights, 1966–1972
- UNESCO World Heritage Convention
- First Optional Protocol to the International Covenant on Civil and Political Rights, 1966
- Convention on the Elimination of All Forms of Discrimination against Women, 1979–1984
- African Charter on Human and Peoples' Rights (African Charter or ACHPR), 1987
- ICOMOS Principles of Recording of Monuments and Groups of Buildings
- ICOMOS Declaration of Human Rights
- Optional Protocol to the International Covenant on Economic, Social and Cultural Rights, 2008

These international protocols deal with issues of interest to the ordinary Kenyan such as human rights and democracy, justice, equity and equality, as well as non-discrimination of all kinds, cultural rights, socio-economic rights and social development. Their significance is their emphasis for the sustainability principle, and also for the exchange of ideas at international fora on global challenges. More importantly, the protocols obligate the Kenyan state to adhere to global standards. They thus act as a template to guide local efforts.

Kenya's challenge in implementing these protocols is hampered by the lack of an effective and adequate framework, however, as we have seen in the laws discussed above. The new Constitution discussed above is nevertheless a step in the right direction.

National policies

Some of the relevant policies in the context of this chapter include:

Millennium Development Goals (MDGs)
The United Nations' MDGs were eight international development goals established in the aftermath of the Millennium Summit of the United Nations (UN), held in 2000 in New York. Following the adoption of the

UN Millennium Declarations, it was agreed that member states would strive to achieve these goals by the year 2015. Along with 189 other UN members, Kenya was a signatory to these goals.

The eight MDGs goals were: to eradicate extreme poverty and hunger; to achieve universal free education; to promote gender equity and empower women; to reduce child mortality; to reduce maternal mortality; to combat HIV/AIDS, malaria and other diseases; to ensure environmental sustainability; and to establish a global partnership for development (United Nations 2015; Nwonwu 2008, 4). Cultural heritage conservation and the way it is practised were capable of playing an important role in ensuring that these MDGs were achieved. However, as per the MDGs Status Report for Kenya 2005, the role of cultural heritage resources and their conservation for helping to achieve some of these – such as eradicating extreme poverty and hunger and sustainable social development – was not clearly stated (Republic of Kenya 2005).

According to a World Bank Report entitled *Kenya Overview* (World Bank 2014), Kenya has managed to meet a few MDG targets, including the reduction of child mortality, near universal primary school enrolment and narrower gender gaps in education. However, the year 2015 came and went without all of the goals being achieved. It can be argued that had the role of cultural heritage and its conservation in Kenya been taken more seriously, most of them might have been achieved to a more successful level.

Vision 2030

Vision 2030 is Kenya's development programme for the period 2008–2030. This national, long-term development blueprint seeks to create a globally competitive and prosperous nation with a high quality of life by 2030. Its aim is to transform Kenya into a newly industrialising, middle-income country, able to provide a high quality of life to all its citizens in a clean and secure environment (Republic of Kenya 2007).

The vision is anchored on three key pillars: economic, social and political governance. Although the role of the tourism industry was one of the areas highlighted as a means of achieving Vision 2030, the specific place where cultural heritage and its conservation can be used to obtain sustainable social development does not stand out. However, the National Museums of Kenya (2009) has developed a Strategic Plan designed to position the institution strategically as a key driver in the country's social and economic development. One of the ways in which the National Museums of Kenya intends to achieve this is by involving diverse stakeholders in promoting the cultural heritage sector in social development. However, without explicit laws to support the plan, its success cannot be guaranteed.

The National Policy on Culture and Heritage (Republic of Kenya 2009) brings out the central role of cultural and natural heritage to the socio-economic and sustainable needs of the country, seeking the inclusion and participation of all its citizens. The Policy perceives cultural diversity to be one of the roots of development not only for economic growth, but also as a means of intellectual, emotional, moral and spiritual existence (Republic of Kenya 2009, 1).

The National Policy on Culture and Heritage has two policy statements. These respectively declare the intention to 'take all necessary steps to ensure the protection and promotion of culture and of cultural diversity among Kenyans' and to 'take all necessary steps to ensure the protection and promotion of the Country's national heritage' (Republic of Kenya 2009, 2).

The National Policy on Culture and Heritage also promises to take appropriate measures to protect, conserve and preserve tangible and intangible national heritage within its boundaries. It highlights the economic dimensions that can be achieved through tourism, employment and other areas of economic potential.

In general, the National Policy on Culture and Heritage is an impressive document. It emphasises the central role of culture and national heritage in Kenya's socio-economic and sustainable development.

Summary, conclusion and recommendations

As we have seen in this chapter, Kenya's new Constitution recognises the central role of ordinary citizens in the country's social development and seeks to safeguard their rights to benefit from their resources. Kenya also has an impressive national policy on culture and cultural heritage that has potential to accrue benefits to ordinary people. The main impediment to these endeavours is the country's weak and inadequate laws. These are not yet in line with the challenges facing ordinary people.

As we have observed, the main impediments to public benefits in cultural heritage are as follows:

- The absence of a specific law dealing with Cultural Heritage Impact Assessment. This puts Kenya's cultural heritage at the mercy of opportunists, looters and vandals who can manipulate administrative confusion – especially between the role of NEMA and the NMK – to disadvantage local communities

- The laws' lack of clarity on how to promote multi-sectoral interests. This would provide opportunities for entrepreneurship and employment, able in turn to empower ordinary people economically and contribute to the social wellbeing of local communities
- The laws are inadequate in promoting partnership and cooperation between government and non-government stakeholders. Heritage can and should benefit all; there is no reason why this aspect is not legislated to create opportunities for local communities
- The laws are weak on strategies for community empowerment to address sustainable livelihoods
- The laws are inadequate in promoting public participation, communication, education and awareness. This is not in tandem with the new Constitution

It is evident from this study that the main impediments to public benefits in archaeological heritage and other types of cultural heritage in Kenya are the weak, inadequate and ineffective laws described above. In this environment, however, the work of heritage professionals – such as those of the NMK, for instance, through their Strategic Plan 2009–2014 – towards making heritage conservation relevant to the wider society is an important step in the right direction (National Museums of Kenya 2009). More efforts in this direction from other institutions and professionals associated with cultural heritage, for instance universities and government bodies, are likely to improve the situation. More importantly, however, policy makers and heritage managers in Kenya need to concentrate more on restructuring the legal and administrative framework in line with the current constitution.

References

Bozeman, Barry. 2007. *Public Values and Public Interest: Counterbalancing economic individualism.* Washington, DC: Georgetown University Press.
Carman, John. 2002. *Archaeology and Heritage: An introduction.* London; New York: Continuum.
Council of Europe. 1992. *European Convention on the Protection of the Archaeological Heritage (Revised).* Strasbourg: Council of Europe. Accessed 29 July 2019. https://rm.coe.int/168007bd25.
Council of Europe. 2005. *Council of Europe Framework Convention on the Value of Cultural Heritage for Society (The Faro Convention).* Strasbourg: Council of Europe.
de la Torre, Marta and Mason, Randall. 2002. 'Introduction'. In *Assessing the Values of Cultural Heritage: Research report*, edited by Marta de la Torre, 3–4. Los Angeles, CA: Getty Conservation Institute.
Dictionary.com. s.v. 'Public Interest'. Accessed 8 January 2018. http://www.dictionary.com/browse/public-interest.
Dümcke, Cornelia and Gnedovsky, Mikhail. 2013. *The Social and Economic Value of Cultural Heritage: Literature review.* Berlin; Moscow: European Expert Network on Culture (EENC).

Matsuda, Akira. 2004. 'The Concept of "the Public" and the Aims of Public Archaeology', *Papers from the Institute of Archaeology* 15: 90–7.

Merriman, Nick. 2004. 'Introduction: Diversity and dissonance in public archaeology'. In *Public Archaeology*, edited by Nick Merriman, 1–18. New York: Routledge.

Merryman, John H. 1989. 'The Public Interest in Cultural Property', *California Law Review* 77 (2): 339–64.

Mwangi, Tabitha W. 2013. *Exploring Kenya's Inequality: Pulling apart or pooling together?* Nairobi: Kenya National Bureau of Statistics (KNBS) and Society for International Development (SID).

National Museums of Kenya. 2009. *National Museums of Kenya Strategic Plan 2009–2014.* Nairobi: National Museums of Kenya.

Nwonwu, Francis. 2008. 'Introduction'. In *Millennium Development Goals: Achievements and prospects of meeting the targets in Africa*, edited by Francis Nwonwu, 1–8. Pretoria, South Africa: Africa Institute of South Africa.

Oloo, Wycliffe and Namunaba, Ibrahim B. 2010. 'Cultural Heritage Impact Assessment in Kenya'. In *Cultural Heritage Impact Assessment in Africa: An overview*, edited by Herman Kiriama, Ishanlosen Odiaua and Ashton Sinamai, 10–27. Mombasa, Kenya: Centre for Heritage Development in Africa.

Republic of Kenya. 1999. *Environmental Management and Co-ordination Act.* Nairobi, Kenya: The National Council for Law Reporting with the Authority of the Attorney General.

Republic of Kenya. 2005. *MDGs Status Report for Kenya 2005.* Nairobi, Kenya: Government of the Republic of Kenya.

Republic of Kenya. 2006. *The National Museums and Heritage Act.* Nairobi, Kenya: Government of the Republic of Kenya.

Republic of Kenya. 2007. *Kenya Vision 2030: A Globally Competitive and Prosperous Kenya.* Nairobi, Kenya: Government of the Republic of Kenya.

Republic of Kenya. 2009. *National Policy on Culture and Heritage.* Nairobi, Kenya: Government Printer.

Republic of Kenya. 2010. *The Constitution of Kenya*, rev. ed. Nairobi, Kenya: The National Council for Law Reporting with the Authority of the Attorney General. Accessed 29 July 2019. https://www.wipo.int/edocs/lexdocs/laws/en/ke/ke019en.pdf.

Stiglitz, Joseph E. 1998. 'Towards a New Paradigm for Development: Strategies, policies and processes'. Prebisch Lecture at United Nations Conference on Trade and Development, Geneva, 19 October 1998.

UNESCO – United Nations Educational, Scientific and Cultural Organization. 2015. 'World Heritage List'. UNESCO World Heritage Centre. Accessed 9 May 2015. http://whc.unesco.org/en/list.

United Nations. 2015. 'We Can End Poverty: Millennium Development Goals and beyond 2015. Background'. Accessed 9 October 2020. https://www.un.org/millenniumgoals/bkgd.shtml.

Wilkinson, Richard and Picket, Kate. 2010. *The Spirit Level: Why equality is better for everyone.* London: Penguin Books.

World Bank. 2013. *Global Monitoring Report 2013: Rural-urban dynamics and the Millennium Development Goals.* Washington, DC: World Bank.

World Bank Press Release. 2013. 'Time for Kenya to Shift Gears to Accelerate Growth and Reduce Poverty'. 17 June 2013. Accessed 9 October 2020. https://www.worldbank.org/en/news/press-release/2013/06/17/time-for-kenya-to-shift-gears-to-accelerate-growth-and-reduce-poverty.

World Bank. 2014. 'Kenya Overview'. Accessed 10 December 2014. http://www.worldbank.org/en/country/kenya/overview.

8

Learning from archives: integrating preservation and access

Nancy Bell and Dinah Eastop

Introduction

This chapter introduces the interdisciplinary approach to conservation (understood as investigation, preservation and presentation) that has been adopted at The National Archives (UK) and links this work to the institution's democratic mandate (The National Archives 2017i). The chapter highlights the underpinning conceptual and practical approaches that are used to make conservation sustainable by integrating strategies for preservation, access and development. It also demonstrates the engagement of community groups in the development of archival records.

In doing so, we first introduce The National Archives, then consider its formal mandate and a case study that shows how an integrated approach can optimise sustainability. We also draw attention to the wide range of resources available on The National Archives website. The discussion focuses on the democratic ethos of The National Archives and explores how this is manifested in practice. The chapter's main conclusion is that the archive sector provides excellent models for managing cultural heritage sustainably in environmental, social and economic terms.

The National Archives is responsible for collecting and preserving UK government records and for making them publicly accessible, traditionally as learning resources. Archives are distinctly different from museums, which offer interpretative experiences. For many years The National Archives was an executive agency of the Ministry of Justice, but since 2015 it has been located within the Department of Digital, Culture, Media and Sport (DCMS). The Department was recently renamed to include Digital in its title, reflecting its acquisition of significant new responsibilities covering the digital sectors – telecommunications, data protection, internet safety, cyber skills and parts of the media and creative industries.

As the government's national archive, it holds a huge range of records. These span 1,000 years, from the Domesday Book (assembled after 1085) to websites, for everyone to discover and use.

The National Archives preserves only a small percentage of the government record. The selection of records for permanent retention is made jointly by staff of all government departments and bodies whose records are deemed public records under the Public Records Act. Guidance on selection and transfer are also provided, together with the operational selection policies for each government department which are available online. Each department is also responsible for determining which records should be designated as open (to the public) on transfer to The National Archives and which should be transferred as closed for a period of time (The National Archives 2017h).

Records selection is an important step in archival practice. Tensions can arise between demands for scrutiny and secrecy. One recent example concerns 'migrated' colonial records related to the suppression of the Mau Mau uprising in Kenya in the 1950s and 1960s (Petersen 2012). These records, from Britain's former colonial governments, were sent to the UK (hence *migrated*) on the eve of decolonisation. The Foreign and Commonwealth Office (FCO) of the British government claimed erroneously that all information it had on the Mau Mau rebellion had been transferred to The National Archives (Cary 2011). This was not in fact the case: the records had not been transferred to The National Archives, which was neither suppressing access nor claiming the records did not exist. It transpired that the records had remained in 'archival stasis' in Hanslope Park, the government's Communications Centre. By appearing to deny the existence of the records, it was claimed that the FCO sought 'to shape the future colonial archive and the realities it would produce' (Elkins 2012).

Such claims underline the importance of government records in understanding both the past and the present, and the way in which histories are generated and sustained. A useful distinction can also be drawn between archives and libraries. The former are characterised as unconscious, reflecting the raw data of policy or procedures, and the latter as conscious, reflecting different interpretations.

For the record. For good

The records held by The National Archives play a mediating role not only between the past and the present, but also between the government of the day and the public. The National Archives has responsibilities both to the British government, which generates the original material, and to the public, who have rights to scrutinise the archived records of government departments. The National Archives must confront the past, the time in which the records were created, and the future, the time for which the records are preserved, while also seeking to meet the needs of its current users. Exposed as it is to these blurring temporalities, The National Archives has adopted an integrated, interdisciplinary approach to achieve these challenging, apparently competing objectives (The National Archives 2017d).

The mandate of The National Archives can be characterised as *For the record. For good*, the title of its Business Plan for 2011–15. The first part of this title, 'For the record', emphasises the importance of preserving 'the record', i.e. the selected, archived records of the UK government. The second part, 'For good', exploits the expression's dual meaning: it can refer both to time and to morality. In the context of The National Archives, 'For good' encompasses both. The Archives' responsibility is to preserve designated material 'for ever' (i.e. a duty of care extending over generations) and also for the 'public good' (i.e. for public benefit).

The ethos of The National Archives is rooted in democratic principles: public access to the records of government is considered paramount to sustain an effective democracy. Openness to scrutiny ('transparency') is demonstrated by The National Archives itself, through the vast amount of information about its policies and practices available (at no charge) from its website. Among this is the business plan noted above (The National Archives 2013b) and reports on conservation research plans and outcomes, as noted below.

Sustaining and adding social value

Conservation has been characterised by its focus on scientific understanding of materials and construction – and more recently by the environment in which collections and sites are maintained. The important role of social sciences in this area is now more widely recognised, as it is important to understand the significance attributed by people to different forms of heritage and in different settings (Jones and Holden 2008). The cultural and social dimension of conservation is widely reported, with examples including Clavir (2002) and Johnson et al. (2005); see also essays in Richmond and Bracker (2009). A notable example of applying social science approaches to the understanding of conservation issues is provided by *Mind the Gap* – a report on an investigation to understand the working culture of collaborative research, and in particular perceived hindrances to such collaboration (Bell et al. 2014). An attitude survey formed the basis for the evaluation. This was informed by a questionnaire, designed to elicit both quantitative and qualitative information and drawing on social science methodologies.

The National Archives has been active in developing relationships between users and potential users of the archival records locally, regionally, nationally and internationally; many projects involve archive users in the development of the records. (A case study described below provides an example of such user engagement.) Known as 'User Participation Projects', these projects highlight the integrated role of users in adding value to the records. Partnerships arise in many ways, ranging from a single enquiry from a member of the public to a wider, proactive outreach strategy. The latter may be linked to anniversaries, for example the expulsion of Ugandan Asians in 1972 (see below).

For over 20 years The National Archives has worked with volunteers. It has enlisted their help upon a wide range of cataloguing; some projects will last for a few months, others continue for several years. The National Archives has recently expanded its volunteer projects online, engaging 'virtual volunteers' to help improve catalogue descriptions by contributing their record knowledge and expertise.

As well as working with local and regional history groups, and with university students, The National Archives uses community partners to attract audiences who are often new to archives. Its outreach staff actively seek new ways of engaging communities with archives, working both on-site and in community settings. Past projects include *Caribbean through a lens,* in which community partners from Leeds to London worked with the team for over 18 months to create powerful exhibitions, reminiscence workshops and events inspired by colonial photographs of the Caribbean (The National Archives 2017a). Another project explored the archival records of the expulsion of Asians from Uganda by President Idi Amin in 1972, enabling exploration of first-hand accounts. Podcasts by those caught up in these events provide moving descriptions of what took place and its consequences; some include a note of optimism in the stories of new lives created in Britain (The National Archives 2012; Orne 2012).

Outreach services include group visits to view the archival records and support for developing ideas for community engagement using archive collections. They may involve hosting workshops or public talks with speakers on diverse histories and free loan of travelling exhibitions on Caribbean, Ugandan Asian and lesbian, gay, bisexual and transgender histories (The National Archives 2017e).

The international reach and impact of the records, as well as the colonial origins of some – and their post-colonial legacy – is illustrated by the following example of links between the UK and Canada. In October 2013 a delegation from the Canada-based Federation of Saskatchewan Indian Nations (FSIN) visited The National Archives to view documents connected to a royal proclamation. The four-day visit was organised to mark the 250th anniversary of the Royal Proclamation by George III, issued on 7 October 1763. This Proclamation is viewed as an important moment in the relationship between First Nations and the Crown – a declaration that established government for Quebec, East Florida, West Florida and Grenada.

The FSIN represents 74 First Nations in Saskatchewan, Canada. Its delegation consisted of 25 Indigenous people including chiefs, veterans, elders and leaders. They met with records specialists at The National Archives and viewed a selection of documents and maps connected to the Proclamation. The delegation's leader, Chief Perry Bellegarde, commented that:

> As Indigenous peoples, it is very important for us to be here because the Royal Proclamation of 1763 represents the first time that the Crown recognised Indigenous peoples' title to lands and territories. The Royal Proclamation is fundamental to the legal framework for First Nations in Canada and is referenced in Canada's constitution. (The National Archives 2013a)

Sustainable in environmental terms

The National Archives has identified and implemented sustainable approaches to conserving the archives in its care and to maintaining its premises. These approaches range from ongoing careful monitoring and control of how space is used to sustaining local bee populations by having beehives in the grounds. Ways have been sought to enhance the environmental conditions of the storage areas (repositories) while also reducing financial and environmental costs. Research was undertaken to develop a building model, known as a Building Environment Simulation (BES), that would simulate the repositories' environmental conditions (primarily their relative humidity and temperature) in order to provide the information needed to optimise building performance, and so to achieve a stable preservation environment with reduced energy use (Ntanos and Bell 2007; Hong et al. 2012; Hong et al. 2011).

This research was initiated by The National Archives' Collection Care Department. The project proved highly effective because it required research collaborations that were intra-institutional, inter-institutional and interdisciplinary. In the first instance, discussions took place within the institution to identify who 'looked after' (i.e. monitored and controlled) the environment of the repositories (for example, the roles of conservators and the building maintenance team). This preliminary investigation established that the two teams used different terminologies, reflecting different professional norms and traditions. Once such differences have been recognised, collaboration becomes much easier and research and development more effective (Eastop and Similä 2007; Similä and Eastop 2016; Bell et al. 2014).

Following this crucial initial stage, The National Archives formed an inter-institutional research partnership with the Centre for Sustainable Heritage at University College London, which had specialist expertise in modelling. Environmental records provided by The National Archives (arising from years of monitoring relative humidity and temperature within the repositories) were used as a basis for developing the BES. The model was constructed for three of the repositories, based on their physical dimensions, material characteristics and the mechanical air-conditioning temperature and relative humidity (RH) settings. When proposals are made to change the building – for example by altering the roof insulation – the BES is used to predict the likely effects, enabling informed cost-benefit analysis and effective use of resources. The National Archives provides information on energy, environment and sustainability on its website; it also offers free online access to research reports. Examples of such reports include 'Environmental Assessment Without Limits at The National Archives' (Ntanos and VanSnick 2010) and *Conservation Research and Development for the National Archives: Strategy and implementation plan 2009–2011* (Ntanos 2009).

The National Archives is committed to improving its environmental performance by reducing energy use and carbon emissions, preventing pollution and reducing waste streams (National Archives 2017c). In 2010/2011, for example, it achieved a higher than average reduction in carbon emissions of 17.7 per cent, exceeding the target figure of 11 per cent set by the Ministry of Justice. Such improvements are not only environmentally friendly, but also cost-effective in both the shorter and longer term. The National Archives works within strict financial controls and has developed commercial services to support its core objectives. Such commercial developments are part of an integrated strategy to optimise the use of public resources.

Integrating preservation and access: a case study

The integrated conservation approach adopted by The National Archives is illustrated in this chapter by one case study. The work involved enhancing the preservation of, and improving access to, a large set of diverse records known as the Board of Trade (BT) Design Register 1839–1991. The Register includes nearly 3 million designs registered for copyright protection by proprietors from all over the world. The geographical spread and diversity of design Representations is remarkable; one example is illustrated here (Fig. 8.1). It is the Representation of a design for a kerchief

Fig. 8.1 Design for a kerchief commemorating Field Marshal Garnet Joseph Wolseley, 1st Viscount Wolseley and the razing of Coomassie in the Gold Coast (now Kumasi, Ghana) in 1887 (Design 282367). © The National Archives.

commemorating Sir Garnet Wolseley and the razing of Coomassie in the Gold Coast (now Kumasi, Ghana) in 1887; the quarter repeat, of a design intended to be printed on cloth, is shown as a print on paper.

The BT Design Register is acknowledged to be an important primary source for understanding trade, commerce and technology (Sykas 2005; Tuckett and Nenadic 2012, 2013), the history of design (Greysmith 1983; Halls 2013; Kramer 2007; Lyons 2005), dress (Levitt 1986) and material culture (Eastop 2015; Riello 2009). It is also recognised to be a source of inspiration for present-day artists and designers (Eastop et al. 2012). Being both a very vulnerable set of records and a highly significant resource for a wide range of potential users, the BT Design Register was identified as a key conservation challenge. External support was therefore secured from The Clothworkers' Foundation to undertake an Options Appraisal in 2010/2011. Some of the recommendations were subsequently implemented as pilot studies in 2012 and 2013. This work was made possible thanks to further external funding from the Arts and Humanities Research Council (AHRC).

The Design Register is made up of two main types of record: Registers, which contain the text record of each design (the registration), and volumes or folders which contain the Representations of the registered designs. Registers record the 'unique' number assigned to each design, the date of registration, the name of the design's proprietor and the proprietor's address. In the earlier series the Representations of the designs are adhered to the pages of large, bound volumes; in the later series they are loose and stored in folders. The Representations take many forms such as drawings, tracings, photographs, samples of cloth or other materials, for example fur, felt, embossed leathers and papers. Complete articles were also submitted as Representations, with notable examples including printed kerchiefs (Riello 2009), gloves (Eastop 2015), straw bonnets and Stevengraphs (Brooks and Eastop 2014). Further information on the Design Register is available from the online catalogue *Discovery* (National Archives 2017g).

As part of the Options Appraisal, the opinions of existing and potential users of the records were sought in order to inform the strategy for preservation and access. Users and potential users confirmed that online delivery of the written records provided in the Registers was a priority. This was duly included as an integral part of the conservation strategy, as online delivery would reduce handling of the volumes. Each registration for the period 1842–1883/4 was transcribed and catalogued. In this context, cataloguing refers to standardising place names and also the addition of the supplementary category 'female proprietor'. The decision was made to highlight female proprietors while transcribing the registers; it is now possible to search under the category 'female proprietor' in addition to the transcribed text of registration. One can thus establish, for example, how many female proprietors registered designs under the 'Lace' category.

The outcome of this transcription project is that more than 700,000 design registrations are now accessible online, in a readily searchable form and available to users free of charge. This huge task was achieved by integrated teamwork. It involved the work of specialist National Archives staff and transcribers employed by a commercial agency (but working on-site at The National Archives and paid via the AHRC grant mentioned above), assisted by volunteer transcribers.

User participation and user-generated content were recognised as important factors in sustaining and informing this work. The Registers contain the majority of the written information, but additional information is provided in text on or alongside some Representations. Examples of this include the details of agents who sought registration on behalf of proprietors, the names of persons or places depicted in some designs (for instance monarchs, buildings and battle scenes) and the numbers allocated to the designs prior to submission to the Design Register (for example studio design numbers). A User Participation Project was initiated to record this additional information, which has been added as metadata to the online records (Fig. 8.2). One example

Fig. 8.2 A volunteer inspecting designs and transcribing information written on or alongside the Representations. © The National Archives.

is the full transcription of the achievements of Queen Victoria's record reign as listed on a printed cotton handkerchief with a design registered in 1897 – the year of her Diamond Jubilee (Design 292206) (The National Archives 2017f).

Another pilot project was undertaken in 2013/14 to explore and exploit the interconnections between museum and archive collections. The aim was to link records in the BT Design Register with collections at York Castle Museum (YCM). Fifteen links were established in this study (supported by the Textile Society [of the UK]). They ranged from printed cotton handkerchiefs, boys' sailor suits and mantlepiece ornaments to holders for balls of wool and Stevengraphs. These links provide precise dating and provenance (for example, the name of the proprietor who registered the design), as well as evidence of the original colour and finish of some products (some of the material in the BT Design Register has been preserved in an unfaded condition). For example, links were established between *Called to the Rescue: Heroism at sea* – a framed Stevengraph preserved at York Castle Museum – and a Representation in the Design Register. The latter retains its vivid colours, having been enclosed in the volume and therefore protected from light exposure, while the version at York Castle Museum provides complementary information in the form of an original label (Brooks and Eastop 2015).

The links made between York Castle Museum and the BT Design Register will be made public via a 'tagging' facility which encourages 'user participation' through the recording of metadata. This facility allows members of the public to add their comments to the online records provided by The National Archives. This facility will be used to link collections at York Castle Museum with those at The National Archives. For example, the draft text of the 100-character tag for the handkerchief mentioned above is: 'Printed handkerchief with same design of Victoria's record reign 1897 at York Castle Museum (THK69)'. This means that people will be able to see designs registered nationally by visiting a regional museum.

Options for the online delivery of the designs themselves (the Representations) were also investigated for both commercial and research purposes; further options were considered. Intuitive Image Browsing (Ward et al. 2008; Eastop 2012) and visual search techniques that imitate the characteristics of human vision were investigated. Measures to encourage use of this design resource (both on-site and online) have been introduced, including 'not-for-profit' reuse of the designs (for example via Creative Commons licensing) and via income-generating services. An online exhibition of 300 ceramic and miscellaneous designs from the Victorian era that were featured in the BT Design Register has already been provided (The National Archives 2017b).

Filming has provided another way of widening public engagement as part of an integrated collection management strategy. Films can draw attention to different aspects of archival practice, as revealed in the work of artist and film-maker Anna Brass. She made three films in 2013 to convey the experience of working with the BT Design Register. In her film *The Volunteer Experience* Brass evokes the rhythm and repetition of page-turning, of unfolding and refolding the Representations of designs in one volume of the BT Design Register (ahrcpress 2013). Another example is the presentation *Material Culture in a Digital World* by Dinah Eastop. This was filmed and included in the outcomes of the Gerald Aylmer Seminar 2013.

Interactive modes of online engagement have been encouraged, such as the posting of selected designs in a form that allows the user to control the lighting. This is achieved via Polynomial Texture Mapping, one application of Reflectance Transformation Imaging (PTM/RTI) (Padfield et al. 2005; Earl et al. 2010; Eastop 2013a; 2013b; 2016; National Archives 2013a; Duffy et al. 2013). Simpler and cheaper alternatives have been investigated at The National Archives, for example 'shape from shading' technology (Gallen et al. 2015).

The application of PTM/RTI at The National Archives complements established measures, such as providing access to the records held there in person and online. It is also just one example of exploiting information and communications technology (ICT) for widening access and user engagement. User consultation, user participation and user-generated content are recognised as important factors in sustaining and informing the work of enhancing access to archival records, and in developing archival resources.

Conclusion

Cross-disciplinary working is fundamental to the operation of The National Archives. The cultural heritage sector and the work of social development have much to learn from one another, as well as from the archive sector. Maintaining long-term public access to government records is the fundamental objective of The National Archives. 'Transparency' in both policies and practices is central to its activities as it

> strives to be an open and transparent organisation ... in addition to responding to Government's requests for particular information to be published, it is our aim to proactively share as much information as possible and make it available on our website. (The National Archives 2017j)

A democratic ethos is fundamental to The National Archives. The practice of government can be held up to scrutiny if primary records are retained and access to them is facilitated, for example by search capacities of ICT and commitments to retaining the ontology of the originating government department and to cataloguing. Specialist archivists and conservators provide advice on the collections and their care. Research undertaken within the conservation team – and more widely – informs historical narratives (for example by understanding developments in the technology of wax seals), handling guidelines (for example by identifying the presence of harmful substances such as arsenic within the records) and, as noted above, the effective use of resources. Conservation work is incremental; it makes step-by-step changes, on a project basis, to enhance both preservation and access. Managers are encouraged not only to deliver more for less, but also to engage more actively with citizens and civil society.

We have argued that The National Archives' ethos of transparency, accessibility and preservation facilitates innovation; this also often crosses traditional disciplinary boundaries. Negotiating every change is undertaken with care, bearing current sensitivities, economics and practicalities in mind. Integration of preservation and access, and an understanding of the social and other benefits of supporting democratic processes through transparency and accessibility to government records, is important for social development, whether at a regional, national or international level. The overarching theme that emerges from this multifaceted and multidisciplinary narrative is that preservation activities add social, economic and environmental value. Demonstration of these social, economic and environmental values can be used as an important tool for advocacy.

References

ahrcpress. 'The Volunteer Experience – Anna Brass'. *YouTube* video, 3:47. Posted 23 April 2013. https://www.youtube.com/watch?v=VpV0fiw8pME.

Bell, Nancy, Strlič, Matija, Thompson, Andrew, Laurenson, Pip, Fouseki, Kalliopi, Dillon, Catherine and McDarby, Frances. 2014. *Mind the Gap: Rigour and relevance in heritage science research*. Kew: The National Archives. See for example p.5. Accessed 27 December 2017. http://www.nationalarchives.gov.uk/about/mind-the-gap.htm.

Brooks, Mary M. and Eastop, Dinah. 2014. '"Linked by Design": Textile collections of York Castle Museum and the Board of Trade Design Register', *TEXT* [Journal of the (UK) Textile Society] 42: 78–80.

Cary, Anthony. 2011. *A Report on Migrated Archives*. London: Foreign and Commonwealth Office, 24 February 2011. https://www.gov.uk/government/uploads/system/uploads/attachment_data/file/32969/migrated-archives.pdf.

Clavir, Miriam. 2002. *Preserving What Is Valued: Museums, conservation, and First Nations*. Vancouver; Toronto: UBC Press.

DemosTV. 2008. 'It's a Material World'. *YouTube* video, 5:30. Posted 27 November 2008. http://uk.youtube.com/watch?v=-c_0eMSBXIk.

Duffy, Sarah M., Bryan, Paul, Earl, Graeme, Beale, Gareth, Pagi, Hembo and Kotouala, Eleni. 2013. *Multi-light Imaging for Heritage Applications*. Swindon: English Heritage.

Earl, Graeme, Martinez, Kirk and Malzbender, Tom. 2010. 'Archaeological Applications of Polynomial Texture Mapping: Analysis, conservation and representation', *Journal of Archaeological Science* 37 (8: August 2010): 2040–50. http://eprints.soton.ac.uk/156253/.

Eastop, Dinah. 2012. 'Presenting Rough and Smooth with Innovative Technology'. In *Taking the Rough with the Smooth: Issues and solutions for decorative surfaces; Postprints of the ICON Textiles Working Group Forum*, edited by Alison Fairhurst, 41–8. London: ICON. CD-ROM.

Eastop, Dinah. 2013a. 'Exploring the BT Design Register: Representing sensory experience online'. *The National Archives* (blog). Published 15 November 2013. http://blog.nationalarchives.gov.uk/blog/exploring-bt-design-register-1839-1991-representing-sensory-experience-online/.

Eastop, Dinah. 2013b. 'Online Exploration of the Rough and the Smooth'. *Supporting Research at the National Archives*. Research e-newsletter (autumn 2013): 2–3. http://www.nationalarchives.gov.uk/documents/research-newsletter-autumn-2013.pdf.

Eastop, Dinah. 2015. 'History by Design: The UK Board of Trade Design Register'. In *Writing Material Culture History*, edited by Anne Gerritsen and Giorgio Riello, 273–9. London: Bloomsbury.

Eastop, Dinah. 2016. 'New Ways of Engaging with Historic Textiles: Interactive images online'. In *Ways of Seeing Early Modern Decorative Textiles*, edited by Catherine Richardson and Tara Hamling, 82–93. *Textile History* 47 (1: special issue).

Eastop, Dinah, Bülow, Anna E. and Brokerhof, Agnes W. 2012. 'Design, Digitisation, Discovery: Enhancing collection quality', *Studies in Conservation* 57 (S1): 96–102.

Eastop, Dinah and Similä, Katriina. 2007. 'Documentation as Process and Outcome'. In *Sharing Conservation Decisions*, edited by Rosalia Varoli-Piazza, 114–17. Rome: ICCROM. http://www.iccrom.org/ifrcdn/pdf/ICCROM_15_SharingConservDecisions_en.pdf.

Elkins, Caroline. 2012. 'The Colonial Papers: FCO transparency is a carefully cultivated myth', *Guardian*, 18 April 2012. http://www.theguardian.com/politics/2012/apr/18/colonial-papers-fco-transparency-myth.

Gallen, Rachel, Eastop, Dinah, Bozia, Eleni and Barmpoutis, Angelos. 2015. 'Digital Imaging: The application of shape-from-shading to lace, seals and metal objects', *Journal of the Institute of Conservation* 38 (1): 41–53.

Greysmith, David. 1983. 'Patterns, Piracy and Protection in the Textile Printing Industry 1787–1850', *Textile History* 14 (2): 165–94.

Halls, Julie. 2013. 'Questions of Attribution: Registered designs at the National Archives', *Journal of Design History* 26: 416–32.

Hong, Sung H., Strlič, Matija, Ridley, Ian, Ntanos, Konstantinos, Bell, Nancy and Cassar, May. 2011. 'Monitoring and Modeling the Storage Environment at the National Archives, UK'. In *ICOM-CC Preprints of the 16th Triennial Conference, Lisbon*, 19–23 September 2011. Paris: ICOM Committee for Conservation.

Hong, Sung H., Strlič, Matija, Ridley, Ian, Ntanos, Konstantinos, Bell, Nancy and Cassar, May. 2012. 'Climate Change Mitigation Strategies for Mechanically Controlled Repositories: The case of The National Archives, Kew', *Atmospheric Environment* 49: 163–70.

Johnson, Jessica S., Heald, Susan, McHugh, Kelly, Brown, Elizabeth and Kaminitz, Marian. 2005. 'Practical Aspects of Consultation with Communities', *Journal of the American Institute for Conservation* 4 (3: Fall–Winter 2005): 203–15.

Jones, Samuel and Holden, John. 2008. *It's a Material World: Caring for the public realm*. London: Demos.

Kramer, Elizabeth. 2007. 'From Luxury to Mania: A case study of Anglo-Japanese textile production at Warner & Ramm, 1870–1890', *Textile History* 38 (2): 151–64.

Levitt, Sarah. 1986. *Victorians Unbuttoned: Registered designs for clothing, their makers & wearers, 1839–1900*. London: George Allen and Unwin.

Lyons, Harry. 2005. *Christopher Dresser: The people's designer 1834–1904*. Woodbridge: Antique Collectors' Club.

Ntanos, Kostas. 2009. *Conservation Research and Development for the National Archives: Strategy and implementation plan 2009–2011*. Kew: The National Archives. http://www.nationalarchives.gov.uk/documents/information-management/conservation-research-strategy-2009-2011.pdf.

Ntanos, Kostas and Bell, Nancy. 2007. 'A Holistic Appraisal of Environmental Conditions in the National Archives, UK'. In *Museum Microclimates*, edited by Tim Padfield and Karen Borchersen, 19–23. Copenhagen: National Museum of Denmark.

Ntanos, Kostas and VanSnick, Sarah. 2010. 'Environmental Assessment without Limits at the National Archives'. Paper presented at the ICOM-CC Graphic Documents Group, Interim Meeting, Copenhagen, 6–8 October 2010. Accessed 27 December 2017. http://www.nationalarchives. gov.uk/documents/information-management/environmental-assessment-without-limits.pdf.

Orne, Jenni. 2012. 'Reaching out – Ugandan Asians 40 Years on'. *The National Archives* (blog). Published 22 October 2012. http://blog.nationalarchives.gov.uk/blog/reaching-out-ugandan-asians-40-years-on.

Padfield, Joseph, Saunders, David and Malzbender, Tom. 2005. 'Polynomial Texture Mapping: A new tool for examining the surface of paintings'. In *Preprints of the 14th Triennial Meeting of ICOM Conservation Committee*, 504–10. London: James & James.

Peterson, Derek R. 2012. *Ethnic Patriotism and the East African Revival: A history of dissent, c.1935–1972*. New York; Cambridge: Cambridge University Press.

Richmond, A. and Bracker, A. *Conservation: Principles, dilemmas and uncomfortable truths*. Oxford: Butterworth-Heinemann, in association with the Victoria and Albert Museum.

Riello, Giorgio. 2009. 'Things that Shape History: Material culture and historical narratives'. In *History and Material Culture: A student's guide to approaching alternative sources*, edited by Karen Harvey, 24–46. Abingdon: Routledge.

Similä, Katriina and Eastop, Dinah. 2016. 'Positioning: Where you stand'. In *Learning Curve: Education, experience and reflection; Postprints of the Forum of the ICON Textile Group*, edited by Alison Fairhurst. London: Birkbeck College. CD-ROM.

Sykas, Philip, A. 2005. *The Secret Life of Textiles: Six pattern book archives in North West England*. Bolton: Bolton Museums, Art Gallery and Aquarium.

The National Archives. 2012. 'Ugandan Asian Events'. http://media.nationalarchives.gov.uk/index.php/category/ugandan-asians-event/.

The National Archives. 2013a. 'First Nations Delegation visits the National Archives'. http://www.nationalarchives.gov.uk/news/880.htm (page discontinued).

The National Archives. 2013b. 'For the Record. For Good: Our Business Plan for 2011–2015'. Accessed March 2013. http://www.nationalarchives.gov.uk/documents/the-national-archives-business-plan-2011-2015.pdf.

The National Archives. 2017a. 'Caribbean through a Lens – Explored!' Accessed 27 December 2017. http://www.nationalarchives.gov.uk/caribbean/.

The National Archives. 2017b. 'Design Registers'. Accessed 27 December 2017. http://www.nationalarchives.gov.uk/designregisters/.

The National Archives. 2017c. 'Energy, Environment and Sustainability'. Accessed 27 December 2017. https://www.nationalarchives.gov.uk/about/energy-use.htm.

The National Archives. 2017d. 'Our Role'. Accessed 27 December 2017. http://www.nationalarchives. gov.uk/about/our-role.htm.

The National Archives. 2017e. 'Outreach'. Accessed 27 December 2017. http://www.nationalarchives. gov.uk/get-involved/outreach.htm.

The National Archives. 2017f. 'Registered design no.292206: Commemorative handkerchief – A souvenir of the record reign of Queen Victoria 1897'. Accessed 27 December 2017. http:// discovery.nationalarchives.gov.uk/details/r/C13375052.

The National Archives. 2017g. 'Registered Designs 1839–1991'. Accessed 27 December 2017. http://www.nationalarchives.gov.uk/records/research-guides/reg-design-trademark.htm.

The National Archives. 2017h. 'Selecting and Transferring Archives'. Accessed 27 December 2017. http://www.nationalarchives.gov.uk/information-management/manage-information/selection-and-transfer/.

The National Archives. 2017i. 'The National Archives'. Accessed 8 November 2017. http://www.nationalarchives.gov.uk/.

The National Archives. 2017j. 'Transparency'. Accessed 27 December 2017. https://www.nationalarchives.gov.uk/about/transparency.htm.

Tuckett, Sally and Nenadic, Stana. 2012. 'Colouring the Nation: A new, in-depth study of the Turkey Red Pattern Books in the National Museums Scotland', *Textile History* 43 (2): 161–82.

Tuckett, Sally and Nenadic, Stana. 2013. *Colouring the Nation: Scotland's nineteenth-century printed cotton textiles*. Edinburgh: National Museums of Scotland.

Ward, Annette A., McKenna, Stephen J., Buruma, Anna, Taylor, Peter and Han, Junwei. 2008. 'Merging Technology and Users: Applying image browsing to the fashion industry for design inspiration'. In *2008 International Workshop on Content Based Multimedia Indexing: Conference proceedings*, 288–95. New York: IEEE Computer Society.

9
Objects and wellbeing: a personal view

Elizabeth Pye

Introduction

In this chapter I explore my pleasure in objects, a feeling strongly influenced by my own background (I come from a family of artists and makers) and my long career in archaeology and conservation. I suggest that objects can be a source of such personal interest and fascination that interacting with them can substantially enhance our psychological wellbeing.

By objects I mean three-dimensional objects, ranging from ceramics, furniture and textiles to tools and machinery. Many of them are designed for physical interaction and all of them may be found in the collections of museums or individuals. The objects may be decorative or mundane; they may have interesting life stories or may conjure up memories; they may be associated with historical events. While memories and stories can be strongly emotive (and, of course, intangible), linked to them is a physical object – and for me the materials and manufacture of objects have a special interest. It is deeply rewarding to explore visible structure and form, tool marks, details of construction or intricacies of decoration. Furthermore, materials may have attractive or informative tactile qualities, particularly evident when objects are being handled.

There is now increasing interest in making this kind of intimate access more widely available to museum visitors. In this chapter I discuss both benefits of handling and the barriers to making it more available.

What is wellbeing?

Wellbeing is agreed to be a difficult concept to define, but it is generally considered to be more than physical health (although this is a very important part). Definitions may include the psychological and social satisfaction derived from a range of factors, among them the enjoyment of creative or cultural activities. This satisfaction contributes to the psychological resources, resilience and vitality needed to face life's challenges, which in turn generate a sense of wellbeing (Galloway and Bell 2006; Michaelson et al. 2009; Dodge et al. 2012; La Placa et al. 2013). Budd (1996, 7) states that 'the experience of a work of art can involve the invigoration of one's consciousness', while Alain de Botton describes visual art as:

> a vehicle through which we can do such things as recover hope, dignify suffering, develop empathy, laugh, wonder, nurture a sense of communion with others and regain a sense of justice and political idealism. (2014, 3)

These views express the kind of stimulation that might be expected to contribute to psychological wellbeing.

Both the visual arts and music can be satisfying intellectually and emotionally. Music has long been considered potentially therapeutic; I have even heard it said that a sick person can be temporarily 'cured' while totally absorbed in listening to music. There is now widespread evidence that visually attractive or relaxing surroundings alleviate stress and shorten recovery time for patients in hospitals – hence the use of bright colours, paintings and sculpture in hospitals. Many examples exist of participatory projects which involve people in the therapy of making their own art (Baron 1996; Staricoff 2004; Clift et al. 2009; Lankston et al. 2010; Thomson et al. 2011; Cameron et al. 2013; Paintings in Hospitals n.d.).

Can museum objects be as satisfying? The idea that involvement with heritage and museums can contribute to happiness has been explored and promoted recently by bodies such as Historic England (2014) and the Heritage Lottery Fund (Ellis 2015). Many museums run participatory projects focused on objects in their collections. Their broad aim is to improve the participants' wellbeing through creativity, social interaction or the generation of new knowledge or skills (for example Roberts et al. 2011; Arts 4 Dementia 2013).

A very interesting research project that involves bringing museum objects into hospitals has shown that handling and discussion of these artefacts can improve patients' experience and relieve anxiety. In so doing, they contribute to individual wellbeing (Chatterjee et al. 2009; Ander et al. 2013; Camic and Chatterjee 2013; Morse et al. 2015, Chatterjee 2016; UCL n.d.a). This has led to the development of the *UCL Museum Wellbeing Measures Toolkit*, currently being tried out across the UK. The toolkit seeks to assess the extent to which involvement in museum activities contributes to participants' psychological wellbeing, and so to inform the design of these activities (Thomson and Chatterjee 2014).

However, in these projects the experience of the object is often mediated at least partly through another person. This facilitator may be a nurse, teacher or outreach specialist. What I am concerned with in this chapter is the individual personal satisfaction to be obtained when exploring an object – a one-to-one relationship between person and object. This type of direct encounter can generate highly absorbing interest, to a level so engrossing that the stresses and strains of life are forgotten – truly a mentally refreshing experience.

What makes objects so fascinating: my personal experience

In what ways are objects so pleasurable, even exciting? Firstly, objects are complex, challenging and multi-dimensional (Kingery 1996; Candlin and Guins 2009; Dudley 2009); many conjure up stories ranging from personal childhood memories to associations with remarkable people or events. They may also impress us by their age, ingenuity or beauty. In this sense objects can be said to possess powerful meanings (Pearce 1994; Peers 1999; Jones 2006; Turkle 2009). These meanings are affected by our own experiences and knowledge, and consequently can be very varied. Such meanings may be deepened and extended by the interpretation offered in a museum, for example, or through our own further investigation. What follows here is a discussion of the engaging and emotive qualities of objects illustrated through my personal experience.

The rich lives of objects

Objects are made, used, admired, damaged, repaired, discarded, discovered, studied, elucidated and sometimes conserved. This richness of circumstance is often described in terms of the object's life story – an individual 'biography' which can itself be a source of fascination (Kopytoff 1986; Gosden and Marshall 1999; Eastop 2000; Alberti 2005; Joy 2009).

Outside the realms of museums and conservation, I have enjoyed two relatively recent publications which epitomise the life story of objects. The first is *The Glass Room*, a novel of 2009 by Simon Mawer, set against the chequered career of a house loosely based on the Tugendhat House designed by Mies van der Rohe at Brno in the Czech Republic. The second is *The Hare with Amber Eyes*, Edmund de Waal's account of the changing fate of his family's art collections, particularly a collection of Japanese netsuke (de Waal 2011). The ebb and flow in the fortunes of the house and the Japanese carvings powerfully illuminate and reflect the turmoil in Europe during the last century.

The contrasting stories of two South African pennies that I own have a particular enchantment (Fig. 9.1). Both coins are dated to 1898 and were probably brought back to the UK by returning soldiers as souvenirs from the South African War of 1899–1902 (the so-called 'Boer War'), but their lives then diverged. One penny was incorporated into the lid of a small silver box (hallmarked London, 1902) and was lovingly cared for and regularly polished. The other was lost or discarded in rural Norfolk where it was unearthed recently, green and corroded – a serendipitous discovery while digging in our garden. Born in the same mint, and apparently valued enough to bring back to England, each then followed an intriguingly different life trajectory. Through their lives the coins changed in perceived value. They started with the same legal and

Fig. 9.1 Two South African pennies dated 1898, showing the effects of very different lives. © Stuart Laidlaw 2011.

monetary value. One could then be said to have become a focus of curiosity, achieving aesthetic historic value; the other lost all value until rediscovered and returned to life (de la Torre 2002; Clifford 2009).

Evocative objects

Some objects are extraordinarily evocative of an historic person or event. I was startled by an encounter with the severely plain greatcoat and black felt hat of Napoleon Bonaparte, which typified the French emperor's often recorded (and still well-known) battlefield image. Displayed among other, far more elaborate military uniforms in the Hôtel des Invalides in Paris, the coat and hat were immediately arresting – I felt as if I had suddenly come face to face with the man himself (Musée de l'Armée Invalides n.d.). This association with Napoleon seemingly remains so powerful that another of his hats sold in 2014 for £1.5 million (BBC 2014).

Even apparently ordinary objects can be endowed with power. In 2011/2012 an intriguing exhibition entitled *Charmed Life: The solace of objects* was held at the Wellcome Collection; it focused on charms and amulets collected in London at the beginning of the twentieth century. These included a range of curiously modified or embellished everyday objects: horseshoes, acorns, fossils, blue beads, shoes. Each item has been invested with the hope or belief that it could somehow mediate on behalf of its owner (Wellcome Collection 2011/2012). It was thought that some objects might ward off the evil eye; others were believed to prevent nightmares or to protect against lightning strikes. Individually and collectively, they told vivid stories of the many challenges faced by the inhabitants of London's poorer areas, and spoke poignantly of the fears and superstitions that beset their owners.

It is easy to forget the astonishing advances in scientific knowledge that have occurred in the last 300 years. The instruments used to extend our knowledge provide a narrative of extraordinary scientific achievements and great leaps in understanding of our world (and now even of parts of space too). The Science Museum in London holds an early compound microscope of the type used by Robert Hooke, dating from the late seventeenth century (Science Museum n.d.). This simple instrument is, for me, a potent example of technological achievement. Such an instrument enabled Hooke to see minute structural features – such as cells in wood – for the first time, and to produce his famous detailed drawing of a human flea (Jardine 2003). Today we take computers and mobile phones for granted, but they enable us to 'think' and communicate in a way not imagined even in my youth: 'My laptop computer is irreplaceable … It's practically a brain prosthesis' (Newitz 2009, 88). These instruments, of course, have their own rapidly accelerating narrative; early models (dating from only a few years ago and now collected by museums) appear amazingly large, clumsy and limited in performance.

Objects may also be potent symbols of political developments today, such as the painted ceramics of Ai Weiwei, the Chinese artist and activist. By dipping ancient pots in modern, industrial and brightly coloured paint, or by painting the familiar Coca-Cola logo on them, he has made a deliberate and forceful statement about globalisation and the destruction of heritage (Artlyst 2011). Any shock I may feel, as an archaeologist and conservator, at this material desecration is overtaken by finding these objects strikingly beautiful. To me this only reinforces their message and causes me to 'regain a sense of ... political idealism' (de Botton 2014).

Stories written in the materials of objects

Encounters with objects can conjure up a range of ideas and emotions. However, when we are looking at objects what we actually *see* is the solid substance and physical form – the product of manufacture. Just as the social/conceptual significance of objects brings us in touch with people's ideas and motives, so does the material evidence of the maker's selection and modification of materials in the creation of an object. This physical aspect of objects is of particular concern to conservators and materials scientists; understanding the material is essential before undertaking conservation processes or investigating early technologies (Caple 2000; Pye 2000). To me, this evidence of making is the most fascinating and absorbing characteristic of objects. Only if we learn to 'read' objects we can begin to understand the nature of material modification and makers' choices. These stories – of ingenuity and empirical knowledge used in choosing and working raw materials, and in shaping, constructing and decorating them – are inspiring in their own right. However, in the study of objects these tangible material aspects seem to be underappreciated. Highlighting this, Ingold says of many discussions about materiality:

> Their engagements are not with the tangible stuff of craftsmen and manufacturers, but with the abstract ruminations of philosophers and theorists. (Ingold 2007, 2)

The material and form of objects can be a rich source of information about both making and makers. Tool marks on wood or stone, joints formed by solder or rivets between metal components, bubbles and flow-lines in glass, dribbles of glaze on ceramics and repairs on textiles all provide insight into how these materials were shaped and modified. This material evidence brings the process of making vividly to life. Spalding and Chapman point out that although the colour and pattern of the Lindisfarne Gospels can be viewed digitally:

> no reproduction allows you to appreciate the uneven thickness of paint in these Gospels, as the artist starts with his brush full and then tails off when his brush is empty. [...] You have the sensation you are looking over the monk's shoulder watching him paint. (Spalding 2002, 66)

For me the use and exploitation of wood holds a particular fascination. This may be because I grew up among the tools and wood shavings of my father's workshop, so that the tools and the marks they leave are familiar and the maker's actions seem almost visible. Or perhaps it is because I feel that wood is often given too little consideration, dismissed as a mundane material. In our early sixteenth-century house there is a stunning decorated main beam, carved with stylised vine trail (Fig. 9.2). Every time I sit beneath it and look up, I marvel at the beam's liveliness and speculate about its maker. This kind of workmanship is a direct encounter between the hand, the tool and the material being transformed; the traces of the

Fig. 9.2 Carved wooden beam, sixteenth century. © Nick Balaam 2011.

process are intimate, not consciously intended for future display. Yet to me the tool marks and inconsistencies of the carving are the visible evidence of a live performance – I only wish that I could see the carver at work!

We often talk about the artist's hand, but to me the hand of the artisan is just as interesting. It is this kind of unregulated work that gives objects their variety and individuality, and makes them pleasurable to view. The design theorist David Pye (my late father) defined such activity as the 'workmanship of risk':

> …in which the quality of the result is not predetermined, but depends on the judgement, dexterity and care which the maker exercises as he works. (D. Pye 1995, 20)

Study of traditional objects demonstrates an impressive and sophisticated empirical knowledge of the distinctive working and durability qualities of different species of wood. Although in today's world of plastics this may not be fully appreciated, wood is in fact a remarkably versatile material (Hoadley 2000). Specific woods have been selected for specific purposes for centuries. Elm (*Ulmus spp.*), for example, has a particularly wavy grain and tends not to split easily, so is traditionally used for situations in which splitting of the wood could be damaging or disastrous – wheel hubs, pulley blocks or chair seats.

The traditional Windsor chair tells an engaging story of understanding material properties and of skill in making (Mursell 2009). Its seat is normally elm, because the insertion of the closely-spaced back struts might risk splitting the seat. Yet the chair also shows understanding of the ability to bend a different type of wood – often yew or ash – by steaming, allowing the maker to create the typical curved back and arms. The anonymous artisans who produced these chairs were immensely adept; they worked by hand, used simple tools and did much of the work by eye. The story of the chairs continues into the twentieth century: when Lucian Ercolani founded his firm Ercol in High Wycombe in 1920, he adopted and adapted the Windsor chair, using the elm seat and steamed curved back (Jackson 2013) (Figs 9.3a and 9.3b). Early Ercol furniture is now much appreciated and fashionable (and expensive).

Memories of making and use contained within the material of objects

Also fascinating are the visible memories of earlier processes sometimes contained ('written') into the physical fabric of objects. In some

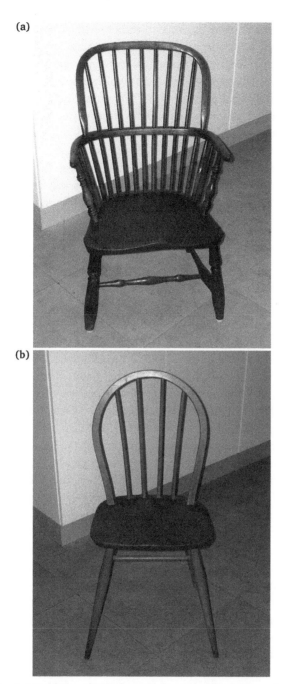

Fig. 9.3 (a) Traditional Windsor chair, probably eighteenth century; (b) Ercol chair made by using similar materials and techniques, twentieth century. Photographs © Nick Balaam 2011.

objects structural features essential to earlier technologies are preserved in the shape of non-functional decoration (a phenomenon known as skeuomorphism). A striking example occurs in pottery from the sixth millennium BC site of Arpachiyah (Iraq) which precisely imitates coiled basketwork (Mallowan and Rose 1935; Wengrow 2001). I can imagine a scene of clay-lined baskets falling into the fire, followed by the realisation that heating clay produces a durable ceramic – and perhaps a process of disguising this strange 'new' material to enable it to gain acceptance. Some finished objects capture a visible memory of a different physical state of the material during the making process, particularly if heat is involved in manufacture. A ceramic object, although brittle when finished, may show finger marks and smears made by the potter while the clay was still moist and mobile before being fired. A cold, hard, iron bar may show distinct hammer marks and ornamental twists worked into the material when it was red hot, soft and malleable.

Stories of use are captured in the form of marks of wear or damage 'written' into the surface of objects. The wear on coins can be particularly evocative, and the extent of this (indicated by loss of metal, and consequently of surface detail) is often used by archaeologists to indicate the length of time during which an individual coin was in circulation. More vividly it evokes the number of hands through which the coins passed, and the number of purses or pockets they shared with other coins. I own some pennies minted in the early years of Queen Victoria's reign (she acceded to the throne in 1837) and known as 'bun pennies' after the young queen's hairstyle (Fig. 9.4). These remained in circulation until the introduction of decimal coinage in 1971. Until then coins of at least five nineteenth- and twentieth-century monarchs were in common circulation – a visible history lesson to children of my generation. Some of my pennies are almost completely smooth, showing just a ghostly outline of Queen Victoria's young head. Such wear represents their heavy use for over a hundred years: what times these coins have lived through and how many hands, of both rich and poor, must have touched them!

Another memory of use (and economy) is captured in the form of repair. Domestic ceramics (teacups, saucers, plates) were often mended using metal staples or rivets. During my childhood I can remember itinerant china menders going from door to door offering to mend cracked or broken crockery. This technique has largely or totally disappeared, but I still treasure some objects mended in this way. When I started my career as a conservator it was customary to remove the staples and use a modern adhesive to form a less visible repair.

Fig. 9.4 Victorian pennies showing the effects of handling and use for over a century. © Stuart Laidlaw 2011.

Now, however, these early repairs are acknowledged as an important part of the object's history. For me they preserve the story of the china menders, arriving by bicycle and using modest equipment to effect remarkably efficient repairs.

Sometimes the story is *literally* written into the object. I own a Greek/Latin lexicon (dictionary) dating from 1738. It was clearly used by schoolboys through the nineteenth century; they wrote in black ink the kinds of things that schoolboys have always written on their books and drew caricatures, presumably of their schoolmasters (Figs 9.5a and 9.5b). This lexicon is one of my favourite possessions, brought to life through these delightful doodles which tell the vivid (and familiar) story of bored but spirited pupils through the ages.

The value of handling objects

I have attempted to explain the range and multifaceted character of objects from which I derive deep psychological satisfaction. Much of this satisfaction is gained through direct physical contact with objects.

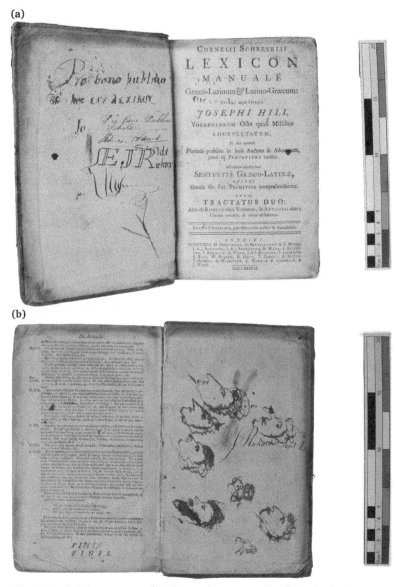

Fig. 9.5 (a) Front page of eighteenth-century Greek/Latin lexicon, with nineteenth-century schoolboy doodles; (b) Back page of lexicon. © Stuart Laidlaw 2011.

This may be through touch – running my fingers over the surface of a sculpture or using fingertips to trace the contours of a carving. It may be through handling – not just touching but using my whole hand (or both hands) to lift and move an object (Wing et al. 2008). I turn an object gently in my hands to catch the light or to explore and discover features not easily seen (grooves inside a pot, a pontil mark on the base of a glass bowl, the lining inside a textile bag) or cautiously to manipulate moving parts. More than this, however, the object becomes a touchstone: I experience its character for myself. I draw meaning from it that may be entirely individual – shaped by my own interests, knowledge and memories – and this enhances my sense of wellbeing.

Touch and handling supplement vision, allowing me to verify and expand on what I see. Through contact I can appreciate weight, temperature or surface texture, and so gain insight into how an object such as a tool may have worked in use. In addition there is the pure pleasure of exploring a beautifully shaped object, an object that is extremely old or one much used – the object comes alive. A thread running through much of de Waal's book is the almost sensuous experience of handling objects. As he says:

> Reaching in and then picking up is a moment of seduction, an encounter between a hand and an object which is electric. (de Waal 2011, 66)

For me, the process of taking my Victorian coins out of their purse, feeling their worn surfaces and laying them out is a tactile reminder of how many times they were counted out in the past, of how many times they changed hands. The coins' size and weight remind me of the much higher relative value they had compared to modern decimal pence.

Conservators, curators and materials scientists handle museum objects routinely (Kingery and Vandiver 1986; Oddy 1996; Caple 2006; McDonald 2008; Pye 2008b). The fascination of working closely with objects is what has brought me and many of us into these professions (and kept us there). We have the freedom to explore objects, to research their lives and to marvel at their intricacies. When we study objects in detail under a microscope, a whole new and intriguing world is opened up. In examining a fragment from the Staffordshire Hoard, a recently excavated cache of Anglo Saxon goldwork, for example, we discover the astonishingly fine pattern impressed on the gold foil set behind the garnets as well as the tiny inconsistencies in the making. The latter presumably resulted from the challenges of working on a very small scale without the types of magnification and lighting now available (Staffordshire Hoard n.d.). Here is certainly a source of wonder.

Experiencing objects in museums

My reactions are entirely personal, shaped by my own background experiences and interests and by my 'reading' of the object's life. Other people may well react in very different ways to the same objects – we each assign our own meanings (or values) to artefacts. An object said to have had a rich life may embody many values, sometimes shifting ones influenced both by its history and by the reactions of people today.

The information that we share with visitors through museum interpretation is a result of academic research and consultation used to investigate these values and establish the significance of an object. This in turn guides many museum decisions about its use and care. However, museum visitors' reactions are personal. They can be, and often are, more varied, idiosyncratic and possibly unexpected than the values identified during academic curatorial research and formalised audience consultation. They are also more difficult to define and pin down (Hein 1998; Falk and Dierking 2000; Hooper-Greenhill and Moussouri 2001; Rowe 2002).

In museums, objects are generally placed out of easy reach or enclosed in protective display cases. Here they seem frozen into immobility, comatose, cut off from visitors. They are selected, positioned and labelled to convey a particular feature of their perceived significance, restricting a visitor's opportunity to make his or her own meaning.

Recognising the problem of distance, the British sculptor Antony Gormley achieved a closer encounter with classical statuary in the State Hermitage Museum in Saint Petersburg. He arranged for the floor levels to be raised to cover the plinths, enabling visitors to encounter the figures almost face to face, person to person:

> We brought the statues down to a more human level ... they were no longer remote ... You can wander through them. (Glover 2011, 5)

This may not have been the way in which the original sculptors intended these works to be seen. However, it provided a new perspective that must have challenged visitors to react in a new – perhaps surprising – way to these classical sculptures.

Through the experimental 'atmospheres project', handling objects was introduced at some National Trust properties. Here visitors were enabled to discover 'the feel' of the living house:

In ... selected rooms, visitors are able to pick things up, examine them, sit on furniture and enjoy sounds and smells. (Cowell 2009)

At Wightwick Manor the billiard room was set as for life in 1900. Visitors could play billiards or read the newspapers and magazines of the day. At Croft Castle the Saloon conjured up an evening party in 1777, with visitors sitting by the fire or playing cards. This kind of interaction brings a historic house to life. It prompts us to imagine what it was like to live there – in a way that simply walking through a room along a carefully prescribed route cannot do.

Increasingly museums holding ethnographic collections – such as the National Museum of the American Indian in Washington, DC – encourage representatives of descendant communities to handle 'their' objects, to care for them in the traditional ways, to reminisce and to demonstrate their use. This can be deeply satisfying and empowering to the visitors. At the same time the Museum gains insight into the objects' meanings and cultural significance (Clavir 2002; Peers and Brown 2003; Feinup-Riordan 2003). Many museums also run special sessions as part of their access and outreach programmes, for example for blind or partially-sighted people or for children, enabling them to handle objects.

Pressure to provide wider access to museums has now prompted re-evaluation of both attitudes to, and benefits of, touching and handling of heritage objects. At the same time a large and fast-developing body of research into virtual handling (haptics) is being conducted. Some of this is being applied to the museum context to enable visitors to handle digital (virtual) objects (Pye 2008a; Chatterjee 2008; Sullivan 2009; see also, for example, Styliani et al. 2009, Carrozzino and Bergamasco 2010). However, the type of extensive, intimate and exciting tactile exploration of the *real thing* (in all its multidimensionality) exercised by curators and conservators is a privilege seldom available to general visitors:

Many contemporary museums are challenging the traditional 'hands off' ethos of the museum with innovative, interactive exhibitions [...] Yet such exhibitions are still exceptions to the rule of sensory restraint which is generally expected to govern the behaviour of museum visitors. Artefacts for the most part are only to be seen, not felt, smelt, sounded and certainly not tasted. (Classen 2007, 896)

Barriers to experiencing objects through touch and handling

Providing access through handling poses a dilemma to conservators and curators alike. A research project undertaken in 2009–10 entitled 'Conservation's Catch 22' characterised the dilemma as follows:

> Access to heritage objects brings social benefit
> Greater access brings greater social benefit
> Greater access brings greater damage
> Greater damage brings reduced social benefit
> (UCL Institute of Archaeology 2009)

During workshops and through using a blog we discovered that many, or indeed most, of the participants were in favour of making objects far more accessible, in particular making them available to touch. With many objects in store (and many of them duplicates), we could surely afford to liberate some more for handling, especially when storage of increasing numbers of objects raises logistical and cost issues (Merriman and Swain 1999; Keene 2005)? Even apparently mundane objects can be a source of enjoyment or wonder (Spalding 2002); liberating them in this way would bring them back to life.

So what stands in the way of providing this type of access more widely? Do we guard our own privilege and pleasure too jealously? Does the nineteenth-century anxiety that public visitors could be rowdy and unclean linger on – so objects still need the protection of glass cases (Candlin 2008)? Despite renewed interest in all the senses (for example Howes 2005; Classen 2005) and research into the emotional effects of touch (Critchley 2008; McGlone 2008; Spence and Gallace 2008), is the reluctance to 'get in touch' with materials compounded by the lingering view that touch is a lower sense, less important (and less inspiring) than lofty visual contemplation?

Of course, a fear of damage to objects is unsurprising and justified. As a result conservators' normal attitude to handling by others has been cautious or even negative. There is also the issue of possible theft; handling sessions need to be carefully supervised and many museums simply lack the staff to do this. However, it is interesting to note that the British Museum introduced handling desks in several of its main galleries, for example the Enlightenment Gallery and the Money Gallery, more than ten years ago. Objects relevant to the gallery are specially selected and the desks successfully operated by well-informed volunteers.

It is perhaps also worth returning to Ingold's (2007) contention that many of us no longer engage with the 'tangible stuff' of materials, but focus rather on the intangible concepts generated by objects. Perhaps there is a lingering feeling that 'brute' materials, and the base processes of making, are less important than elevated 'artistic expression'. Over the last few years, however, there seems to have been renewed interest in materials and making. An example of this is UCL's Institute of Making which seeks to be 'a cross-disciplinary research club for those interested in the made world' (UCL n.d.b). Although based in the UCL Engineering department, the Institute assumes that the properties of materials and the processes of making are exciting and relevant to many disciplines and individuals.

An important reason for our caution about handling must be that we do not know enough about the effects of handling heritage objects – artefacts no longer in regular physical use, made of materials that may be in the process of gradual change (for instance the corrosion of metals, embrittlement of plant fibres, and so on). As yet we know little about what kinds of museum objects, in what kinds of condition, are affected by what kinds of touch or by what frequency of contact. The unavoidable need to accept exposure of museum objects to light, pollution and to temperatures comfortable for humans has generated huge amounts of research, making it possible to assess the risks involved with reasonable confidence (Ashley-Smith 1999). There is certainly scope for similarly targeted research into the effects of touch and handling on heritage materials.

In the engineering field a huge and expanding body of research exists into methods for inspecting surfaces at a microscopic level. Some of these techniques are now being explored for investigation of heritage objects such as paintings (Costa 2012; Jiang 2012; Manfredi et al. 2014). We need to harness some of this research to evaluate the effects of handling. Laser scanning, 3D imaging and microscopic techniques are already used to record shape and surface topography of heritage objects (for example Hess and Robson 2010; Simon et al. 2011; Stanco et al. 2011). Some of these techniques could be applied to detecting and recording minute surface changes, indicating early effects of wear or corrosion not yet possible to detect by the naked eye. Research would need to explore the physical and cumulative effects caused by contact and friction during touch and handling, as well as any chemical effects caused by substances on hands or on gloves. With this knowledge, we could work with and manage the risks of handling, enabling curators and conservators to make a more informed selection of objects to be made available for handling. Selection could be made in much the same way as objects are selected for display or for loan.

It would thus require an understanding of the material, an estimation of the object's likely ability to withstand a particular type and length of exposure to handling and an agreement on how much change would be acceptable. Just as objects are 'retired' from display or from being sent on loan, so they would be used for handling for only a limited time.

Conclusions

For many of us, objects of all kinds stimulate curiosity, interest and enjoyment; access to objects can be exciting and absorbing, and thus can enhance our psychological wellbeing. Our reactions are personal and varied, but it is the material object and its physical features that conjure curiosity and wonder, memories and ideas. The greatest stimulus is gained from the intimate exploration afforded by touch and handling – objects seem to come alive in our hands and reveal their character. However, this is still a privilege available to relatively few. Visitors are expected to look but not to touch; curators and conservators fear damage despite knowing relatively little about the effects of touch on objects. Yet we have access now to highly sensitive instruments capable of measuring the slightest surface change and monitoring the gradual (or rapid) development of surface damage, so there is scope for fruitful research on this topic.

Quite rightly, conservators aim to preserve objects for future generations to enjoy. However, this resolve should not be at the cost of limiting pleasure to people now. It is striking that as long ago as the mid-nineteenth century, when concern was expressed about the safety of paintings in the National Gallery, housed in polluted central London, a High Court judge argued that the enjoyment of visitors was actually more important than the long-term survival of a painting (Conn 2010, 10).

Archaeologists often refer to heritage as a finite resource. This is, of course, true of objects and structures made in the past – the same are not being created now. However, on a rather different level, heritage is being constantly added to – through new discoveries, through replication and through the distancing of time (Holtorf 2001). Even the stuff of my childhood is unfamiliar and fascinating to younger generations – and has become highly evocative for me (the Bakelite telephones I grew up with, the washing machine my mother used and the clothes we all wore 50 years ago are now featured in museum collections). The acknowledged enjoyment of objects, and this continual renewal of our heritage resource, should encourage us to evaluate the risks of physical access and liberate more objects for exploration through touch and handling.

Acknowledgements

In affectionate thanks to Jonathan Ashley-Smith, Fran Balaam, Nick Balaam, Hazel Gardiner, Stuart Laidlaw, Irit Narkiss, Isolde Olcayto, Renata Peters and Dean Sully – all of whom have in some way inspired or supported the creation of this chapter.

References

Alberti, Samuel, J.M.M. 2005. 'Objects and the Museum', *Isis* 96 (4: December): 559–71.

Ander, Erica, Thomson, Linda, Noble, Guy, Lanceley, Anne, Menon, Usha and Chatterjee, Helen. 2013. 'Heritage, Health and Well-being: Assessing the impact of a heritage focused intervention on health and well-being', *International Journal of Heritage Studies* 19 (3: March): 229–42.

Artlyst. 2011. 'Ai Weiwei Takes On Coca Cola In New London Exhibition'. *ArtLyst*. Published 18 September 2011. Accessed 2 January 2018. http://www.artlyst.com/articles/ai-weiwei-takes-on-coca-cola-in-new-london-exhibition.

Arts 4 Dementia. 2013. *Reawakening the Mind: Evaluation of Arts 4 Dementia's London Arts Challenge in 2012: Arts interventions to re-energise and inspire people in the early stages of dementia and their carers*. London: Arts 4 Dementia. Accessed 29 July 2019. https://arts4dementia.org.uk/a4d-reports/a4d-report-reawakening-the-mind/.

Ashley-Smith, Jonathan. 1999. *Risk Assessment for Object Conservation*. Oxford: Butterworth-Heinemann.

Baron, Jeremy H. 1996. 'Art in hospitals', *Journal of the Royal Society of Medicine* 89 (9: September): 482–3.

BBC. 2014. 'South Korean Buys Napoleon's Hat for 1.9m Euros'. News item, 16 November 2014. Accessed 2 January 2018. http://www.bbc.co.uk/news/world-europe-30074931.

Budd, Malcolm. 1996. *Values of Art: Pictures, poetry and music*. London: Penguin Books.

Cameron, Marsaili, Crane, Nikki, Ings, Richard and Taylor, Karen. 2013. 'Promoting Well-being through Creativity: How arts and public health can learn from each other', *Perspectives in Public Health* 133 (1: January): 52–9.

Camic, Paul M. and Chatterjee, Helen J. 2013. 'Museums and Art Galleries as Partners for Public Health Interventions', *Perspectives in Public Health* 133 (1: January): 66–71.

Candlin, Fiona. 2008. 'Don't Touch! Hands Off! Art, Blindness, and the Conservation of Expertise'. In *The Power of Touch: Handling objects in museum and heritage contexts,* edited by Elizabeth Pye, 89–106. Walnut Creek, CA: Left Coast Press.

Candlin, Fiona and Guins, Raiford, eds. 2009. *The Object Reader*. London; New York: Routledge.

Caple, Chris. 2000. *Conservation Skills: Judgement, method and decision making*. London; New York: Routledge.

Caple, Chris. 2006. *Objects: Reluctant witnesses to the past*. London; New York: Routledge.

Carrozzino, Marcello and Bergamasco, Massimo. 2010. 'Beyond Virtual Museums: Experiencing immersive virtual reality in real museums', *Journal of Cultural Heritage* 11 (4: October–December): 452–8.

Chatterjee, Helen, ed. 2008. *Touch in Museums: Policy and practice in object handling*. Oxford: Berg.

Chatterjee, Helen. 2016. 'Museums and Art Galleries as Settings for Public Health Interventions'. In *Oxford Textbook of Creative Arts, Health, and Wellbeing: International perspectives on practice, policy, and research*, edited by Stephen Clift and Paul M. Camic, 281–9. Oxford: Oxford University Press.

Chatterjee, Helen, Vreeland, Sonjel and Noble, Guy. 2009. 'Museopathy: Exploring the healing potential of handling museum objects', *Museum and Society* 7 (3: November): 164–77. Accessed 29 July 2019. https://journals.le.ac.uk/ojs1/index.php/mas/article/view/145.

Classen, Constance, ed. 2005. *The Book of Touch*. Oxford: Berg.

Classen, Constance. 2007. 'Museum Manners: The sensory life of the early museum', *Journal of Social History* 40 (4): 895–914.

Clavir, Miriam. 2002. *Preserving What is Valued: Museums, conservation and First Nations*. Vancouver; Toronto: UBC Press.

Clifford, Helen. 2009. 'The Problem of Patina: Thoughts on changing attitudes to old and new things'. In *Conservation: Principles, dilemmas and uncomfortable truths*, edited by A. Richmond and A. Bracker, 125–8. Oxford: Butterworth-Heinemann, in association with the Victoria and Albert Museum.

Clift, Stephen, Camic, Paul M., Chapman, Brian, Clayton, Gavin, Daykin, Norma, Eades, Guy, Parkinson, Clive, Secker, Jenny, Stickley, Theo and White, Mike. 2009. 'The State of Arts and Health in England', *Arts & Health: An international journal for research, policy and practice* 1 (1): 6–35.

Conn, Steven. 2010. *Do Museums Still need Objects?* Philadelphia: University of Pennsylvania Press.

Costa, Manuel F.M. 2012. 'Optical Triangulation-Based Microtopographic Inspection of Surfaces', *Sensors* 12: 4399–420.

Cowell, Ben. 2009. 'Creating the Right Atmosphere: For people and for collections', UCL Institute of Archaeology. Last modified 11 November 2009. Accessed 2 January 2018. http://www.ucl.ac.uk/conservation-c-22/conference/ben_cowell.

Critchley, Hugo. 2008. 'Emotional Touch: A neuroscientific overview'. In *Touch in Museums: Policy and practice in object handling*, edited by Helen Chatterjee, 61–74. Oxford: Berg.

de Botton, Alain. 2014. 'Alain de Botton's Guide to Art as Therapy', *Guardian*, 2 January 2014. Accessed 2 January 2018. http://www.theguardian.com/artanddesign/2014/jan/02/alain-de-botton-guide-art-therapy.

de la Torre, Marta, ed. 2002. *Assessing the Values of Cultural Heritage: Research report*. Los Angeles, CA: Getty Conservation Institute. Accessed 29 July 2019. https://www.getty.edu/conservation/publications_resources/pdf_publications/values_cultural_heritage.html.

de Waal, Edmund. 2011. *The Hare with Amber Eyes: A hidden inheritance*. London: Vintage Books.

Dodge, Rachel, Daly, Annette P., Huyton, Jan and Sanders, Lalage D. 2012. 'The Challenge of Defining Wellbeing', *International Journal of Wellbeing* 2 (3): 222–35.

Dudley, Sarah, ed. 2009. *Museum Materialities: Objects, engagements, interpretations*. London; New York: Routledge.

Eastop, Dinah. 2000. 'Textiles as Multiple and Competing Histories'. In *Textiles Revealed: Object lessons in historic textile and costume research*, edited by Mary M. Brooks, 17–28. London: Archetype.

Ellis, Liz. 2015. 'Heritage and Positive Mental Health', *Heritage Lottery Fund* (blog). Published 4 April 2015. Accessed 29 July 2019. https://www.heritagefund.org.uk/blogs/how-heritage-good-your-mental-health.

Falk, John H. and Dierking, Lynn D. 2000. *Learning from Museums: Visitor experiences and the making of meaning*. Walnut Creek, CA: AltaMira Press.

Feinup-Riordan, Ann. 2003. 'Yup'ik Elders in Museums: "Fieldwork turned on its head"'. In *Museums and Source Communities: A Routledge reader*, edited by Alison K. Brown and Laura Peers, 28–41. London; New York: Routledge.

Galloway, Susan and Bell, David. 2006. *Quality of Life and Well-being: Measuring the benefits of culture and sport: Literature review*. Edinburgh: Scottish Government. Accessed 2 January 2018. http://www.scotland.gov.uk/Publications/2006/01/13110743/0.

Glover, Michael. 2011. 'Antony Gormley – Of Gods and Men in St Petersburg', *Independent*, 23 September 2011. Accessed 2 January 2018. http://www.independent.co.uk/arts-entertainment/art/features/antony-gormley--of-gods-and-men-in-st-petersburg-2359163.html.

Gosden, Chris and Marshall, Yvonne. 1999. 'The Cultural Biography of Objects', *World Archaeology* 31 (2: October): 169–78.

Hein, George E. 1998. *Learning in the Museum*. London; New York: Routledge.

Hess, Mona and Robson, Stuart. 2010. '3D Colour Imaging for Cultural Heritage Artefacts'. In *International Archives of Photogrammetry, Remote Sensing and Spatial Information Sciences*, Vol. XXXVIII (Part 5): 8–292. Newcastle upon Tyne: Commission V Symposium.

Historic England. 2014. *Heritage Makes You Happy*. Published 12 November 2014. Accessed 2 January 2018. https://historicengland.org.uk/whats-new/news/heritage-makes-you-happy.

Hoadley, R. Bruce. 2000. *Understanding Wood: A craftsman's guide to wood technology*. Newtown: Taunton Press.

Holtorf, Cornelius J. 2001. 'Is the Past a Non-renewable Resource?' In *Destruction and Conservation of Cultural Property*, edited by Robert Layton, Peter G. Stone and Julian Thomas, 286–97. London; New York: Routledge.

Hooper-Greenhill, Eilean and Moussouri, Theano. 2001. *Making Meaning in Art Museums 2: Visitors' interpretive strategies at Nottingham Castle Museum and Art Gallery*. Leicester: Research Centre for Museums and Galleries.

Howes, David, ed. 2005. *Empire of the Senses: The sensual culture reader*. Oxford: Berg.

Ingold, Tim. 2007. 'Materials against Materiality'. *Archaeological Dialogues* 14 (1): 1–16.

Jackson, Lesley. 2013. *Ercol: Furniture in the making*. Ilminster: Richard Dennis.

Jardine, Lisa. 2003. *The Curious Life of Robert Hooke: The man who measured London*. London: Harper Collins.

Jiang, Xiangqian. 2012. 'Precision Surface Measurement', *Philosophical Transactions of the Royal Society A* 370 (1973: July): 4089–114.

Jones, Siân. 2006. '"They Made it a Living Thing Didn't They"…: The growth of things and the fossilisation of heritage'. In *A Future for Archaeology: The past in the present*, edited by Robert Layton, Stephen Shennan and Peter Stone, 107–26. London: UCL Press.

Joy, Jody. 2009. 'Reinvigorating Object Biography: Reproducing the drama of object lives', *World Archaeology* 41 (4: December): 540–56.

Keene, Suzanne. 2005. *Fragments of the World: Uses of museum collections*. Oxford: Elsevier Butterworth–Heinemann.

Kingery, W. David, ed. 1996. *Learning from Things: Method and theory of material culture studies*. Washington, DC: Smithsonian Institution Press.

Kingery, W. David and Vandiver, Pamela. 1986. 'Studying Ceramic Objects'. In *Ceramic Masterpieces: Art, structure, technology*, 279–93. New York: Free Press.

Kopytoff, Igor. 1986. 'The Cultural Biography of Things: Commoditization as process'. In *The Social Life of Things: Commodities in cultural perspective*, edited by Arjan Appadurai, 64–94. Cambridge: Cambridge University Press.

Lankston, Louise, Cusack, Pearce, Fremantle, Chris and Isles, Chris. 2010. 'Visual Art in Hospitals: Case studies and review of the evidence', *Journal of the Royal Society of Medicine* 103 (12: December): 490–9.

La Placa, Vincent, McNaught, Allan and Knight, Anneyce. 2013. 'Discourse on Wellbeing in Research and Practice', *International Journal of Wellbeing* 3 (1): 116–25.

McDonald, Sally. 2008. 'Exploring the Role of Touch in Connoisseurship and the Identification of Objects'. In *The Power of Touch: Handling objects in museum and heritage contexts*, edited by Elizabeth Pye, 107–20. Walnut Creek, CA: Left Coast Press.

McGlone, Francis. 2008. 'The Two Sides of Touch: Sensing and feeling'. In *Touch in Museums: Policy and practice in object handling*, edited by Helen Chatterjee, 41–74. Oxford: Berg.

Mallowan, Max and Rose, John Cruikshank. 1935. 'Excavations at Tall Arpachiyah, 1933', *Iraq* 2 (1): i–178.

Manfredi, Marcello, Bearman, Greg, Williamson, Greg, Kronkright, Dale, Doehne, Eric, Jacobs, Megan and Marengo, Emilio. 2014. 'A New Quantitative Method for the Non-Invasive Documentation of Morphological Damage in Paintings Using RTI Surface Normals', *Sensors* 14 (7): 12271–84.

Mawer, Simon. 2009. *The Glass Room*. London: Little Brown.

Merriman, Nick and Swain, Hedly. 1999. 'Archaeological Archives: Serving the public interest?', *European Journal of Archaeology* 2 (2: August): 249–67.

Michaelson, Juliet, Abdallah, Saamah, Steuer, Nicola, Thompson, Sam and Marks, Nic. 2009. *National Accounts of Well-being: Bringing real wealth onto the balance sheet*. London: New Economics Foundation. Accessed 2 January 2018. http://b.3cdn.net/nefoundation/2027fb05fed1554aea_uim6vd4c5.pdf.

Morse, Nuala, Thomson, Linda J.M., Brown, Zoe and Chatterjee, Helen. 2015. 'Effects of Creative Museum Outreach Sessions on Measures of Confidence, Sociability and Well-being for Mental Health and Addiction Recovery Service-users', *Arts & Health* 7 (3): 231–46.

Mursell, James. 2009. *Windsor Chairmaking*. Ramsbury: Crowood Press.

Musée de l'Armée Invalides. n.d. 'Musée de l'Armée Invalides'. Accessed 2 January 2018. www.musee-armee.fr/en/english-version.html.

Newitz, Annalee. 2009. 'My Laptop'. In *Evocative Objects: Things we think with*, edited by Sherry Turkle, 86–91. Cambridge, MA: Massachusetts Institute of Technology.

Oddy, Andrew. 1996. 'Jewelry under the Microscope. A conservators' guide to cataloguing'. In *Ancient Jewelry and Archaeology*, edited by Adriana Calinescu, 185–97. Bloomington, IN: Indiana University Press.

Paintings in Hospitals. n.d. 'Paintings in Hospitals'. Accessed 2 January 2018. http://www.paintingsinhospitals.org.uk .

Pearce, Susan M., ed. 1994. *Interpreting Objects and Collections*. London; New York: Routledge.

Peers, Laura. 1999. '"Many Tender Ties": The shifting contexts and meanings of the S BLACK Bag'. In *The Cultural Biography of Objects*, edited by Chris Gosden and Yvonne Marshall. *World Archaeology* 31 (2: October): 288–302.

Peers, Laura and Brown, Alison K., eds. 2003. *Museums and Source Communities: A Routledge reader*. London; New York: Routledge.

Pye, David. 1995. *The Nature and Art of Workmanship*, rev. ed. London: Herbert Press.

Pye, Elizabeth. 2000. *Caring for the Past: Issues in conservation for archaeology and museums*. London: James & James.

Pye, Elizabeth. 2008a. *The Power of Touch: Handling objects in museum and heritage contexts*. Walnut Creek, CA: Left Coast Press.

Pye, Elizabeth. 2008b. 'Understanding Objects: The role of touch in conservation'. In *The Power of Touch: Handling objects in museum and heritage contexts,* edited by Elizabeth Pye, 121–38. Walnut Creek, CA: Left Coast Press.

Roberts, Samantha, Camic, Paul M. and Springham, Neil. 2011. 'New Roles for Art Galleries: Art-viewing as a community intervention for family carers of people with mental health problems', *Arts & Health: An international journal for research, policy and practice* 3 (2: September): 146–59.

Rowe, Shawn. 2002. 'The Role of Objects in Active, Distributed Meaning-Making'. In *Perspectives on Object-Centered Learning in Museums,* edited by Scott G. Paris, 19–36. Mahwah, NJ: Laurence Erlbaum Associates.

Science Museum. n.d. 'Robert Hooke Type Compound microscope'. Accessed 2 January 2018. http://collection.sciencemuseum.org.uk/objects/co8592773/robert-hooke-type-compound-microscope-compound-microscope-microscope.

Simon, Camille, Huxhagen, Uwe, Mansouri, Alamin, Heritage, Adrian, Boochs, Frank and Marzani, Franck S. 2011. 'Integration of High-Resolution Spatial and Spectral Data Acquisition Systems to Provide Complementary Datasets for Cultural Heritage Applications'. *IS&T/SPIE Electronic Imaging Meeting*, January 2010, San Jose, United States, 7531 (1: November): 1–9.

Spalding, Julian. 2002. *The Poetic Museum: Reviving historic collections*. London: Prestel.

Spence, Charles and Gallace, Alberto. 2008. 'Making Sense of Touch'. In *Touch in Museums: Policy and practice in object handling,* edited by Helen Chatterjee, 21–40. Oxford: Berg.

Staffordshire Hoard. n.d. 'Staffordshire Hoard'. Accessed 2 January 2018. www.staffordshirehoard.org.uk.

Stanco, Filippo, Battiato, Sebastiano and Gallo, Giovanni. 2011. *Digital Imaging for Cultural Heritage Preservation: Analysis, restoration, and reconstruction of ancient artworks*. Boca Raton FL: CRC Press.

Staricoff, Rosalia L. 2004. *Arts in Health: A review of the medical literature: Research Report 36*. London: Arts Council England.

Styliani, Stella, Fotis, Liarokapis, Kotsakis, Kostas and Petros, Patias. 2009. 'Virtual Museums, a Survey and Some Issues for Consideration', *Journal of Cultural Heritage* 10 (4: October): 520–8.

Sullivan, Paul. 2009. 'Feeling Our Way: Towards a shared approach to object handling in the public galleries', University College London. Accessed 22 April 2015. http://www.ucl.ac.uk/conservation-c-22/conference/paul_sullivan.

Thomson, Linda and Chatterjee, Helen. 2014. 'Assessing Well-Being Outcomes for Arts and Heritage Activities: Development of a museum well-being measures toolkit', *Journal of Applied Arts & Health* 5 (1): 29–50.

Thomson, Linda J.M., Ander, Erica E., Menon, Usha, Lanceley, Anne and Chatterjee, Helen J. 2011. 'Evaluating the Therapeutic Effects of Museum Object Handling with Hospital Patients: A review and initial trial of wellbeing measures', *Journal of Applied Arts & Health* 2 (1: April): 37–56.

Turkle, Sherry, ed. 2009. *Evocative Objects: Things we think with*. Cambridge, MA: Massachusetts Institute of Technology.

UCL – University College London. n.d. a. 'Heritage in Hospitals'. Accessed 2 January 2018. https://www.ucl.ac.uk/culture/projects/heritage-hospitals.

UCL – University College London. n.d. b. 'Institute of Making'. Accessed 2 January 2018. http://www.instituteofmaking.org.uk.

UCL Institute of Archaeology. 2009. 'Conservation's Catch 22'. Accessed 2 January 2018. http://www.ucl.ac.uk/archaeology/research/directory/catch_22.

Wellcome Collection. 2011/2012. 'Felicity Powell – Charmed Life: The solace of objects; exhibition 6 October 2011–26 February 2012.' Accessed 29 July 2019. https://wellcomecollection.org/exhibitions/W-GYiBEAAK61cRK1.

Wengrow, David. 2001. 'The Evolution of Simplicity: Aesthetic labour and social change in the Neolithic Near East', *World Archaeology* 33 (2: October): 168–88.

Wing, Alan, Giachritsis, Christos and Roberts, Roberta. 2008. 'Weighing up the Value of Touch'. In *The Power of Touch: Handling objects in museum and heritage contexts,* edited by Elizabeth Pye, 31–44. Walnut Creek, CA: Left Coast Press.

Index

Aboriginal peoples and art 11, 31; *see also*
    Indigenous peoples
    national Aboriginal organisation 34
    peoples and art 11, 31
    'Preserving Aboriginal Heritage'
        (conference, 2007) 40
access integrated with preservation (case
    study of UK National Archives) 147–51
aesthetics 7–8, 32–3, 127
African resources 4–5, 131
ageing
    accelerated 88–9, 96
    properties of materials 91–3
Ai Weiwei 160
American Institute of Conservation
    (AIC) 32–3
Amin, Idi 144
animal bones, analysis of 117
Anishnaabe First Nations 41
Appelbaum, Barbara 14
Appropriate technologies (publication) 89
archaeological heritage 131, 139
    definition of 127–8
    destruction of 132, 134, 160
archival deposition 106–7, 113–18, 122
archives 141–52
    as distinct from libraries 142
Arpachiyah pottery 164
art, works of 12, 32, 156
artisans 162
artist's intention (maker's intention) 12, 13
authority of museums and heritage
    institutions 24
Avrami, Erica 15

Baltimore meeting (2011) 55
Barakat, Sultan 47
Beardsley, Monroe C. 12
Bellegarde, Perry 145
Bernstein, Bruce 10
best practice, dissemination of 117
Bickerton, Craig 121
Birzeit Historic Centre Project (2007–2011)
    4, 72–82
    local council input to 82
    overall objective of 78
Bishop Grosseteste University (BGU-UK) 108,
    110, 119
Blades, Nigel 90
Board of Trade (BT) Design Register
    (1839–1991) 147–51
Bonaparte, Napoleon, coat and hat of 159

'bottom-up' processes 7, 122
Bozeman, Barry 128, 132
Brandi, Cesare 8, 15
Brass, Anna 151
British dominance 19–20
British Museum 170
Budd, Malcolm 156
Building Environment Simulation (BES)
    model 145–6
built environment 66–71
Burra Charter (1999) 70–1

Canada 30–1, 34–6, 40, 145
Canadian Assembly of First Nations 34
Canadian Conservation Institute (CCI)
    31–2, 40–1
Canadian Museums Association 34
capacity-building 61–3, 108
cataloguing of finds 107, 111, 114, 116–7,
    144, 148
ceramic objects 164
Charmed Life (exhibition, 2011–2012) 159
china menders 164–5
Classen, Constance 169
codes of ethics and practice 30, 32, 37, 85, 88
coins 158–9, 164–7
    identification of 117
collaborative working (collaboration) 1–4, 7,
    10–11, 18–20, 23, 35–6, 40–2, 47
    between universities and community groups
        108, 119–22
collections
    access to 170–2
    care of 85–6, 99
    worthiness to join 15
Collections Council of Australia (CCA) 35–6
collective action 67–8
colonial
    records 142, 144–5
    rule 2, 6–7, 18
'Common Ground' land management
    initiative 42
communication skills 21–2
communities of practice (CoP) 70
community archaeology groups 105–23
    failed projects of 107
    relations between 119–20
    sustainability of 120
community involvement in a project 4,
    70–4, 78–9
    benefits from 67, 69–70, 121–2
'condition' of material fabric 14–15

conscientisation (Freire) 18
conservation
  aim of 14–15
  characteristics of 143
  context-dependent nature of 9, 14
  at the crossroads of many disciplines 23
  definition of 15
  linking people with people 30, 42, 44
  never-ending process of 23
  new theory generated by 24
  and participation 9–11
  potential impact of 17
  practices of 11–13
  process 8–9, 13, 15, 24
  revealing the truth 15
  social dimension of 143–4
  subfields of 36
  theoretical basis for 8
  power of 15–16, 24
'conservation-grade' materials 88, 90, 93, 99
conservation practice
  as a catalyst for networking and further
    activity 68–9
  community involvement in 71
  promoting learning 70
  relationship with social development 67
conservation professionals
  attitudes of 37, 47
  concern with public benefit 126
  formerly operating in relative professional
    invisibility 16
  freedom to explore and study objects 167,
    169, 172
  as an independent profession 7, 87
  lack of management skills 71
  need for more engagement in debate 36
Conservation's Catch 22 (research project,
  2009–2010) 170
context-specific technologies 89
controversial decisions 22
corrosion of iron objects 115
cost-benefit analysis 95, 99, 146
Council for British Archaeology (CBA) 106–7
Council of Europe 71
  Framework Convention on the Value of
    Cultural Heritage for Society (2005)
    126, 129
Covid-19 169
Cranmer Webster, Gloria 31, 33
critical reflection 18
critical thinking 56
Croft Castle 169
cross-disciplinarity 1–3, 7–11, 151
cultural constructs 35
cultural districts 68–9, 138
cultural diversity 66, 138
cultural heritage 126–7, 133–9
  benefits from 126
  definitions of 126–7
  destruction in Iraq 48
  as distinct from natural heritage 126,
    135, 138
  impediments to gaining public benefit
    from 138–9
  importance of 46, 63
  management of 71, 141
  safeguarding of 134–5

and social development 137, 151
  use of a country's resources without
    compensation 133
cultural property, conflict between *use* and
  preservation of 32, 36–9, 50–3
cultural sensitivity 10
cultural values 30, 33
curators becoming facilitators 34

de Botton, Alain 156
decision-making processes 7–17, 20, 24, 85,
  97, 100
Deisser, Anne-Marie 10
de la Torre, Marta 126
de Waal, Edmund 158, 167
disease, fighting of 137
display cases 168
doctors, conservators compared with 40
Domesday Book 142
doodles 165–6
Drayman-Weisser, Terry 56
Dümcke, Cornelia 129
dust, protection against 91–3
Dykstra, Steven W. 12

eco-museums 34
education 4, 53, 62–3, 119, 131, 137
  'banking' concept of 19
elm wood 162
empowerment 7, 18, 71, 134
engagement
  of the community 5, 70–1, 118, 121, 123,
    141, 144–5
  different forms of 24, 72
  online 151
English language, use of 50, 58
entertainment in museums 34
environmental impact assessment (EIA) 134–5
Erbil 48–9, 62
Ercolani, Lucian (and Ercol furniture) 162–3
ethical concerns 86, 133; *see also* codes of
  ethics and practice
European museum model 20
evocative objects 159–60
experiential learning 70
expertise 21, 53, 58

fabric of objects 162
Facebook 42, 60
'fake news' 19
Feagin, Susan L. 13
field-walking projects 105–6
First Aid to Cultural Heritage in Times of Crisis
  (FAC) methodology 61
First Aid for Finds (publication) 115
First Nation communities 41–3
follow-up assessments 72
Freire, Paulo 3, 7, 18–24

Getty Conservation Institute (GCI) 71
glass cases in museums 170
globalisation of heritage 85
Gordon, Cesar 11
Gormley, Antony 168
government records, importance of 142–3
Grant, Howard 22
Gurga Ciya, Kurdistan 86

Halland Regional Museum, Sweden 68
handling of objects 155, 165–72
  barriers to 170–2
  need for research on 171–2
  use in teaching 56
'hands off' ethos of museums 169, 172
haptics 169
Helmer, Joyce 43
Hepworth, Paul 56
heritage
  different types of 126–7
  as a finite resource, but one which is
    constantly being added to 172
heritage conservation
  benefits from 129–32
  challenges and opportunities offered by 1–2
  commitment to and interest in 69, 79–80
  link with societal concerns 66, 125–6
Heritage Health Index 97
Heritage Lottery Fund (HLF) 108, 110, 156
heritage wardens (in Kenya) 135
Hinduism 37–9
Hinemihi meeting house, London 11
Historic England 156
historical districts 66, 72
Hooke, Robert 159
hospitals 156–7
human rights 2–5, 133

impartiality, professional 16–17
inclusion, policy of 2
Indigenous peoples 3–4, 10, 18, 22, 33–6, 145
individualism, economic 132
industrial districts 68
inequality 130–3
information and communications technology
    (ICT) 151–2
infrastructure development 74
Ingold, Tim 160, 171
intangible 3, 71, 138, 171
intellectual capital 70
intentional fallacy 12
intentions of an object's maker 12–13
interdisciplinarity 5, 141, 143, 151–2
International Council of Museums
    (ICOM) 94, 99
International Institute of Conservation (IIC) 32
International Monetary Fund (IMF) 130
internationalisation 85
internet access 36, 43, 91
interpretation, concept of 12
Iraq, developing the heritage preservation
    community in 58–60
  State Board of Antiquities and Heritage
    (SBAH) 49
Iraqi Institute for Conservation of Antiquities
    and Heritage (IICAH), Erbil 4, 46–63
  Advisory Council 49
  change from capacity-building to disaster
    preparedness (2014–2016) 61
  educational programmes and didactic
    method 50–5
  formal curriculum reviews 55–8
  funding and management of 48–9, 63
  institutions using the facilities of 59
  mission and importance of 48, 53, 60
  reconciliation through education 60

'Islamic State' (ISIS) 48, 60–1
Iwasa, Noriaki 16–17

Jigyasu, Rohit 90

Kenora 41
Kenya 5, 125–39
  abundance of resources 131
  challenges faced by 130
  Constitution (2010) 125, 133, 136
  cultural sites in 131–2
  Environment Management and
    Coordination Act (EMCA, 1999) 134
  Mau Mau uprising in 142
  National Bureau of Statistics 130–1
  National Museums (NMK) 131, 135–9
  National Museums and Heritage Act (2006)
    126–7, 134–6
  National Policy on Culture and Heritage
    (2009) 138
  New Development Paradigm 132
  regional or global protocols and conventions
    signed by 136
  social development in 125, 137–8
  Vision 2030 (development
    programme) 137–8
Khorsheed, Abdullah 49, 63
knowledge
  hierarchisation of 21
  power conferred by 20
Kreps, Christina F. 35
Kurdistan region 49, 61
Kurdistan Regional Government (KRG) 48

labelling of objects 115
life stories of objects 157–8
Lincolnshire 4, 114–15
  Archaeological Archive 116
Lindisfarne Gospels 161
listening 22, 41
loaning out of museum objects 31–6
local practices 10
Lombardy 69

McCue, Duncan 42–3
McDermott, Richard A. 70
McIntyre, Alice 23
McMullen, Ann 21
maintenance work 69, 76, 81–2
Marxist theory 132
Mason, Randall 126
'master trainers' 58
material fabric of objects 8
  source of information 160–5
materials and making, interest in 171
materials used in conservation
  availability of 91
  specialised 86–9
Matsuda, Akira 128
Mawer, Simon 158
meanings of objects 17
Melville, Duncan 121
Messinger, Ruth W. 41
Michalski, Stefan 98
microscopes 159
Mies van der Rohe, Ludwig 158
Millennium Development Goals (MDGs) 136–7

Mind the Gap (report, 2014) 144
'minimum intervention' concept 14
monitoring of stored collections 97–100
mortality rates 137
motivation, intrinsic 70
Muhawi, Farhat Y. 74–5
Murray Pease Report (1964) 13, 32
Museum of Anthropology (MOA), University
    of British Columbia 31, 38–9
museum climate specifications 88
museum objects 156, 168–9
museum values 30
museums
    changes faced by 33–5
    need for wider access to 169, 172
music 156

Namunaba, Ibrahim 134
National Gallery, London 172
National Museum of the American Indian
    (NMAI) 10
National Trust 168–9
Native Americans 35
natural heritage 126, 134–5, 138
    and natural environment 134
networking 68, 121
'neutrality' 11, 15–17
New Mexico Museum, Santa Fe 10
'new museology' 34
The New Yorker 37
Newitz, Analee 159–60
Nimrud Rescue Project (2017) 61–2

objects
    definition of 155
    material and form of 160–1
    pleasure in and fascination with
        155–68, 172
    'reading' of 160
Oddy test 88–9, 96, 100
    alternatives to 89
Oloo, Wycliffe 134
'Open Lab and Road Show Project' 4, 108–23
    aims and observed benefits of 108, 117–23
    evaluation of 118–19
    foreseen outcomes of 113–19
    timing of meetings 111
    unforeseen outcomes of 119–22
    weaknesses of 123
optimal treatment of conserved objects 14
outreach activities 119, 144, 269

packaging materials 93, 97–8, 114–16
paleontology 131
Palestine 66–84. *See also* Birzeit Historic
    Centre Project
participation in heritage activities
    benefits from 69–72, 78, 121–2, 156–7
    by all citizens of Kenya 132–3, 138
    by archive users 144
    by communities 34–5
    and conservation 9–11
    economic value of 121–2
    sometimes only happening in theory 23
participatory action research (PAR) 7, 18
'Participatory Processes and Conservation
    Practices' (survey, 2013) 2

partnership 20–1
    between the government and stakeholders
        in heritage conservation 139
    global, for purposes of development 137
people-centred approaches 91
political activism 6
pollution control 90, 93
postcolonial world 3, 7, 24
post-conflict situations 47, 53, 60
post-excavation processes 106–10, 113, 117,
        120, 122
    support needed for 108
postmodernism 132
poverty and poverty reduction 130–1, 137
power structures 7, 24
practitioners in heritage conservation 89–90
preservation of heritage 35–6, 39–43
    examples of 40–3
'Preserving Aboriginal Heritage' (conference,
        2007) 40
Prevention in Museums in Africa (PREMA)
        initiative 86
preventive conservation 8, 10, 75, 79, 81
    curriculum of 50
    effectiveness or efficiency 78–9, 98–9
    standards 87
private interests 129
private practice in conservation 37
professional attitudes and practices 47
provenance 6–7
psychological wellbeing through involvement
        with museum activities and artefacts
        157, 172
public, 'general' 128, 130–3
public benefits from heritage 129–30
    intrinsic and *instrumental* 129
public interest 128–9
    theory of (Bozeman) 132
public spending on professional input to
        heritage activities 123
public values 128–9

Quebec Declaration on the Spirit of Place
    (ICOMOS, 2008) 71
questions, direct asking of 22

Rashid, Qais 62
reconciliation 1, 46, 47, 60, 61
reflection and reflective practice 9, 23–4; see
        also critical reflection
Re-Org methodology 90, 94
repatriation of museum objects 42
restitution debate 17
re-treatability 13
'reversibility' principle 13
risk management 61, 90
Riwaq (NGO) 72–82
'road show' activities 113
Robson, James P. 42
Ruskin, John 15

Sah, Anupam 39–40
Said, Edward 19–20
Saint Petersburg State Hermitage Museum 168
Salomon, Frank 11
San Cristobal de Rapaz, Peru 11
Sarr, Felwine 6

Saskatchewan 35–6, 145
Savoy, Bénédicte 6
Schumacher, Fritz E. 89
Science Museum, London 159
scientific approach to heritage conservation 91
selling of artefacts 48
Shekhar, Ashok 37
Shiva named as a plaintiff in a legal case 37
silence, culture of 19–20
skeuomorphism 164
skills
    brought to a project 120
    development of 113, 117–18, 122
Sloggett, Robyn 17
Smith, Richard D. 13
Smithsonian Institution 61–2
Snyder, William M. 70
social capital 68, 70
social development in the United Kingdom
    143–4, 151–2
social dynamics 67–9
'The Social Impact of Cross-disciplinary
    Conservation' (conference, 2014) xiii
social media 42
social orientation of conservation 3, 24
social values 85
'soft-diplomacy' 46
South African pennies 158–9
Spalding, Julian 161
Staffordshire Hoard 167
stakeholders 34–40, 126, 129, 139
standards: for archaeological processes 37, 116
    global 86, 136
state institutions 128
stewardship of collections 6
Stiglitz, Joseph E. 132
Stone, Tom 40
storage facilities and materials 90, 93–8, 107,
    114, 116
subjectivity 8
Sully, Dean 11
sustainability 4–5, 66–9, 82, 85–6, 88, 90–1,
    133–9, 141
    environmental 145–7
    of future archaeological projects 117–18
    key principle of 97
    of local heritage groups 120
    planning models for 90

tangible benefits 129
technology transfer 89
Temple of the Tooth Relic 10
Tepe Marani, Kurdistan 86
terminology 88
territorial capital 66–7
terrorism 62
testing of materials 96–9
Tomlinson, Zoë 108
'top-down' projects 122
training 3–4, 53, 86, 114
'transparency' 151
'tribes' in New England 21
trickle-down economics 131

Triple Bottom Line accounting 86
trust 68

Uganda 130
United Kingdom National Archives 5, 141–52
    Collection Care Department 146
    democratic ethos of 141, 143, 152
    environmental performance of 146
    fundamental objective of 151
    selection of records for 142
    use of film by 151
    user participation at 144, 151
United Kingdom Department of Digital,
    Culture, Media and Sport (DCMS) 142
United Nations
    Educational, Scientific and Cultural
        Organization (UNESCO) 66, 71–2, 89–90,
        97, 131–2
    HABITAT 72
    see also Millennium Development Goals
Universal Declaration on Cultural Diversity
    (UNESCO, 2001) 66
University College London (UCL)
    Centre for Sustainable Heritage 146
    Institute of Archaeology 170
    Institute of Making 171
    Museum Wellbeing Measures Toolkit 157
university resources 108–10, 119, 123
user consultation, user participation and user-
    generated content 151

values 15–16
values-based planning 90
Venice Charter (1962) 85
verbalism 23
Victoria, Queen 149–50, 164
Vienna Memorandum (UNESCO, 2005) 71
Viñas, Muñoz 7, 14
Viollet-le-Duc, Eugène Emmanuel 15
visual art 156
vocabulary, use of 22
volunteers, use of 105–6, 144, 170

wellbeing 30, 40, 121–2, 156–7
    definition of 156
    psychological 157, 172
    social 133
Wellcome Collection 159
Wenger, Etienne 70
Wheatley, Daniel 121
Wightwick Manor 169
Wijesuriya, Sri Lanka 10
Wimsant, William K. 12
Windsor chairs 162–3
'win-win' situations 37
Wolseley, Garnet 147–8
women's empowerment 137
wood, use of 161–2
World Bank 130, 137

York Castle Museum 150

Zuni community 33

Lightning Source UK Ltd.
Milton Keynes UK
UKHW021459200221
379073UK00002BA/12